NEGOTIATING
<small>WITH THE</small> SOVIETS

NEGOTIATING
WITH THE SOVIETS

RAYMOND F. SMITH

An Institute for the Study of
Diplomacy Book

INDIANA UNIVERSITY PRESS
Bloomington and Indianapolis

Manufactured in the United States of America

Library of Congress Cataloging-in-Publication Data

Smith, Raymond F.
    Negotiating with the Soviets / Raymond F. Smith.
        p.   cm.
    ''An Institute for the Study of Diplomacy Book.''
    Bibliography: p.
    Includes index.
    ISBN 0-253-35285-1.—ISBN 0-253-20535-2 (pbk.)
    1. United States—Foreign relations—Soviet Union. 2. Soviet Union—Foreign relations—United States. 3. Diplomacy. I. Title.
JX1428.S65S54   1989
327.73047—dc19   88-46014
                                                           CIP

1 2 3 4 5 93 92 91 90 89

*This book is dedicated to those who,
one day at a time,
are seeking progress,
not perfection.*

CONTENTS

PREFACE

From 1976 to 1979, I was assigned by the State Department to the United States Embassy in Moscow, the first year as a consular officer, the last two years as a political officer. Two of the most lasting impressions from this rich experience were, first, that often we did not negotiate as effectively with the Soviets as I thought we should and, second, that many Americans assigned to the Embassy departed disillusioned and far more hostile toward the Soviet Union than when they arrived. Often, the most disillusioned and hostile were those who had arrived with the greatest expectations. I thought there might be a connection between the two—that both the negotiating failures and the disillusionment grew out of the Soviets' failure to behave the way we expected them to.

A few years later, from 1982 to 1984, I headed the bilateral section of the Soviet desk in Washington. During that time, I probably had more frequent face-to-face contact with Soviet embassy officials than anyone else in the U.S. government. Many of these contacts were informal negotiations, and they were supplemented by several rounds of formal negotiating sessions on consular and administrative issues which I headed on the U.S. side. I tried to put into practice a few of the ideas I had developed on negotiating with the Soviets.

These experiences were the initial stimulus for this book. It starts with the premise that if we are going to negotiate effectively with the Soviets we need to try to see the world through their eyes. That does not mean adopting their world view, nor does it mean adopting a cultural relativism which does not permit us a preference for our own values. It means recognizing that, while we share with Soviet citizens many values common to all mankind, our historical experiences have also produced some fundamentally different values and expectations. For the purposes of this book, the sum of those differences can be described as distinctive negotiating styles.

There have been a lot of descriptions of how the Soviets negotiate. While there is some of that perforce here as well, the fundamental aim of this book is to get beneath the how, to try to develop an understanding of why the Soviets negotiate the way they do. That deeper understanding, I believe, will enable us to negotiate more effectively with the Soviets, without the disillusionment and hostility to which the experience often gives rise.

This book is based fundamentally on the first-hand experience mentioned above. The primary research and writing were done during a 1986–1987 sabbatical from the State Department. During the editing, updating, and redrafting process, which extended through 1988, I drew on additional first-hand experience: as the Soviet advisor on the State Department's Policy Planning Staff; as Deputy Director of the On-Site Inspection Agency, which included organizing and taking part in several rounds of negotiations on implementing the INF Treaty; and currently as political counselor at the U.S. Embassy in Moscow, which has to date included several months of filling in as Deputy Chief of Mission and several brief stints as Chargé d'Affaires.

The numerous interviews I conducted while researching this book were primarily with people with first-hand experience in negotiating with the Soviets. Many, though by no means all of them were and still are government officials. For that reason, our interviews were conducted on a background basis, which meant that I could not identify them, except generically. I have also drawn on a wide variety of written material. Some of it is anecdotal, reminiscences of experiences with the Soviets which I believe are illustrative. Other material ranges from academic scholarship in Soviet studies through Russian history to philosophy and ideology. The object of it all, I ask the reader to remember, is a deeper understanding of Soviet negotiating behavior. The practitioner, I hope, will sit down better prepared to negotiate and later walk out of the room more successful, or at a minimum less frustrated.

The State Department, an intelligent employer in this regard, has a senior training program, which permitted me to take the time to write this book. I had the good fortune to be selected for the Department's Una Chapman Cox Foundation program, and therefore benefited from a generous stipend to cover research and travel costs. The Foundation has been a good friend of the Foreign Service and I hope that this book can be taken as at least a small indication that the friendship has been beneficial. Georgetown University's Institute for the Study of Diplomacy was my professional home for a year, a comfortable, congenial and stimulating place to work.

I want to thank the many colleagues in government who gave me the benefit of their experience and ideas and the many persons outside of government who were equally generous with theirs. A number of persons read and commented on drafts of this book. I would particularly like to thank Ambassador David Newsom, whose comments prompted me to undertake a significant change in the structure of the presentation. Associate Dean Allan Goodman, of Georgetown University's School of Foreign Service, and my friend and Soviet affairs colleague Dick Combs also provided valuable critiques. Kevin Jack Riley, Julie Ruterbories, and Lynn Hindes provided valuable research assistance. The book benefited from a careful editorial review by Indiana University Press and, specifically, by Jo Burgess. Last, but not least, my thanks to Ann Miller, who encouraged me to take the risk. I am, of course, solely responsible for the contents. The views expressed do not necessarily represent those of the U.S. government.

Negotiating with the Soviets

CHAPTER 1

NEGOTIATING WITH THE SOVIETS

> To those who think that Soviet leaders, officials,
> and experts are people like us, let me say that
> if I have learned anything from my study of the
> Soviet Union, it is that the Soviets are not
> like us.
>
> —Seweryn Bialer, *The Soviet Paradox*

ON JUNE 22, 1941, THE ANNIVERSARY OF NAPOLEON'S INVASION
of Russia, the German army invaded the Soviet Union. Its initial successes on the
eastern front at least matched those it had previously achieved on the western. Its
armies pushed apparently effortlessly deep into Soviet territory. Within ten days,
the entire seacoast up to Tallinn had been taken. Smolensk fell by July 16. By the
end of August, the Nazis' 6th Army had broken through on the Don front and
was moving toward the Volga; Stalingrad was in danger of falling. Stalin, seemingly demoralized by news of the invasion, disappeared from public view for
days. His first public pronouncement was not until July 3, eleven days after the
beginning of the invasion.[1]

To the United States and Great Britain, the invasion represented both an enormous opportunity and a potentially grave danger. The Soviet Union, the largest
country in the world, a country with a stirring Russian martial history of tena-
cious and ultimately successful defense of its territory against foreign invaders,
could be an ally of incalculable value. But a Soviet Union quickly defeated and
forced to sue for peace, as France had been, would be almost as great an asset to
Hitler. Secure on his eastern flank, as he could never have been while Stalin
brooded in the Kremlin, Hitler would be free to turn even greater assets toward
England than was possible before the invasion. Keeping the Soviet Union in the
war immediately became an almost overriding interest of Germany's two significant remaining Western opponents. But memories of the Molotov/Ribbentrop pact
were fresh. Soviet determination to resist Hitler was in doubt, and, as German
military successes followed one upon another, so was Soviet ability.

Two early diplomatic missions to the Soviet Union—the Hopkins mission of
July 29–31 and the Harriman/Beaverbrook mission of September 28–October 2—

were intended to assess Stalin's determination and the Soviet Union's staying power, to encourage the Soviets to stay in the war, and to offer them all possible material help for that purpose. Hopkins, after two long meetings with Stalin, came away "confident of Soviet staying power in the war and impressed by Stalin's strength of personality, firmness of decision, and totality of control."[2] Hopkins's report, added to the manifest U.S. national interests in the matter, led President Roosevelt to promise economic assistance to the Soviet Union in its struggle against Hitler.

German military successes continued unabated over the next two months. By the time of the Harriman/Beaverbrook mission, the Germans were only thirty miles from Moscow. They were to get closer yet. The monument marking the furthest advance of the German army, using the potent symbol of a gigantic tank trap, stands on the outskirts of Moscow, between the city and its principal international airport. Harriman and Beaverbrook were under instructions to discuss establishment of a program of support for the Soviet armed forces, support that would not simply be limited to the present crisis but would continue until Hitler's defeat. Because of Roosevelt's concerns about public and congressional opposition to aiding the Soviet Union, Harriman had the additional and unenviable task of attempting to extract from the Soviets a public commitment to greater religious freedom.

The two missions, and particularly the latter, set a pattern for Western/Soviet negotiations that was generally followed throughout the war. One element of it was Stalin's ability to take and hold the moral high ground. By asking Hopkins in July for an American army to help fight the Germans on Soviet soil and then asking Beaverbrook for a similar commitment in September—a request neither country felt in a position to meet—Stalin was able to assert that his country was bearing a disproportionate share of the burden of fighting Hitler, that his country was bleeding while the United States and Britain stood on the sidelines. His repeated requests over the next three years for the opening of a second front, probably genuine enough in substance, also had the same effect. It is a position the Soviet Union maintains to this day, and one that in terms of the actual losses suffered by each of the Allies, is not without some objective merit.

Stalin also showed himself to be particularly adept at exploiting sudden changes of mood to leave his negotiating partners/adversaries off-balance, confused, and vulnerable. His first meeting with Harriman and Beaverbrook lasted for three hours. It was frank and cordial, even friendly. Stalin discussed the Soviet military situation and his needs. He reiterated his request for a British army in the Ukraine. In what was apparently the only discordant note at the meeting, he responded sharply to Beaverbrook's suggestion that British troops might be sent to the Caucasus by saying the war was not there, but in the Ukraine.[3] Harriman raised the issue of religion in the Soviet Union and the effect that negative public opinion on this issue could have on aid to the Soviet Union. Stalin responded with little apparent interest, evidently suggesting that this was an issue better addressed to subordinates. Beaverbrook and Harriman left the meeting feeling that it had gone extremely well and confident that they would have a successful mission.

The second meeting was a dose of cold water. Stalin was rude, insulting, and contemptuous of the paucity of the Western offers of help. He accused the British and Americans of wanting to see Hitler defeat the Soviet Union. Harriman was puzzled about why Stalin behaved this way, but he understood that one motive could be Stalin's belief that this tactic would enable him to extract more assistance. Despite Harriman's intellectual understanding that Stalin's behavior could simply be a negotiating tactic, he and Beaverbrook left the meeting deeply depressed and concerned that their mission might end in failure. They did, before leaving, ask Stalin for a third meeting, and to their great relief, he agreed.

Beaverbrook, convinced that the third meeting would be a repetition of the second and wanting to distance himself from the disaster, asked Harriman to lead off the following day. Stalin again drastically altered his mood; this time he was businesslike and reasonable. The three men methodically reviewed the list of items the Soviets had requested, and Harriman explained how far the United States and Britain could go to meet the requests. Stalin acknowledged that he was pleased with the offers of assistance. The meeting broke up in a friendly way, with Stalin's invitation to the Western delegates for dinner the following evening. Harriman was moved to the belief that "if we came through as had been promised, and if personal relations were maintained with Stalin, the suspicion that has existed between the Soviet Government and our two governments might well be eradicated."[4] Harriman did not again raise the religious question with Stalin and admitted later that Roosevelt was unhappy with his failure to get any substantial concession from the Soviets on the subject.

Stalin is generally given high marks for his negotiating effectiveness in these early encounters. As Joseph Whelan put it:

> Though the Soviet Union was then facing its greatest peril in its brief history as the German armies were approaching within 30 miles of Moscow, and though its needs for Allied assistance in great quantities were immediate and most acute, still Stalin was the tough-minded negotiator who could and did, by employing the tactic of abuse, throw off balance his negotiating adversaries. By placing them on the defensive, he reversed the roles of petitioner and donor, thus creating a psychological mood and relationship that could give greater assurance that his needs would be met. Perhaps on no other occasion was Stalin able to demonstrate more dramatically this historic Russian negotiating tactic of successfully using diplomacy to create a negotiating position of strength out of one of weakness.[5]

The pattern thus established, of Soviet domination of the moral high ground, rapid and dramatic shifts of mood from extreme cordiality to extreme hostility, and Western failure to extract Soviet concessions in return for Western help, continued throughout the war.

About forty-five years later, a middle-rank American diplomat at the START talks in Geneva faced a Soviet counterpart of ambassadorial rank and many years of diplomatic experience.[6] This disparity was partly counterbalanced by the fact that the Soviet was new to the strategic arms talks, whereas the American had been involved in the issues for some years. It was clear, nevertheless, that in terms of diplomatic protocol, the Soviet was far senior. Their first couple of working sessions were uneventful. The Soviet strode into the next one, however, breathing fire and brimstone. He delivered a forty-five minute attack on the U.S. position and intentions, scathing in tone and, in the American's view, slanderous in content. The American, no shrinking violet, replied with forty-five minutes in the same vein on the Soviet position, ending by saying that the exchange had been strikingly dissimilar to those the two had had before, that he doubted that continuing along this line was useful, but that if the Soviet side wished to he was perfectly prepared to accommodate them. There was never a repetition of this kind of tirade.

The American START negotiator—an arms control specialist, not a Soviet expert—instinctively took the right tack in responding to his counterpart's behavior. His far more experienced predecessors in 1941 did not. Neither proceeded on the basis of a correct understanding of Soviet negotiating behavior and neither, therefore, had an effective strategy for dealing with it. The START negotiator had no strategy. His gut reaction happened to be the right one in that particular circumstance; in another circumstance, faced with a different aspect of Soviet negotiating behavior, his gut reaction would be just as likely to be wrong. Harriman and Beaverbrook had a strategy, but it was the wrong one because it was premised on a misunderstanding of Stalin's motivations. Stalin's behavior, they believed, stemmed from deep suspicion of Western motives and intentions. If those suspicions could be laid to rest, the groundwork would be established for a close relationship among partners struggling together as equals to rid the world of the menace of Hitler. The strategy, therefore, was to give Stalin whatever he asked for, within the limits of the possible, and not to press him for any quid pro quo.

These incidents typify the haphazard, ill-informed approach the United States has generally taken to negotiating with the Soviet Union. It is not that our negotiators have lacked talent or dedication. It is rather that their talent and dedication have not been accompanied by any real effort to see the world through Soviet eyes. At best, they may have been exposed to a few books or articles on how the Soviets negotiate, manuals on avoiding negotiating pitfalls. They are unlikely to have asked, or to have been told, *why* the Soviets negotiate the way they do. And that is the crucial question. If we do not ask it and attempt to answer it, we will continue to substitute our own psychological or ideological projections for Soviet reality.

The Soviet view of negotiations differs profoundly from ours. Some Americans would deny the accuracy of that statement. Others would appear to accept its accuracy but would deny it any place in negotiating practice. Still others would embrace it fervidly, trumpeting their interpretation of the differences as demonstrating the impossibility of serious negotiations. We must replace these views with an understanding that there is a distinctive Soviet negotiating style, that many of the Soviet negotiating tactics which have been observed repeatedly (how the Soviets negotiate) arise from that style, and that both style and tactics have their roots in a Soviet and Russian experience that in many ways touches the Western experience only tangentially. There is no reason for us to be in the position of President Carter, who, following the invasion of Afghanistan, confessed his disillusionment, saying that the invasion had caused him to completely reassess his views about the Soviet Union. Despite its surface opaqueness, the Soviet Union is not Churchill's "riddle wrapped in a mystery inside an enigma." Rather, it is a product of its historical experiences, sharing many elements of commonality with all of mankind, bearing many variants of the uniqueness that marks this species and its creations. We may never be able to predict its behavior precisely, any more than we can be certain of the behavior of another human being. We can, however, understand the sources of its conduct. Doing so will affirm the possibility and necessity of negotiation and will equip us to conduct the process more effectively. We have a responsibility to do so, a responsibility that comes with superpower status in a nuclear age.

The sources of Soviet negotiating conduct lie in the Russian political culture and in the pervasive variant of Marxist-Leninist ideology that justifies the status of the country's current ruling class. Where ideology and political culture are mutually reinforcing, we can expect to find particularly strong drivers of Soviet negotiating conduct. Where they are at odds, there will be greater variability. The Russian political culture is dominated by authoritarianism and risk-avoidance. While Western societies were slowly and painfully evolving toward a system that limited political authority and guaranteed individual rights, the small ruling class in Russia maintained, some would argue even increased, its hold on power. No conception of individual autonomy arose. The individual was, at most, an element of his community; at least, the chattel of his rulers. While Western society was developing an ethic of risk and reward, Russian society, operating always under pressure and at the margins of survivability, preferred the safety of the known, however unsatisfactory, to the perils of change, which promised progress but might as likely deliver disaster.

Marxism-Leninism reinforces traditional Russian authoritarianism, while imposing a twist on its tendency toward risk-avoidance. Leninism provided the adaptation that permitted Marxism to flourish in the Russian political culture. However dedicated Lenin's Bolsheviks may have been to the overthrow of the existing order, their party was quintessentially authoritarian and, therefore, well-suited to the Russian political landscape. As a revolutionary, Lenin could hardly help being a risk-taker. In fact, he was constantly frustrated by the conservatism of many of his fellow revolutionaries, exhorting them to push to the limits of the possible. But in contemporary Soviet society, risk-avoidance has reasserted itself, combining with the traditions of Russian authoritarianism to produce a reliance on control to produce progress while minimizing risk.

The role of authority, the avoidance of risk and the necessity for control are vital to understanding Soviet negotiating behavior. They provide the context within which the specific issues on the table are negotiated, whether the negotiators are two Soviet citizens at the collective market or Soviet and American diplomats in Geneva. Context and content are the elements of any negotiation. Our predispositions lead us to emphasize content and to slight context. The Soviets are the opposite. As a result, we frequently talk past one another. Americans focus on the words, Soviets on the pauses. Societies differ in the degree to which they consider the context of transactions important. We Americans tend to be low-context people. We focus on the substantive issues, on what is being said: "Just the facts, ma'am." The Soviets are considerably higher-context.[7] Issues involving authority, risk, and control, and how they affect the relationship among the negotiating parties, are so important to them that it may be difficult for them to get to the subjects on the agenda until those issues are resolved. In fact, though perhaps not on a conscious level, those often are the real issues to a Soviet negotiator. Americans, impelled by democratic impulses, are disdainful of form, downplay its importance, and seek to divorce it from substance. To a Soviet, form and substance are inextricably linked.

With all of these differences, is it any wonder that our efforts to negotiate with one another frequently break down in mutual bafflement and anger? The greater wonder, perhaps, is that we manage periodically to stumble toward agreements that serve our interests and, more often than not, to live up to them. We can do better than this. We can negotiate more effectively with the Soviets if we understand them better. To understand is not to accept or, even, to condone. It is a tool, like any other form of human knowledge, which hopefully we can use for the good of mankind. The beginning of understanding is willingness—willingness to stand outside of our own framework, to try to see the world through other eyes. Authority, risk-avoidance, control—the sources of a distinctive Soviet negotiating style. What are the elements of that style? How does it manifest itself in Soviet negotiating tactics? What are the historical and ideological roots of this negotiating behavior? Once we have addressed these questions, we can turn our attention to the contemporary Soviet Union and the phenomenon of Mikhail Gorbachev. What is changing in the Soviet Union today, and what remains the same? For our specific purposes here, we need to look at how authority, risk-avoidance, and control are viewed in contemporary Soviet society, for changes in these core concepts could effect major changes in Soviet negotiating behavior.

Finally, what does all of this mean for us? What are the elements of an effective American negotiating strategy? There is no requirement that, having understood the Soviet negotiating style, we adapt our own to it. On the contrary—that style arises out of Soviet values, many of which are antithetical to our own. And we must not delude ourselves that many of the world's intractable problems are going to dissolve before a more informed, more coherent approach to dealing with the Soviet Union. Our responsibility is to do the best we can on the things we can affect. Two of those things are our understanding of the Soviet Union and our own negotiating behavior.

CHAPTER 2

CHAMELEONS, SAUSAGES, AND SOVIET NEGOTIATING STYLE

> Ty nachalnik, ya duryak; ya nachalnik, ty duryak. [You're the boss, and I'm an idiot; I'm the boss, and you're an idiot.]
>
> — Russian saying

HIERARCHY

SOVIET RESTAURANTS ARE NOT KNOWN EITHER FOR THEIR culinary accomplishments or for their variety. But, until the recent arrival of co-operatives, they were the only game in town. As a diplomat serving in Moscow, or as a visiting tourist, you may find yourself planning an evening out at one of them. The Aragvi, for example, has been the site of some notable meetings. Imagine yourself driving up to the Aragvi one evening. You have phoned ahead for reservations. For a long time, if you were an American diplomat, you would also have carried with you a letter to the restaurant on embassy letterhead, embossed with the embassy seal, asserting that you were indeed American diplomat so-and-so for whom a reservation had been made for that evening. One notable accomplishment of the 1980 Olympics in Moscow was the dropping of that requirement, but, with or without the letter, you would run into a situation something like the following.

As you get out of your car, you notice that the door to the restaurant is closed and that there is a line of people waiting outside. There is one thing you need to understand straight off. If you get into that line, your chances of getting fed are slim to none. So, armed with the knowledge that you have a reservation, you feign not to notice the line, march boldly up to the door, and turn the knob. The door is locked. Looking through the window, you notice that an elderly man in some sort of uniform is sitting in a chair about twenty yards from the door. His back is turned to the door. You knock. No response from the elderly gentleman. You knock louder. Still no response. Surely he must have heard your second knock, which was as loud as you could make it without seeming rude and peremptory. What do you do now?

You may not know it, but you have begun a negotiation with a Soviet doorman. Thus far, it has been typical of transactions that go on between Soviets all over the country countless times each day. How you handle it from this point will determine whether you eat in the Aragvi tonight. Your choices are to get back into your car and drive away, to slink back into the line, to continue to knock politely, or to change your style. I advise the latter. Making a careful judgement of how much force it will take to break the window of the door, you should pound on it repeatedly with just a bit less force. If you are persistent, this kind of pounding will attract the doorman's attention—and his wrath. He will storm over to the door, call you a hooligan, and threaten to have you arrested if you don't get lost. You should ignore his words, tell him roughly that you have a reservation, that you are a foreigner and a damned important diplomat to boot, and that if he doesn't get this bloody door open right now he is going to have the Foreign Ministry and the entire Soviet bureaucracy landing on him like a ton of bricks (or as close as you can come to this with your less than perfect command of Russian—form triumphs over content here).

Without further ado, the doorman unlocks the door and ushers you inside, assuring you that he did not realize that you had a reservation. Evidencing no sign of the fact that you have just been shouting at one another, he politely escorts you to the cloakroom, points out the entrance to the dining room, and heads back to the door to give a tongue-lashing to some unfortunates outside who, having observed your style of gaining entrance, are assaying a more timid version of the same. Having disposed decisively of them, he heads back to his chair, passing you on the way with a friendly, man-to-man comment about the uncultured types outside. At this point you can either condescend barely to notice him or respond in kind with a friendly remark about what a tough job he has. Either way you are in, although the alternatives have vastly different implications for the nature of any further transactions, as we shall see.

The successful negotiation you have just conducted illuminates some characteristic features of the Soviet negotiating style. The most important of these is the highly developed Russian sense of whether the transaction in which they are engaged entails hierarchical relationships or not and the vastly different expectations that accompany the two kinds of transaction. Ronald Hingley, in his excellent study, *The Russian Mind,* illustrates the characteristic by reference to Chekhov's story, "Fat and Thin." Two old school friends meet accidentally after many years. While exchanging warm and hearty greetings, they discover that the fat one has reached the higher echelons of the Table of Ranks, while the thin friend is still consigned to the lower reaches. As soon as this becomes clear, "friendly communion abruptly gives way to condescension on one side and awed sycophancy on the other."[1] Hingley sees the tendency for a single individual or group to alternate between one extreme position and its opposite, or even, somehow, to occupy two or more seemingly mutually exclusive positions simultaneously as a Russian specialty.[2] Russians' expectations of behavior in relations that are based on authority differ glaringly from their expectations of personal relationships. "In all relations which are not defined as leader and led, superordinate and subordinate . . . Russians . . . demand the most absolute equality in their personal relationships. It would appear that Russians do not conceive of any intermediate positions: there is either complete equality, or complete superordination and subordination."[3] They are thus, Hingley argues, doubly polarized; first between wholly authority-free and wholly authority-dominated situations; second, within the latter only, between total domination and total submissiveness.[4]

Let's revisit the Aragvi, bearing what we have just learned in mind. The doorman clearly perceives the relationship between him and persons trying to get into the restaurant as hierarchical, with him in the dominant position. The Russians (or acculturated non-Russian Soviet citizens) standing in line outside share that perception. They are in a submissive posture, hoping at some point to be able to wheedle their way into the restaurant, perhaps if a few more diners are needed to meet the nightly quota. You convinced the doorman that you were in the position of authority, not him; he instantly adjusted his behavior accordingly, and with no apparent resentment. After ensuring that you were well taken care of, he went back to the door, reasserted his authority over those who remained and went out of his way to attempt to draw you into a we/them alliance with him against the "uncultured types" outside. Why the latter gesture? Having been convinced that as long as the relationship with you remained a hierarchical one, he would be on the subordinate side, the doorman sought to shift his relationship with you onto the personal level, where expectations of complete equality would prevail. Depending on your response, he would either have been emboldened to continue the effort or would have accepted his relegation to the subordinate category.

The Aragvi visit was hypothetical, but not purely. It was a composite of numerous similar exchanges the author had during a three-year tour at the American embassy in Moscow and during several subsequent visits to the country. Does it suggest that boorishness is the way to get things done with the Soviets? Of course not. But it does suggest that if you want to get things done with them it behooves you to be sensitive to how they perceive the nature of the relationship and, if necessary, to adjust your behavior accordingly. As one student of cross-cultural communication put it:

> People anywhere in the world master hundreds of what we came to call "situational dialects" which are used in specific situational frames. . . . One should not only speak to people in their language but in situations with which they are familiar and feel at ease, and which are appropriate to the transaction. . . . The bus driver, the counterman, and the man in the control tower all appreciate it if you use their particular [situational dialects] properly.[5]

Likewise for the doorman at the Aragvi. Americans are generally uncomfortable with the kind of behavior I have described. While we often pay lip service to the idea that Russians are different from us, this is an area in which our own outlook is so thoroughly ingrained that it is difficult for us to step outside of it. Unwittingly, we impose our frame of reference on the situation and on our negotiating counterparts. I am convinced that we need a strong sense of our differences in this area if we are to negotiate successfully with them and avoid potentially major mistakes.

It can be argued with some accuracy that a sensitivity to authority relationships is characteristic of the population of any authoritarian state. Yet even among such populations the Russians seem *primus inter pares*. And some careful observers believe that, while most authoritarian states have been gradually evolving toward less arbitrariness, the history of Russia is one of movement in fits and starts toward ever greater authoritarianism.[6] Authoritarian institutions have been a dominant leitmotif of the Russian political culture, a theme we will revisit when we look more closely at the political culture. For now, we need to develop a fuller understanding of how this trait impacts on the Soviet negotiating style.

Observers differ on when and why Russians developed their characteristic view of authority relationships. Contemporary writers on Soviet society, from Robert C. Tucker to Stephen F. Cohen, agree that major aspects of the Soviet outlook can be traced to Tsarist times. Tucker highlights his view that "the Soviet political mind . . . is not simply Soviet; in many ways it is a Russian political mind."[7] Cohen considers the Tsarist past an important part of the legacy that must be understood in evaluating the Soviet experience.[8] But for a detailed treatment of this legacy, it is generally necessary to turn to some of the older writers, whose focus was more on the Russian past than on the Soviet present.

Some of those writers see the reign of Peter the Great as a watershed. Nicholas Vakar argued that the immediate historical background of Soviet society was the history of the Muscovite state—usually dated from the fourteenth century through the formation of the empire in 1721. He believed that during the time of Peter and of Patriarch Nikon, Great Russian history essentially divided into two, a history of the small sophisticated urban upper classes and that of the immense rural mass.[9] Tsardom did not condition the population to accept Bolshevik authoritarianism. Rather, Russian habits of obedience have been the cause of political autocracy. The autocrat was the image of authority that each peasant child learned to accept in the family, where his first and most durable political concepts were formed.

Sociologist Dinko Tomasic argued that the interests of the Church, the State, and the landlord were joined with the establishment of serfdom in the sixteenth century in "strengthening the power of the Father and of the village elders and sponsoring in the peasant family and in the village community, dominance-submission relationships, absolute power and dependence, blind obedience and self-abnegation."[10] The Bolshevik revolution, led by a faction of the upper classes and bearing the strong influence of Western ideas, was itself subordinated to a second revolution from within—a revolution under Stalin in which the values and expectations of peasant society, hearkening back to the Muscovite state, became dominant in the Soviet Union.[11] The Russian philosopher Nicholas Berdyaev shared this view, at least in substantial part,[12] while Hingley traced the roots of Russian authoritarianism even further back—to the period of the Tatar yoke beginning in 1240.

> Before a Russian prince or princeling could ascend his throne he was compelled to journey to Tatar headquarters at Saray on the lower Volga, there to make obeisance to the Khan and to undergo various humiliations before receiving, if he found favor, a patent to rule. The system put a premium on extreme sycophancy toward the Khan, combined with extreme treachery toward competing princelings—a process of natural selection which only the most cunning, ambitious and obsequious could hope to survive.[13]

Hingley and Vakar may both have been right. Muscovite society's initial expectations about the nature of authority relationships might have grown out of the prince's dealings with the Khan. Just as the prince groveled before the Khan, so the rest of Muscovite society groveled before the prince, and so on down through society to the humblest peasant. The split between the educated and upper classes and the peasants caused these expectations to be frozen in Russian society until the late nineteenth century, a period during which most of Europe was slowly evolving toward a different set of expectations.

Historical explanations do not exhaust the theories about Russians' attitudes toward authority. The "swaddling hypothesis" was an early attempt to bring psychoanalytic techniques to bear on the Russian psyche. The sociologist Geoffrey Gorer found in the Russian practice of tightly binding infants, to the point that they could not move their limbs, a possible source of Russian expectations of superordination/subordination in authority relationships, as well as "a general tendency to 'test' authority; if it is not firm and consistent, it will be first disregarded and then cast off."[14] Drawing primarily on historical material, Tomasic reached a similar conclusion about the Russian tendency to test authority: "in disputes, if the settlement be distinct and pre-emptory, he will be satisfied, whether the sentence is favorable or unfavorable, wise or unwise. If there be hesitation, he immediately becomes intractable."[15]

While each of these theories is fascinating in itself, their importance for understanding the Soviet negotiating style is that they converge around the same point. Whether because of the Tatar influence, the influence of peasant society, the practice of swaddling infants, or for some other reason, Russians are acutely conscious of hierarchical issues in a relationship, and their expectations of behavior differ dramatically depending on how they see those issues in any given relationship. This tendency is not simply one of historical interest. In discussing the contemporary Soviet Union, former *New York Times* Moscow correspondent Hedrick Smith writes that "for Russians the instinctive question is: 'who is stronger and who weaker'; . . . any relation becomes a test of strength." Smith draws on a number of experiences from his own time in Moscow to illustrate the point. "If a person bumps into someone or has an accident, he is ready to stand up for himself," a young professional woman told him. "But if he finds out the other one is some official, say, from the District Party Committee, the next moment he is bowing and fawning and trying to avoid trouble." "Put a Russian in charge of a little plot of ground or a doorway somewhere," a scientist related, "and he will use his meager authority over that spot to make life hard on others."[16]

The other side of this dominance/submission struggle, however, is a concern for equality. When two students of Soviet negotiating behavior conclude that "the Soviets are very sensitive to being treated as equals of the United States,"[17] the inference might be drawn that what was being discussed was some variant of diplomatic "face." That would be wrong. What is primarily involved here is a gut-level reaction to the fear that the alternative to a relationship of equality is one of hierarchy in which the Soviet Union would be dominated. If that is the alternative, the "instinctive" Russian reaction is to attempt to put the relationship on a different footing. Robert Jervis gives an interesting example of how Bismarck played on this Russian tendency for some major stakes.

> After Germany's support for Austria in the Balkan crisis of 1877 had alienated Russia, Bismarck sought to bring her back into the alliance. To do this, he did not make overtures to the tsar, but instead made a pact with Austria to show Russia that the path of hostility toward Germany was not an easy one. Bismarck made Russia choose between friendship on German terms and a high level of hostility by fore-closing the course that Russia preferred. This policy was successful (i.e., Russia returned friendship for German hostility) because Russia saw how much harm would come to her if Bismarck turned sharply against her.[18]

It is far from clear, however, that it would be a natural Russian tendency to opt for a relationship of equality over one in which the Russian was the dominant partner. A recent Soviet emigré with whom I discussed these issues shared the following revealing anecdote. While at the university, he shared a room with another Soviet, and the two became good friends. The roommate was subsequently selected to be on the institution's Komsomol committee. Within two weeks, the roommate's behavior toward his friend had changed to that of a boss.

Robert Bathurst has done a series of negotiating simulations using Soviet emigrés to play the Soviet parts and Americans to play the American. He has been struck by the different styles the two delegations demonstrated in choosing their leaders. The Americans would typically discuss and agonize over the issue for hours and would frequently wind up choosing as leader a person not particularly experienced in U.S.-Soviet negotiations or knowledgeable about the Soviet Union. The Soviets, on the other hand, did not go through a selection process. They all "knew" on the basis of their commonly accepted standards of status or authority who the leader would be without discussion and acted accordingly. An American who has been active in negotiating private exchange agreements with the Soviet Union recalls discussing with his Soviet counterpart one day the American understanding of consensus and how we go about changing it. After explaining the process of changing a consensus among Americans, he asked how Soviets do it. "We try to change the leader's mind," was the reply.[19]

Stalin's treatment of Harriman and Beaverbrook takes on a different meaning when seen in this light. From what we know of Stalin, no one could have recognized more acutely than he, or have been more uncomfortable with, the fact that he desperately needed U.S. and British material help to survive. He was weak, potentially friendless, and under all-out attack. But his goal was not simply to get as much material support as he could. It was equally to establish that although he was the demandeur, he would not be dominated. His harsh verbal attacks were a classic example of a Russian attempt, by verbal intimidation, to reverse what the Russian himself sees as an objectively inferior position. It can easily be argued that this was nothing more than smart negotiating tactics in the circumstances, that any good negotiator, in any culture would have tried similar tactics. Where, then, is the distinctively Russian characteristic? The argument has some merit, but also misses some important points. The point is not whether Stalin was a good negotiator. History can judge that, and will probably judge that he did well at aggrandizing his country's power and influence, albeit at frightful cost. But why did he choose this particular negotiating style? Given U.S. and British interest in helping him, a fact he could hardly have been unaware of, a variety of other approaches might have reached the same goal. The simple explanation is that he chose the negotiating style with which he was comfortable and which his own experience had shown him was likely to achieve his goals. Whatever questions of material aid might have been on the table, the key underlying issue was the relationship being established among the parties. He had to show that he would not be dominated, despite his objectively weak position. Being Stalin, the alternative of a relationship of equality was not one that had great appeal for him.

A clear understanding of the importance of the Russian perception of hierarchy might have led Harriman and Beaverbrook to expect that their initial meetings with Stalin would not be about three allies attempting to find the best way of overcoming a common adversary, but about who was going to be dominant and who subordinant among the allies themselves. Would their negotiating behavior have been changed thereby? Perhaps not, given how overriding were fears of a separate Stalin/Hitler peace. Moreover, we should not forget that two lower-ranking negotiators were dealing with a *de facto,* if not *de jure,* chief of state, never a situation conducive to equality of verbal fireworks. At a minimum, they might have been less plunged in gloom after their second meeting with Stalin. But more importantly, having a better grasp on what Stalin's behavior was about might have led them to stand more firmly on obtaining some quids for U.S. and British support. We know from Harriman's memoirs that President Roosevelt was unhappy that nothing had been obtained on the issue of religious freedom. Nothing substantive was obtainable, of course, given the nature of the Soviet system, but something more in the way of a public posture, which is what the president's political needs were, might have been achieved. After the second meeting, the subject was not raised with Stalin again. On more strictly military matters, the Soviet refusal to supply information to support their requests for materiel might have been overcome, thus establishing a sounder basis for cooperation throughout the war.

If, as we have suggested and as we shall try to demonstrate later in more detail, Soviet sensitivity to hierarchy derives from deep roots in the political culture and is reinforced by major aspects of Marxism-Leninism,[20] we should not be too quick to see Stalin's negotiating behavior as uniquely Stalinesque, or as simply effective tactics. An underlying issue for Soviet negotiators, particularly in the early stages of a negotiating relationship, may frequently be to determine whether or not the relationship is going to be hierarchical and, if it is, who is dominant. The tough, aggressive behavior that Westerners have noted as characteristic of some Soviet negotiators may, as in Stalin's case, be part of an effort to reverse an objectively weak position, or it may be designed to test the strength and determination of the adversary. Gorer argued that the expectation of complete dominance/submission in a relationship coexists with a general tendency to "test" authority. If it is not firm and consistent, it will be first disregarded and then cast off.[21]

Russians frequently test one another in the early stages of a relationship. It is not uncommon for two Russians to get into an argument shortly after they have gotten to know one another. If both argue long and hard for their respective points of view, however the argument comes out, their friendship has the possibility of deepening. If, however, one gives in too easily, they are not likely ever to become friends. The winner will not respect the loser for having given in so readily. Perhaps more importantly, he will not trust him. How can a man's word be good, if his mind can be changed that easily? And if I can change his mind that easily, so can someone else.[22] A Russian expects another Russian to have strong opinions, but at the same time understands completely the difference between expressing them in a situation involving hierarchy and one that does not, a characteristic that Americans often consider hypocritical (a subject to which we will return in the section below on mood changes). But what seems in private conversation to an American to be a reasonable respect for the other person's opinion, may appear to a Russian as, at best, wishy-washy, at worst, contemptible. In referring to a man she didn't like, a Russian woman said, "He has no opinions of his own. . . . He is like a sausage: what you stuff him with—this he carries around."[23] Let us allow Lenin to have the last words on this: "Every man with convictions . . . writes 'provocatively' and expresses his views strongly. Only those who are accustomed to sit between two stools lack 'provocativeness'."[24] "I love to hear people scold—it means they know what they are doing and have a line to follow."[25]

General John R. Deane's memoirs of his service in Moscow during World War II give several colorful illustrations of the early testing he experienced by his Soviet counterparts. His first call on Soviet Chief of Staff General Antonov was particularly striking:

> I have never had a reception of more studied coldness. There was not the slightest spark of cordiality as he shook hands and asked me to be seated. [Antonov then went on to berate Deane about U.S. efforts in Italy.] By this time I had become

thoroughly chilled except under the collar and recited a few plain truths. I pointed out that we had liquidated Rommel's forces in Africa, forced Italy out of the war, taken on a second front in the Pacific without the help of our great Red Ally, and, at the same time, run the gauntlet of the German submarine menace to deliver supplies to Russia. With that he asked me if I had any further business, indicating that our conference was concluded. This time when we shook hands there were two pairs of eyes which belied any cordiality in the process. My subsequent meetings with General Antonov were extremely pleasant, and I attained the utmost admiration for his intelligence and ability.[26]

Deane instinctively took the right approach in responding to the testing by Antonov. If he had not stood up for himself, and his country, if he had bent over backward to be "reasonable," his subsequent meetings with Antonov would not have been "extremely pleasant."

The chronological gap from World War II to the START talks is roughly forty years, a momentous four decades in both Soviet and world history. Several members of the U.S. START delegation have suggested to the author that issues of national negotiating style may play a less important role in these negotiations than in some others. Their reasoning is that both delegations are very closely tied by the negotiating instructions from their capitals. Moreover, since the issues involved are the most vital aspects of national security, the outcome will depend almost exclusively on a very cold-eyed calculation of national interests and risk. This may be true in terms of the bottom line of any agreement, but style may still play a significant role in the negotiating process, including on such hardly inconsequential issues as how long it takes to get an agreement.

It seems clear that at least some Soviet delegates to the START talks are highly conscious of hierarchical issues and do test their American counterparts, as the anecdote in the previous chapter illustrated. Americans have also found themselves on the other side of the seniority gap. A former member of the U.S. START delegation of ambassadorial rank who had a Soviet counterpart of lower rank found that the two were never able to establish a comfortable working relationship. The Soviet behaved very deferentially toward the American but was clearly uncomfortable with the relationship and referred several times to how difficult the situation was for him because of their disparity in ranks. He was stiff and awkward even on social occasions, except those he attended with his wife, the daughter of a very high-ranking Party official. When his wife was present he was relaxed and comfortable, evidently basking in the reflected glow of her father's rank.[27]

Jonathan Dean had some revealing things to say on this subject about Soviet behavior at the Mutual and Balanced Force Reduction (MBFR) talks in Vienna.

Soviet negotiators in the MBFR talks maintained very good self-control except when they considered . . . that an effort was being made to pressure the Soviet position or that the Soviet Union was not being given adequate respect as a country. Such suspicions were often accompanied by emotional outbursts (sometimes contrived for tactical impact, but more often quite genuine) to the effect that the Soviet Union was not a defeated power and that it categorically refused to negotiate under ultimatums.[28]

There may be a tendency at this point to consider Soviet sensitivity to issues of hierarchy to operate only at the margins of international negotiations, or only in marginal negotiations. This reasoning would argue that perhaps in the Stalin era, when the age-old Russian traits of insecurity, inferiority, and suspicion of foreigners were operating at historically high levels, issues of hierarchy lay close to the surface in all international negotiations, but in the modern era, in dealing with a Soviet Union that has long-since attained nuclear parity with the United States, such issues are much less important. It is never easy to determine the precise mix of motivations and pressures that drive a negotiating partner or adversary. And in the case of the Soviet Union, cultural and political differences, as well as the Soviet concern for secrecy, multiply the differences. In any particular negotiation, the task of the statesman, and of the scholar, is to make the best possible judgment about those issues. The inherent imprecision of the task is what adds the element of art to the elements of skill and knowledge necessary to the effective negotiator.

In dealing with the Soviet Union, any negotiator who is not actively aware of hierarchical issues and considering whether they are an underlying element in Soviet negotiating behavior runs the risk of misunderstanding some fundamental elements of the actual negotiating process. The Cuban missile crisis is an excellent example in point. It is almost universally considered the most dangerous crisis ever to occur between the two nuclear superpowers, the closest the world ever came to all-out nuclear war. Those who lived through those days in October 1962 are unlikely to forget them. I was a college freshman at the time, recently out of the army. I remember an acute sense of fear, anguish, and powerlessness; a belief that the world stood on the edge of catastrophe; a conviction that at any moment I might see a mushroom cloud going up over my city; a realization that if that occurred I would probably die, but that even if I survived it would be to live in a devastated world. And I remember the relief when Khrushchev announced that the missiles would be taken out of Cuba, and the pride in my country and its president for having acted with both firmness and moderation in meeting the challenge the missiles represented.

The nature of the crisis and the feelings it aroused account for the fact that it is perhaps the most studied single event in contemporary history. Numerous memoirs by participants highlight the crisis, analyze the U.S. decision-making process and detail the memoirist's own role.[29] Scholars have dissected the crisis from a variety of analytical frameworks.[30] In brief, the crisis arose from a Soviet decision, apparently taken in May 1962 to place sixty-four intermediate-range missiles and medium-range missiles in Cuba. The work was carried out in secret. Senator Keating's charges from July onward that missiles were being sent to Cuba tended to be dismissed as politically motivated, but reports began to multiply in September and early October. The Soviet Union unequivocally denied at the highest levels that it was placing any offensive weapons in Cuba and clearly understood that any missile capable of reaching U.S. soil and carrying a nuclear weapon would be considered, by definition, offensive by the United States. The Soviets have explained their action as a response to the U.S. threat to Cuba, as a means of deterring an American invasion of the island.[31] American observers, aware of the overwhelming U.S. superiority in intercontinental ballistic missiles and of Khrushchev's efforts to hold down the military budget, believe that a major motivation was to find a quick and cheap way of redressing the Soviet Union's strategic inferiority. Pulling off such a bold coup would have had a variety of political benefits as well: casting doubt on U.S. will and determination, potentially dividing the Western alliance, giving the Soviet Union a psychological edge in other areas of competition throughout the world.

Clearly, successfully installing and maintaining the missiles would have brought the Soviet Union a broad variety of military and political advantages in its competition with the United States. The potential benefits are not in doubt. The real question is why the Soviet leadership, and particularly Nikita Khrushchev, believed it could get away with such an audacious move. The missile decision stands out in Soviet post-1945 foreign policy as a uniquely high-risk endeavor. The Soviet leaders have shown themselves to be extremely cautious about military forays beyond their borders, particularly those that would carry a risk of confrontation with the United States. Their actions in Hungary, Czechoslovakia, and Afghanistan demonstrate more their intense insecurity about developments in their Eastern European empire and on their other borders than a penchant for far-flung military adventurism.

The sources of Soviet miscalculation lay in U.S. actions toward Cuba and interactions with the Soviet Union in the period leading up to the May 1962 decision. The poor planning, inept execution, and insufficient U.S. support early in the Kennedy administration for the Bay of Pigs invasion of Cuba seems to have made a great impression on the Soviet leadership. According to a member of the National Security Council staff at the time, Kennedy's efforts to get a summit meeting with Khrushchev had gone unanswered prior to the Bay of Pigs. Quickly thereafter, the Soviets replied affirmatively and made arrangements for the June 1961 Vienna summit.[32]

By all accounts, the Kennedy/Khrushchev meeting in Vienna was an extremely difficult one. Kennedy's objective was to convince Khrushchev that the United States and the Soviet Union could work together to resolve common problems.[33] Khrushchev was tough, unyielding, brutal, threatening.[34] Transcripts of the first day's meetings convinced Kennedy's advisors that the Soviet first secretary was seeking to humiliate the president, that he believed that this young, privileged scion of a wealthy family could not compete in the same league with a Soviet leader who had fought his way to the top during, and had survived, the Stalin era.[35] The issues on the agenda for the two leaders included, on the first day, military security and Berlin and, on the second, Laos. But just as Kennedy had an underlying objective for the meetings, so, it appears, did Khrushchev. His was to establish that his relationship with Kennedy was not one of equality, but of hierarchy, and that he, Khrushchev, was the dominant party in the relationship.

The failure of the two leaders to communicate was not only a case of conflicting objectives, it was also a classic example of low- and high-context communications and communicators failing to understand one another.[36] Kennedy's message was primarily in what he said, that the two countries needed to find a way to work together. Khrushchev, operating from a high-context framework, believed that what was important was not the words, but the meaning of Kennedy's behavior in the context of the relationship. Kennedy was weak and capable of being dominated. Kennedy, expecting a transaction based primarily on the positions stated by the two leaders, failed to appreciate the even greater importance of Khrushchev's objectives in terms of the broader relationship issues on the latter's underlying agenda.

Kennedy and his advisors convinced themselves that the president's more assertive performance during the second day's discussions of Laos demonstrated to the Soviet leader that he was not going to cow the president. Soviet behavior during the rest of that summer suggests otherwise. Construction of the Berlin wall and resumption of atmospheric nuclear testing continued the aggressive international posture that Khrushchev had displayed at Vienna. After close study of Soviet political infighting during this period, some authors have suggested that the Berlin wall and nuclear testing decisions were the result of a more hard-line faction in the Soviet leadership pressuring Khrushchev.[37] Evidently such major international decisions would have been subject to debate within the Politburo and might well have been used by one or the other faction in its political struggles. There are rarely satisfactory single-factor explanations of Soviet behavior. An understanding of the domestic context of Soviet foreign policy is essential. At the same time, how Soviet internal struggles manifest themselves on the international scene is very likely to be affected by the Soviet leaders' perceptions of the opportunities and risks, of the correlation of forces. Moreover, we should be aware and cautious about a Western tendency to attribute aggressive Soviet foreign policy actions to sources other than the top Soviet leader. This has been done with every Soviet leader, including Stalin, and, while it could be true in specific cases, generally contradicts what we know about how the Soviet system operates. There is little in Khrushchev's background, personality, or behavior to suggest that he would have been averse to aggressive foreign policy moves.

The Soviet decision to put missiles into Cuba, the belief that the United States would ultimately acquiesce, can scarcely be understood except in the context of a fundamental miscalculation about U.S. will. Charles "Chip" Bohlen, former U.S. ambassador to the Soviet Union, attended the first meeting of the Executive Committee, or Excom, as it came to be known, before departing to take up his duties as ambassador to France (Ambassador Llewellyn Thompson subsequently replaced him as the one Soviet expert on the Excom). He saw it as a challenge that required a firm U.S. response, referring in discussions to the Lenin adage:

"If you strike steel, pull back; if you strike mush, push forward." Some of the U.S. leaders who were on the seventeen-member Executive Committee, an ad hoc body established by Kennedy to handle the crisis, saw the Soviet decision as a fundamental misestimation, or underestimation of Kennedy.[38] Kennedy's own initial reaction—"He can't do this to me."—showed a gut-level understanding that he was facing a personal challenge from the Soviet leader. But the evidence for this is more than circumstantial or inferential. Arkady Shevchenko, the highest-ranking Soviet official ever to defect to the United States, says that Khrushchev planned, by installing the missiles rapidly and secretly, to confront the United States with a *fait accompli,* which the United States would not dare to counter for fear of unleashing nuclear war.

> To a substantial degree, such premises were based on Khrushchev's assessment of Kennedy's personal qualities as President and statesman. After the Vienna summit, Khrushchev concluded that Kennedy would accept almost anything to avoid nuclear war. The lack of confidence the President displayed during both the Bay of Pigs invasion and the Berlin crisis further confirmed this view.[39]

Shevchenko had occasion to hear Khrushchev hold forth personally on his view of Kennedy. At the end of 1961, while Shevchenko was attending a meeting in the office of Khrushchev's personal assistants, the Soviet leader entered and "immediately began to lecture us about Kennedy's 'wishy-washy' behavior." Khrushchev concluded: " 'I know for certain that Kennedy doesn't have a strong backbone, nor, generally speaking, does he have the courage to stand up to a serious challenge.' "[40]

There was no disagreement among American leaders about U.S. objectives in this crisis. The missiles had to be gotten out of Cuba at the least possible risk of war between the United States and the Soviet Union. The Excom considered three options: a diplomatic offensive focusing on the United Nations; a blockade; or a preemptive air strike to destroy the sites. Only the latter two appear to have gotten substantial consideration. After days of intensive debate, the Excom voted eleven to six to recommend to the president imposition of a "quarantine" on Cuba—a blockade by another name to satisfy concerns about avoiding a U.S. action that under international law would constitute a *de facto* declaration of war. The rest is history.

Much of the writing on U.S. decision-making in the crisis has focused on the debate between "hawks" and "doves." Even allowing for the utility of short-hand, this terminology appears particularly inapt in this case. A recent reprise of the crisis has suggested that owls (presumably as in "wise as an") be added to the Excom aviary.[41] The real "dove" option, a diplomatic campaign to get the missiles removed, was put forward by Adlai Stevenson. The Excom as a whole seems to have accepted that this response would be inadequate and ineffectual. Both "hawks" and "owls" accepted that some military response by the United States would be needed to demonstrate the seriousness with which the United

States viewed the missile installation. There were a variety of arguments against a preemptive strike. Robert Kennedy was particularly concerned about its morality. There was confusion about how much assurance the military could give that the missiles would be destroyed. The president believed it essential not to humiliate Khrushchev, to give him a way out of the crisis short of military action. He was convinced that if backed into a corner from which there was no alternative but a humiliating retreat, Khrushchev would have to react, as Kennedy would have under similar circumstances.[42] There was grave concern that the Soviets might react by challenging the exposed Western position in Berlin.[43]

The blockade alternative was far from risk-free. None of the missile sites was yet operational at the time they were discovered. While the crisis played itself out, several became operational, placing the United States in actual jeopardy of an attack that before had been only a prospective possibility. For the purposes of this study, however, the key question is not the strictly military one. The U.S. objective—to get the missiles out with the least risk of war—was appropriate. But the appropriate U.S. actions to attain that objective depended fundamentally on a correct assessment of Soviet motivations and objectives. The recent reanalysis of the crisis by James G. Blight, Joseph S. Nye, Jr., and David A. Welch trenchantly makes this point. The authors agree that knowing one's enemy, his view of a crisis and what is at stake, "largely determines which strategies are appropriate and effective and which are not." Misinterpreting these factors can be dangerous because "the same strategies would elicit very different responses and would carry with them very different risks" if our analysis of an adversary's view of a crisis differed substantially from the adversary's actual view.[44]

We have argued here that the Soviet belief that this very risky, but potentially highly rewarding, action could succeed stemmed from a mistaken perception of Kennedy. Khrushchev considered Kennedy to be weak-willed and easily dominated. He believed that he had dominated him at Vienna and that this had established the basic nature of the relationship. The military correlation of forces might be all to the favor of the United States, but more than military might entered into the overall correlation of forces. The Soviet Union had a unique opportunity to utilize its position of moral dominance to effect a far-reaching change in the correlation of world forces, at manageable risk and at low expense. The risk was manageable first, because of Kennedy and second, because the only threat to Soviet vital interests—a U.S. attack on the homeland—was several steps removed from the initial Soviet action, emplacing the missiles. The Soviet leadership could act to ensure that threat never materialized, by acting at any of the intervening steps to neutralize it. Kennedy's concern to maintain control of the process was more than matched by that of the Soviet leadership, which was pursuing the optimizing strategy that Alexander George has discussed, but with no intention of exposing the Soviet Union to a U.S. attack.[45]

If, indeed, Khrushchev in particular, or the Soviet leadership in general, believed this assessment, believed that Kennedy's concern about the dangers of nuclear war was so overwhelming that he would shrink from a major Soviet challenge, then it was vitally important for the United States in this crisis to change that perception. A tentative U.S. response would reinforce that misperception and encourage the Soviets to escalate the confrontation, to force the United States to face the prospect of nuclear war. This would have been totally compatible with a Soviet determination not to allow itself under any circumstances actually to be drawn into war over this issue. By this standard, as by many others, a response that relied solely on diplomatic persuasion would have been totally ineffectual, in fact, dangerous in reinforcing Soviet misperceptions. The Soviet response to the quarantine suggests, to this observer, that it also was interpreted as indicating U.S. weakness and uncertainty. Khrushchev rejected any thought of compromise, was hard-line and threatening. To ensure that there was no mistaking the message, the Soviets conveyed variants of it via three different channels: a message from Khrushchev to Kennedy, a statement in Pravda, and a meeting between Khrushchev and some U.S. businessmen who happened to be in Moscow. Soviet ships continued toward Cuba, and a rush effort to complete the missile sites began.

The Soviet decision several days later not to challenge the U.S. blockade was equivocal. Round-the-clock work on the missile sites continued. The U.S.-Soviet confrontation continued to escalate as the Soviet missile sites became operational and the United States positioned an invasion force in southern Florida. Soviet agreement to remove the missiles came only at the eleventh hour, and only when they were convinced that an invasion of Cuba was imminent. Only unmistakable evidence of U.S. willingness to invade Cuba, despite the fact that Soviet missiles on the island were now targeted on American cities, convinced the Soviet leadership that it had erred fundamentally in its assessment of the situation. Once it was convinced, once it had made the necessary reassessment, it quickly took the steps necessary to abate the crisis while trying, as would be expected, to extract whatever marginal advantage it could still gain.

U.S. actions did not, in fact, correspond with the president's intention not to back Khrushchev into a corner, not to humiliate him, but to leave him a way out. The United States defined this situation as a U.S.-Soviet confrontation and slowly, painstakingly, and before the entire world, turned the screws on Khrushchev until he had the choice of standing by and watching Cuba be invaded and occupied by the United States, declaring war, or retreating. The Soviets chose to retreat and, despite their efforts to put the best face on it, were in fact humiliated. As one put it: "You will never do this to us again."[46]

Was there a lower risk alternative for the United States? Yes, there was. A preemptive air strike against the still uncompleted missile sites would have forced an immediate Soviet reassessment of the misjudgements that led them to undertake installation of the missiles. Instead of a U.S.-Soviet confrontation, the issue would have been defined as a U.S.-Cuban confrontation. The United States, both before and since, has confronted Soviet Third World allies without bringing the world close to nuclear war, or even, for that matter, noticeably embarassing the Soviet leadership. A message to Khrushchev could have told him of the strike and its limited goals, of the determination not to allow completion of the sites; it could have reassured him that the United States did not want to turn this into a U.S.-Soviet confrontation and did not intend to invade Cuba; it could have warned him of the dangers of turning this into a U.S.-Soviet confrontation, as would surely happen if any missiles were launched against the United States and could result from unwise Soviet steps in other parts of the world, particularly Berlin. The Soviets, having no intention of putting their own territory at risk in this situation, would have been only too happy to trumpet this as an unprovoked U.S. attack on a defenseless Third World country and extract whatever propaganda value they could. The U.S. fear that they would retaliate against Berlin was misplaced. The Soviets fully realized the dangers of Berlin; in fact, as the crisis unfolded, the Soviet U.N. ambassador said his country was not going to be drawn into that American trap.[47] Although Soviet citizens would have died in the air strikes, that would not have affected the Soviet response. It is doubtful that they would even have publicly acknowledged the presence of their nationals at the sites.

What of the morality of U.S. air strikes, a subject which by all accounts preoccupied Robert Kennedy? One person, an American U-2 pilot, died during the Cuban missile crisis. Many more would have died in preemptive air strikes. The overriding U.S. objective was to get the missiles out at the least risk of nuclear war. U.S. actions must be judged against that objective. The author of this book has spent his professional career as a diplomat, driven by the conviction that solutions other than violence must be found to international conflicts. But statesmanship in this imperfect world admits of few absolutes. The paradox of the Cuban missile crisis is that the least dangerous alternative to handling it would have involved an initial response with a high military component. The most dangerous alternative, the purely diplomatic one, carried the gravest risk for an even higher-level U.S.-Soviet confrontation later. U.S. vacillation, particularly if in the end some or all of the offensive Soviet weapons remained in Cuba, would have further reinforced the belief in the Kremlin that the objective situation, including the nature of U.S. leadership, reduced to manageable proportions the risks of further Soviet foreign policy steps that under other circumstances would have been considered foolhardy. If Cuba had succeeded, Berlin would have been next.

The outcome of the Cuban missile crisis was therefore not as bad as it might have been. The Soviet reassessment that accompanied the crisis resulted in a decrease in confrontations, conclusion of the ABM Treaty, and an improvement in the tenor of relations, which laid the groundwork for detente. But in the humiliation the Soviets suffered lay also the seeds of the destruction of detente. The Soviet determination never again to be so humiliated produced a massive, fifteen-year build-up in strategic weaponry that, with Soviet actions in the Third World during the 1970s, produced a U.S. reaction against detente and a determination to reassert itself in the world. While a Soviet strategic weapons program would have continued in any case during the period, it is questionable whether in the face of competing priorities it would have continued for as long, or been as extensive, absent the remembered humiliation of Cuba.

Hindsight, it may be argued, generally provides better vision, although in this case the author suspects that many readers, accustomed to the conventional interpretation that the United States handled the Cuban missile crisis brilliantly, may question that assumption. But the point of this book is that there are certain characteristics of Soviet negotiating behavior that do not require the benefit of hindsight to consider. Soviet objectives in the crisis can be understood on simple grounds of national interest. Successful installation of the missiles would have produced a range of benefits for Soviet foreign policy objectives. But the Soviet decision to take such a risky step, the assessment that the risks were manageable, that it should depart from its customary low-risk activities at distances beyond those of its Eastern European empire, that the United States could be brought to accept this step with all of its far-reaching consequences, requires something more than simply a calculation of national interests. Nor, despite the scholarship of Jonnsson,[48] is an explanation in terms of Soviet domestic hawk and dove conflicts fully persuasive. In the Cuban missile crisis, the United States was facing expectations of negotiating behavior arising from deep roots in the Russian political culture and reinforced by Leninist tenets. "Chip" Bohlen, in quoting the Lenin adage "If you strike steel, pull back; if you strike mush, push forward," understood this, as perhaps did his replacement as the only Soviet expert on the Excom, Ambassador Thompson. Thompson's participation on the Excom was certainly considered invaluable by the other members.[49] But the implications of this for the U.S. response were not fully grasped. The Americans, knowing that ultimately they would do whatever they had to in order to get the missiles out of Cuba, considered the quarantine an appropriate response, combining the right level of toughness and flexibility. The Soviets saw it as mushy. They probed until they found the steel beneath. And while they probed, the U.S.-Soviet confrontation escalated to unprecedentedly dangerous heights.

In the Cuban missile crisis, the "hawks" were right, but for the wrong reasons. Their primary focus on the military balance in the crisis might have been dangerous if applied to another crisis at another time, when the Soviet analysis of what was at stake differed. The "doves"—and recent information suggests that President Kennedy was a closet dove throughout the crisis[50]—were even more dangerously wrong, since their approach would have virtually assured even further Soviet risk-taking, in situations that could have brought us stumbling into a war that neither side wanted. And the "owls" were not wise but near-sighted and lucky. They brought only one Soviet expert into their inner councils and "found the Soviets almost entirely inscrutable"[51] throughout the crisis. The Soviets were not inscrutable. They were merely different. Instead of considering this possibility, the president and his advisors tried repeatedly to force Soviet actions into an American framework. The actions never fit, to the predictable bafflement of the American decision-makers.

The lesson of this is not that the United States should respond militarily whenever it sees itself challenged by the Soviet Union. But any U.S. negotiator, at any level, from the president on down, should expect, particularly if new or in the early stages of a negotiation, to be tested by that person's Soviet counterpart. In any negotiation with a Soviet, the American negotiator should be aware that there may be a hidden agenda. Your Soviet counterpart may ostensibly be dealing with the issues at hand, but beneath that he may be trying to determine your seriousness, your determination, whether the relationship is going to be one of two professionals dealing with one another as equals, or whether one is going to dominate the other. This is not inevitable. It does not always happen. But it happens often enough that a U.S. negotiator who is not alert to it and prepared with a strategy for dealing with it may find the negotiation going astray without knowing why. Kennedy should have been briefed to expect this at Vienna, particularly after the Bay of Pigs fiasco. It should have been a major component of the Excom's deliberations during the Cuban missile crisis.

COMPROMISE

Ideology and political culture contain reinforcing elements that make compromise difficult for Soviet negotiators. This is not to say that Soviet negotiators are not realists enough to know that compromise is necessary if agreement is to be reached. But compromise with the class enemy is a necessity, not something that is simply accepted as part of the negotiating process. Lenin declared that "Marxism does not altogether reject compromises. Marxism considers it necessary to make use of them, but that does not in the least prevent Marxism . . . from fighting energetically against compromises. Not to understand this seeming contradiction is not to know the rudiments of Marxism."[52] Compromise is part of the historical dialectic. Its justification is as an essential element of a shift in the correlation of forces in favor of socialism, not as an end in itself.

Americans are often mildly amused when a Soviet negotiator says "Let's do business," since business is presumed to be an essentially capitalist concept. But it is easier for a Soviet negotiator to contemplate doing business with a capitalist, with the implications of trading favor for favor, than to contemplate compromise with a capitalist. Lenin's injunction "not to make political concessions to the international bourgeoisie . . . unless we receive in return more or less equivalent concessions . . . "[53] is a mandate to trade rather than an invitation to compromise. Bryant Wedge and Cyril Muromcew's analysis of Soviet negotiating behavior in the SALT negotiations led them to conclude that the "Soviet equivalent for compromise is to be found in bartering, especially when quantitative values are involved. Any concession has to be on a quid pro quo basis."[54]

Compromise, in Russian eyes, opens the gateway to domination. The word in Russian, *kompromis,* is not a native Russian word and, to the Russian mind, tends to have more the flavor of what a Westerner would understand as "to be compromised'' than to make reciprocal concessions to arrive at a mutually agreeable or beneficial agreement. A Soviet negotiator will, therefore, tend to disguise his side's compromises behind verbiage or bluster, or to decline to admit that his side's position has changed. Alternatively, he will trumpet a compromise as an enormous concession and go on the offensive, demanding an equal or greater compromise from the other side in return. As one practitioner put it, the Soviets "generally offer concessions slowly and reluctantly, trying to make their opponents very grateful for even the slightest concession, and trying then to extract further concessions in exchange for every one they offer." Another notes that the Soviets have something of a counting mentality about concessions that elicits some highly predictable behavior about major meetings on arms control. "There is always a Soviet concession and they always want a U.S. concession back." In a similar vein, Jonathan Dean found in U.S.-Soviet arms control negotiations that "Soviet negotiators are decidedly close-fisted with their negotiating assets. . . . They carefully husband negotiating resources, demanding a formal quid pro quo for every move and refusing to go further until NATO participants respond with a move of their own. Even a small Western move may suffice to fulfill the requirements of this rather mechanistic reciprocity, which does not seek to weigh the relative importance of moves made by either side."[55] This counting mentality in negotiations is something that I also have experienced. It is an aspect of Soviet negotiating that we will come back to, since awareness of it can be an asset in the closing phases of a negotiation.

The Soviet attitude toward compromise is essentially a subset of their views toward hierarchy. If the relationship is hierarchical, and the issue of dominance/submission has not yet been resolved, the offer of compromise is a sign of weakness.[56] The other party will naturally go on the attack, seeking to exploit it and to definitively establish dominance. Robert Jervis touched on this issue in his discussion of the "spiral" model of international relations.

> The most obvious embarrassment to the spiral model is posed when an aggressive power will not respond in kind to conciliation. Minor concessions, the willingness to treat individual issues as separate from the basic conflict, and even an offer to negotiate can convince an aggressor that the status quo power is weak. Thus in 1903 Russia responded to British expressions of interest in negotiating the range of issues that divided them by stiffening her position in the Far East, thus increasing the friction that soon led to the Russo-Japanese War.[57]

It is not necessary to assume that Russia was, or the Soviet Union is, always and everywhere an aggressive power in order to assert that history, culture, and ideology combine to produce a real tendency to see concessions as a sign of weakness rather than as an occasion for reciprocation.

Moreover, if right is on your side, if you are "living in Truth," compromise is not only weakness, it is morally wrong. A Soviet emigré sees the Soviet view of compromise as follows:

Compromise is a bad word in the Soviet Union. In this, ideology reinforced cultural traditions. The traditional view of how a person should be is principled, strong, honest. Ideology reinforces this with the notion of no compromise with the class enemy. To call something a principled, uncompromising position is a compliment. In the West, it would be called rigid. There is a belief in Russia that there is one Truth, and that you are supposed to try and achieve it, not compromise it. This is reinforced by Marxism/Leninism.[58]

An American diplomat who has negotiated extensively with the Soviets, both during service in Moscow and on international delegations, believes that this is an area of fundamental difference between U.S. and Soviet negotiators, which may have its origin in dialectics. "We look at negotiations as a way of compromising differences to get at a mutually agreeable solution. A Soviet negotiator, negotiating with the class enemy, looks at it as a way to gain unilateral advantage, sometimes by getting an agreement favorable to his side, sometimes by not getting an agreement. There is a different view on the nature of compromise."[59] This difference obviously is a potential source of a variety of problems, including the problem for the U.S. negotiator of whether or not his Soviet counterpart has, in fact, offered a concession. At the Geneva START talks, the Soviet side often has difficulty in making a concession and calling it that.[60] The Americans, believing they may have heard something new, will press the Soviets on the point. The Soviets tend to obfuscate in such circumstances, and the fact that they have, in fact, changed their position only becomes clear over the course of repeated sessions. For the U.S. side, this produces problems in how to report the initial Soviet move, whether or not the United States should respond and, if so, how.[61]

I have found in my own dealings with the Soviets that they respond to U.S. concessions by immediately going on the offensive, by pressing for more. Near the end of a round of Consular Review Talks in Moscow in June 1984, the U.S. delegation, which I headed, conceded on one of three outstanding Soviet agenda items. The Soviet negotiator instantaneously went on the attack, saying that an agreement could be reached if the United States would simply accede to the Soviet position on the remaining two items. He chose to ignore the fact that previous agreement had been reached to leave the remaining two Soviet items out of the package then being discussed. My concession evidently meant that the United States wanted to reach an agreement, but how badly did it want one? How much farther were we willing, or could we be pressed, to go? This could be interpreted either as evidence of the fact that the Soviets are smart negotiators, or that they are innately duplicitous. I believe, rather, that it is an element of their negotiating style. It may be taught, but the teaching "takes" because it reinforces some gut-level predispositions.

During the most crucial days of the Cuban missile crisis, Soviet Embassy Counselor Aleksandr Fomin met several times with John Scali, the ABC's State Department correspondent, apparently on instructions of the Soviet government. Fomin, who urgently requested to see Scali on the afternoon of October 26, outlined terms for a settlement of the crisis that were identical in substance to those contained in the much-discussed Khrushchev letter received later that evening. The Soviets would remove the missiles under UN inspection and Khrushchev would agree not to reintroduce them in return for a public promise by the American president not to invade Cuba. Expressing his deep concern that war might break out, Fomin urged Scali to find out immediately from his friends at the State Department whether the United States would look favorably on such a proposal. He asked Scali to call him day or night on this matter of vital importance. Secretary of State Dean Rusk authorized Scali to tell Fomin the United States saw real possibilities in the proposal, but that time was short. When the two met the same evening, Fomin was anxious to be assured that Scali's message was authoritative, that it came from sufficiently high in the government to be taken as an official view. Finally assured of this, Fomin was not content simply to transmit the response to his government. Even at this crucial moment, which he himself had described as fraught with the danger of war, Fomin went immediately over to the offensive. He asked Scali why, since there was to be inspection of the Cuban bases, there should not also be inspection of the U.S. bases in Florida, from which an invasion of Cuba might be launched. There is no way of knowing whether Fomin was under instructions to raise this point provided the United States responded positively to the Soviet proposal or whether he was freelancing. Either way, the important point for the present discussion was the immediate impulse, in response to a positive U.S. move, to ask for more. If the other side shows signs of give, probe until you find its limits. In this case, Scali told Fomin he did not know how the United States would respond but, speaking as a journalist, thought the idea would be rejected. He stressed the time urgency of the situation, which prompted Fomin to leave in such haste that he left a five dollar bill for a thirty cent check.[62]

The implications of this for American negotiators are obvious. They should expect the Soviets to go on the offensive when the United States makes concessions and should have their counter-strategy prepared. The Soviets expect that we will go on the offensive after they have made a concession. They anticipate this by following a concession with an offensive of their own, demanding as much or more from the other side in return for what they have done. We, on the other hand, expect, if not gratitude, at least understanding and have a tendency to get our backs up about being pushed after we have made a concession. This is particularly so if we have made the concession without asking anything specific in return in order to set the right "tone" for our discussions. Instead of a better tone, we find a worse one and are bewildered, disillusioned, angry, or some combination thereof. Nathan Leites, however, would advise that:

> It is inconceivable to Bolsheviks to offer unilateral concessions to groups viewed as actual or potential enemies in the expectation that this will "pay off" later by inducing more favorable attitudes in the enemies. They rather expect the enemy to behave according to their own requirements of themselves: having been granted an advantage, he will reinforce his push for more.[63]

This is one of the aspects of Soviet negotiating behavior that Hannes Adomeit considered confirmed without qualifications by his analyses of the Berlin crises of 1948 and 1961.[64] And, from the perspective of Herbert York, a practitioner: "In the Soviet viewpoint, the worst mistake that one of their negotiators can make is to offer a concession that is not reciprocated."[65] It is not just a tactical mistake. An unreciprocated concession reeks of weakness and invites attack. That is what a Soviet negotiator's cultural experience tells him. It would be hard to be clearer on this point than Lenin was: "In politics a voluntary cession of 'influence' proves such impotence in the ceding element, such flabbiness, such lack of character, such meekness, that . . . only one thing can be 'concluded': he who gives up something voluntarily is 'worthy' of being deprived not only of his influence but also of his right to exist."[66] Experience with Western negotiators may eventually teach the Soviet negotiator that this is not necessarily the case, but his "natural" response to an uninvited concession will normally be the opposite of Western expectations. The correct Western response in these circumstances is firmness, not indignation. The Soviet is trying to find out whether the concession indicates your entire position is mushy. That is both his learned and his "natural" reaction to a concession. When he finds that the rest of your position is firm, he will usually back off.

MOOD CHANGES

Western negotiators have frequently commented on the capacity of their Soviet counterparts to shift quickly from one mood to another, from extreme friendliness to extreme hostility. The sudden switch, the *volte-face*, figures frequently in Russian myths and folklore.[67] Khrushchev epitomized this trait in his public persona. The experiences of Harriman and Beaverbrook with Stalin demonstrate that sudden switches of mood were not only typical of Stalin, but used by him, perhaps consciously, even in the most crucial of international negotiations. Whelan calls these the "tactics of abuse."[68]

The switch from extreme friendliness to extreme hostility may be striking to foreign observers, but, in my view, it is only one example of a broader Soviet characteristic—the ability to switch rapidly and easily from one mood or mode of operation to another. Geoffrey Gorer and John Rickman believe that it is a typical Russian trait to oscillate suddenly and unpredictably from one attitude to its contrary—from violence to gentleness, from excessive activity to passivity, from indulgence to abstemiousness.[69] The example of the Soviet doorman, with which this chapter began, is another illustration of this capacity. He shifted instantly, with no apparent internal conflict or lingering ill-feeling, from a position of asserting dominance to one of accepting submission. While the example was fictional, years of experience in and with the Soviet Union have convinced me that it was also typical. I share Hingley's view that it is not so much the capacity for friendliness and hostility, both in extreme degree, that distinguishes Russians from non-Russians, "as the apparent ease with which they can make the transition from one condition to the other."[70] In his book, *The Soviet Political Mind*, Tucker briefly discusses the "dual Russia," the controlling, commanding state and the passive, subordinate population, and its recapitulation in the dual personality of the Russian functionary.[71] Earlier writers pursued this image in more depth.

Wright Miller traced this behavior pattern all the way back to the exigencies of Russia's harsh climate which, he believed, "encouraged habits of labor and life which were bound to persist: the old pattern of dumb plodding interspersed with furious bouts of activity, the old tendency for too many people to help at peak times, while for long intervening periods individuals dribbled along as best they could. These alternations have been one of the most distinctive features of Russian life." Authority relationships may also have played a role. Every Russian had to be capable of shifting instantaneously from dominance to submission depending on the person with whom he was interacting. Even the lowliest peasant, Vakar argued, was the undisputed master within his own hut.[72]

It is obviously a bit difficult to establish that this behavior pattern can be traced back to climate or to early Russian authority relationships. What is important is to accept that it is not simply a learned negotiating tactic. It goes deeper than that, and it did not have its origins with the Bolshevik revolution. Leites argued, on the contrary, that Bolshevism seeks to counter this Russian tradition of accepting violent swings in mood and activity. While the writer Maxim Gorky might say that "happiness and sorrow are neighbors within us; their interchange happens with such swiftness as to be imperceptible," a trained Bolshevik would be expected to act not from emotion but from an informed, dialectical analysis of the situation, from "consciousness" that produces mastery over the situation and over oneself.[73] "Consciousness" allows Soviet negotiators to use mood swings to their advantage in negotiations at times, but they are an important component of the Soviet negotiating style not so much because they are consciously chosen as because the impulse to choose them arises from roots deeper than conscious choice. And the Soviet negotiator's ability to switch with apparent ease from one strong mood to another is less a matter of conscious mastery of emotion than a deeply imbued cultural trait.

That this is an important component of the Soviet negotiating style seems clear from the frequency with which both academic students of the subject and participants in negotiating comment on it. Tony Bishop, a British Foreign Office Soviet expert, refers to the numerous recorded examples of negotiations in which Soviet policies have been reversed overnight. "Soviet delegations," he notes, "tend to carry off this *volte-face* without embarrassment and to be able to deliver necessary concessions rapidly."[74] American negotiators interviewed in the course of this research commented repeatedly on this trait, one referring to Soviet negotiators as "chameleons." This can be disconcerting. Americans like to know who their Soviet counterpart "really" is. If he does a sudden 180 degree shift, which position does he actually believe? That, of course, is the wrong question. The "real" Soviet negotiator is both men, and he is able to shift easily from one position to another in situations that would be psychologically uncomfortable for most Americans. Neither position, in the consciousness of the Soviet negotiator, involves a put-on or a show. Hedrick Smith has nicely caught the flavor of this trait:

> In their authoritarian environment, from childhood onward Russians acquire an acute sense of place and propriety. They conform to their surroundings, playing the roles that are expected of them. With a kind of deliberate schizophrenia, they divide their existence into their public lives and their private lives, and distinguish between "official" relationships and personal relationships. This happens anywhere to some degree, of course, but Russians make this division more sharply than others because of political pressures for conformity. They adopt two very different codes of behavior for their two lives—in one, they are taciturn, hypocritical, careful, cagey, passive; in the other, they are voluble, honest, direct, open, passionate.[75]

To be a chameleon in Soviet life is not shameful; it is natural. To be a sausage, on the other hand, is contemptible.[76]

Observers have frequently commented on the Soviet tendency to put extreme proposals on the table, to stick doggedly to them through extended negotiations, and ultimately to modify them quickly and substantially. American proposals, by contrast, have traditionally been considerably closer to what the United States would accept as a bottom line. This is an area in which personality and institutional imperatives are both related and mutually reinforcing. American proposals, particularly in weighty international negotiations such as the SALT and START talks, have been through a lengthy interagency negotiating process before being tabled. Usually, they have also been through NATO consultations. Finally, they must be capable of withstanding public scrutiny if they should become public (and the assumption must be made that they will). All of this tends to move proposals toward a generally accepted (in the West) standard of reasonableness. It is also psychologically comforting to U.S. negotiators. They may not agree with every jot and tittle of a proposal, but the process through which it has gone is likely to leave it intellectually defendable, at least within the community of opinion the negotiator finds relevant.

There is clearly an interagency clearance process for such proposals in the Soviet Union, although we know much less about it than we would like to. There are no allied consultations of any significance, and concern about public disclosure does not exist. The institutional process can produce proposals that are outrageous in content, but that have propaganda or positioning value. Soviet negotiators appear to have no difficulty in presenting such proposals and defending them ardently for extended periods, knowing full well that eventually all of their efforts in defense of the proposals will be swept away. One American diplomat, who lived in the Soviet Union for some time, described this in terms of a

Russian tribal mentality. What the world thinks of their behavior does not matter. There is no higher appeal than upholding the interest of the tribe.

When the interests of the tribe are identified with those of all mankind, which they are in Marxism-Leninism, then the Soviet negotiator is likely to have little difficulty in defending and then abandoning any particular proposal while still feeling that he is "living in Truth." Self-interest—the crucial importance of holding onto one's position—would demand of even the most cynical of Soviet negotiators the mentality of a weathervane. But cultural predispositions and ideological conditioning provide substantial buffers against any winds of self-doubt. Your Soviet negotiating counterparts are far more likely to see themselves as behaving honorably, which fortunately also accords with their personal interests, than to be consciously aware cynics.

The ingrained Russian capacity to bear sharp mood shifts easily is reinforced by some of Lenin's teachings on the necessity, at times, for retreat. A Soviet should resist retreat, should continue the struggle for as long as possible. But when an objective analysis of the correlation of forces demonstrates that the alternative to retreat is annihilation, retreat becomes not only a necessity, but also a duty. Retreat is often sudden, and often accompanied by a final paroxysm of verbal fireworks, a final effort to avoid the necessity for retreat. But when the decision is taken that retreat is necessary, it must be carried through without equivocation. Writing in *Izvestiya* on the Brest-Litovsk Treaty, Lenin said: "We need no self-deception. We must courageously look the bitter, unadorned truth straight in the face. We must measure fully, to the very bottom, that abyss of defeat, dismemberment, enslavement, and humiliation into which we have now been pushed."[77]

Retreat differs from compromise in the feelings it arouses. Retreat is humiliating because it requires acceptance that one has been dominated by the adversary. Compromise is shameful because it involves abandoning principles, no longer living in Truth. Russian history often required both and developed a psychological mechanism to make them easier to bear. Leninist dialectics provided an intellectual justification for bearing them. An essential retreat is a milestone on the path to eventual victory. The Berlin crises of 1948 and 1961 demonstrated, in the view of one careful observer, the Soviet tendency both to resist any encroachment and to retreat before superior force.[78]

As on so many other issues, the Cuban missile crisis illustrates the Soviet tendency to shift positions. The Soviet government announced loudly and repeatedly that it would not comply with a U.S. blockade and warned on October 23, at the highest level, that any U.S. effort to interfere with Soviet ships would be met by the measures necessary to protect Soviet rights. On October 24, Soviet ships approaching the blockade line stopped, and many subsequently headed back home. Khrushchev's famous letter of October 26, offering withdrawal of the Soviet missiles, was followed the next day by a letter radically altering the offer, and on the day after that, by agreement to withdrawal along the lines of the original letter. While circumstantial evidence suggests the second letter should never have been sent (it appears to have been a Foreign Ministry draft that was in the final stages of the clearance process when it was superseded by Khrushchev's personally written letter), the Soviets let the two contradictory letters stand, leaving to the United States the decision of how to deal with the contradiction.

Awareness of the Soviet capability of shifting positions rapidly and easily can be a useful asset to an American negotiator. An American diplomat with whom I spoke told me of an occasion when the head of his delegation delivered an unusually strong statement on the Soviet position at a conference, replying to a Soviet attack on the U.S. position. The Americans wondered how the Soviets would react, since there was a luncheon scheduled immediately afterward between the two delegations. As it turned out, the luncheon was completely friendly. There was no indication during it that any of the exchange of charges and counter-charges had even taken place. Another U.S. negotiator argued that the Soviets expect the United States to reject outrageous Soviet proposals firmly. They will fight long and hard for their position, but not be upset when it is necessary to move on to something else. Americans, he believes, tend, by contrast, to get more emotionally wrapped up in the position they are presenting or defending. Interestingly, this is exactly what Robert Bathurst found in his simulations of U.S./Soviet negotiations. The Americans, playing the U.S. negotiators, would develop an earnest, morally defensible position and wind up frustrated and angry because the Soviet negotiators, played by Soviet emigrés, were not interested in it.[79]

In 1983 and 1984, I headed the U.S. delegation for two rounds of Consular Review Talks with the Soviets. The talks had begun in 1976, had gone through a number of previous rounds without ever reaching an agreement, and had on one or two previous occasions broken down in acrimony, leading to an actual deterioration in how the two sides treated the very consular and administrative matters the talks were intended to improve. I knew that some of the exchanges were going to be acrimonious. Some of the issues on our agenda involved human rights matters on which we wanted and needed to take a strong stand. The chances that the Soviets would agree to any of our proposals for improvements on those issues were slim to none. For their part, the Soviets had some agenda items on the security of their personnel in the United States about which they had strong views. Since as far as they were concerned there was no such thing as enough security for their people, I saw no way for us to satisfy them on these issues. Other issues, involving visa categories and processing times, were potentially reconcilable.

Since I was aware of the Soviet capability to shift easily from one mood to another, I proposed dividing the agenda into two sets of issues—functioning of missions and visas—and to address them in separate meetings. The Soviet side accepted the suggestion, which allowed us to shout at one another as necessary during the functioning of missions meetings, take a break and come back to a businesslike discussion of visas. A number of other factors came together which contributed to the fact that we were finally able in 1984, after eight years of on-and-off negotiating, to sign an agreement; but I am convinced that the negotiating process was helped along considerably by the simple agenda step that enabled us to take advantage of the Soviet ability to shift moods easily and to cultivate the same ability on the U.S. side.

Several U.S. negotiators whom I interviewed remarked that Soviets expect that when they put extreme proposals on the table, the other side will reject them firmly. That done, the Soviets have no difficulty moving on in the negotiations on a more realistic basis. A striking example of this from World War II occurred during the Molotov/Harriman discussions on arrangements for taking the Japanese surrender. The Soviet Union had just entered the war against Japan. Molotov told Harriman that the Allied powers should reach an agreement on the candidacy or candidacies of the Allied High Command to which the Japanese were to be subordinated. Molotov floated the idea that both General MacArthur and Soviet General Vasilievsky might be joint Supreme Commanders. As Deane put it:

> After making sure of what Molotov had in mind, Harriman said that the U.S. had carried the main burden of the Pacific war for four years and had kept the Japanese off Russia's back, that the Soviet Union had been in the war but two days and that it was only just that an American should be the Supreme Commander—any other solution was unthinkable. The Soviets later that day accepted that arrangement and MacArthur as the Supreme Commander.[80]

Deane goes on to say that "the firm attitude taken by Harriman successfully repelled the first postwar bid on the part of the Soviet government to extend its influence over the future of Japan. . . . I think a victory must be credited to Harriman because any vacillation at the start would have been the opening wedge to some unfortunate compromise."[81] Deane is absolutely correct. This would have been a classic blunder if it had taken place, and Harriman was exactly right in taking the line that he did. Although the Soviets are often ready to move quickly away from unreasonable demands if they meet a firm rejection, they will dig their heels in and insist upon some accommodation to their request if the initial reply is vacillating.

What accounts for the fact that if they face a firm rejection quickly the Soviets are often prepared to move away from an unacceptable position, whereas if the response is equivocal their position becomes much more encased in concrete? We can, to begin with, refer again to the Russian tendency to test authority, accepting it if it is firm, attempting to overthrow it if it is vacillating. A position that is firmly stated is not only psychologically compelling, it is powerful because it appears based on conviction, on principle. An equivocal statement reflects a lack of conviction, which can and should be attacked, exploited to your side's advantage.

COUNTERPUNCHING

There is a saying in Russian, "Initiative is punishable." The sense of this combines with a negative view of compromise and an ease in rapidly changing moods to make counterpunching a distinctive element of the Soviet negotiating style. Tony Bishop describes as characteristic of the Soviet negotiating style "passivity, fear of responsibility; adherence to formalities and standard formulations; avoidance of spontaneity or taking unauthorized initiatives."[82] One American diplomat attributed this to the fact that most Soviet negotiators are lackeys, the products of an authoritarian system, trained, and at ease, in obeying orders. Stalin's rule was both capricious and bloody, traits unlikely to encourage initiative. A Soviet writer caught the flavor of it in his story of a one-armed Khan. The Khan commanded a portrait. The first artist painted him as he was, with one arm, and lost his head for insulting the Khan. The second painted him with two arms, and lost his head for painting over reality. The third hit upon the right approach and saved his head. He painted the Khan in profile, naturally from the armed side.

American negotiators found their Soviet counterparts during World War II no more eager to volunteer information than the Khan's artists must have been to paint his portrait. General Deane found U.S. efforts to establish joint planning with the Soviets for the Pacific war frustrated by the inability of the Soviet military delegates not only to make any firm agreements, but even to take up a new subject without getting prior clearance from above. They could not answer even the most inconsequential questions at the meetings in which the questions were asked.[83] While a sense of secrecy and suspicion of foreigners (traits to be considered in the following section) may have played some role in this, one is left with the feeling that self-preservation was the key element. The Soviet negotiator was there to hear what the Americans had to say and to volunteer nothing. If you said anything other than what you had been instructed to say, you could wind up dead.

Counterpunching was a distinctive characteristic of Stalin's personal negotiating style, even though he was presumably free from his subordinates' fear of reprisal for showing initiative. He regularly spent his first meeting drawing out his U.S. or Western interlocutors and his second hammering them for the inadequacy of their proposals. His previously discussed ability easily to orchestrate extreme mood swings made this negotiating style not the reactive and defensive one it could have become in other hands, but in fact dominating and effective.

Reluctance to take initiatives did not begin with the Stalin era, nor did it end with it. The fawning on one side and patronizing on the other described in Chekhov's story "Fat and Thin" illustrates not only the characteristic Russian attitude toward authority relations described previously, but also one aspect of the character of the Russian *chinovniki*, or bureaucrats. A Soviet emigré, calling Chekhov the psychologist of *chinovniki*, suggested that the behavior the artist described was much more common in the Soviet Union, a society of *chinovniki*, than in pre-Revolutionary Russia. Chekhov saw it as contemptible, a departure from normal Russian traditions, and described it as such.[84] Others would argue that the extent to which service to the state was the source of status in Tsarist Russia produced strong impulses toward *"chinovnichestvo"* long before either Marx or Lenin.[85] Soviet society, at a minimum, accentuated traits that clearly existed in pre-Revolutionary Russia, whether or not they were denigrated. And *chinovniks* do not take initiatives; they follow orders.

Contemporary U.S. negotiators are virtually unanimous in describing their Soviet counterparts as reluctant to take the initiative. Sloss and Davis describe the Soviet expectations that the United States will make the first concrete proposal a characteristic element in their negotiating style. Jonathan Dean found that "in the MBFR talks and in the day-to-day drafting of the Berlin negotiations as well, even after larger issues had been resolved, Soviet negotiators showed a pronounced tendency to allow or even urge the United States to take the lead and then to react to these leads."[86] Yulii Kvitsinsky, the Soviet negotiator who took the famous "walk in the woods" with Paul Nitze, was described by most of my interlocutors as a distinct exception to the Soviet norm. Nitze himself pointed out to me that Kvitsinsky would go farther than most Soviets, but not all that far. During their final walk, after Nitze had changed his proposal to accord with a suggestion by Kvitsinsky, Nitze said the proposal was now a joint paper. Kvitsinsky agreed, but said he would tell his government that it was Nitze's paper and Nitze could tell Washington it was Kvitsinsky's.[87] My own experience is that it is practically a standard mode of operation for Soviet diplomats, when they do offer negotiating ideas, to try to elicit an expression of interest from their American counterpart and, if they succeed, to say that they will report the American's idea to their government.

Soviet institutional practices reinforce this reluctance to take the initiative.[88] American negotiators with whom I spoke questioned whether their Soviet counterparts knew what their government's fallback position was. Either they did not know it, and therefore had no choice but to simply keep repeating the same position until they received a new position, or they did, but the consequences of prematurely giving ground were so severe that their negotiating posture was the same—to keep repeating the same position until they got explicit permission to move from it. Seriousness in negotiations is shown in Soviet eyes not simply by how elegantly you argue your case, but by how persistent you are in pressing it. Writes Leites:

> Only when, and always when, protracted attempts or conclusive analysis have fully proved a certain advance to be impossible or inexpedient must the attempt to secure it be temporarily abandoned. . . . Determined, prolonged and fruitless insistence is thus usually . . . both a necessary and a sufficient condition of final sudden withdrawal.[89]

To move from a position after arguing interminably for it is not only psychologically easier for a Soviet negotiator than for a Western one, as the discussion on mood changes indicated, it is also an indication that you have fought hard for your side. In the SALT talks, Wedge and Muromcew found that "once a proposal has been firmly stated it is repeated endlessly. Repetition is evidently regarded as a significant means to make a point; this becomes clear in Soviet responses to Western denials. To be believed, the Russian expects a denial to be made over and over again. A single unemphasized denial means little."[90]

You do not lose by finally changing your position. You win by demonstrating your seriousness. Your adversary will have contempt for you if you give in easily, respect if you have fought hard. Of equal importance, your superiors, upon whom you are totally dependent for a position of enormous prestige and practical benefits in the Soviet context, are most unlikely to reprove you for being too tough in your negotiations with the class enemy. Moreover, the longer you hold out, the more likely it is that the other side will make a move that you can use advantageously.[91]

Soviet negotiators expect the other side to stick as determinedly to its position as they do to theirs. Failure to do so can lead to misinterpretation. Max Kampelman describes the necessity for this as follows: "If we raise an issue eleven times and there is no response or rejection of the issue and if it is important to us and we don't raise it the twelfth time—that becomes significant to the Soviets. Because we have dropped the issue, the Soviets conclude that it's not important for us any more."[92]

In his analysis of the nuclear test ban negotiations, Christer Jönsson found that the typical pattern was Soviet commitment to a principle, calls for U.S. commitment to the principle, and after a period of time, efforts to convince the United States that it, in fact, had committed itself to the principle. For example, "the Soviet Union committed itself to the quota principle, refused to be drawn into a discussion of figures until the United States, too, had made a commitment to the principle, and after several months proclaimed that it interpreted the absence of U.S. objections to the quota idea as an agreement in principle."[93]

American negotiators find this aspect of the Soviet negotiating style both tedious and pointless. As one U.S. START negotiator told me, "It is amazing how many times they can go over the same ground using what seems to us incredibly stale rhetoric. They do this on issues which they present as involving high principles, but which when you get down to actual agreement do not matter worth a damn." An American may be tempted to see this failure to take initiatives and the willingness to repeat the same position in the same words ad nauseam as not even negotiating, or at least not negotiating seriously. But in Soviet hands, these traits have been combined into a counterpunching style of negotiating that the Soviet negotiator considers serious indeed, and which at times has proven disconcertingly effective.

FACTS AND EMOTIONS

Soviet concern for secrecy is legendary. While I was posted in Moscow, I got to know many Jewish refuseniks—persons who had applied for and been refused permission to emigrate. The usual reason given by the authorities for refusal was that they were in possession of state secrets. This was news to most of them. One of the refuseniks, an electronics engineer, told me the story of his refusal. He asked the authorities how he could possibly be in possession of state secrets. In the first place, the field in which he worked was television. In the second, the Soviet Union was ten to fifteen years behind the West in the field. "That," he was told, "is the secret." This story sounds apocryphal to Western ears. It is not. I knew the man well. He finally received exit permission in the fall of 1987, about fifteen years after he first applied.

Like many other Soviet traits, this one is rooted in the Russian past. Western visitors to Russia throughout the centuries have told tales of the suspicion with which they were viewed, the obstacles put in the way of contact with everyday Russian society. The Soviet practice of reserving entire apartment buildings for foreigners has its origins in Peter the Great's establishment of a separate section of the city for them to live in. The Russian concern that outsiders not learn how they really live, how their system really functions, has not lessened under Soviet leadership. Writes Edward Keenan:

> Indeed, one of the characteristic operative features of this system is, whether one is dealing with the sixteenth century or with the twentieth, the rule "Iz izby soru ne vynesi" (literally, "Do not carry rubbish out of the hut") remains in operation: i.e., one does not reveal to non-participants authentic information concerning politics, political groupings, or points of discord. Like several other rules of this culture, this rule of conspiratorial and mutually protective silence (in modern offical parlance "neglasnot") is quite normally adhered to even during the bitterest of political conflicts.[94]

Hingley makes a suggestion worth considering on this issue. In keeping with his sense that Russians generally tend to oscillate between polar extremes, he posits that Russian secretiveness is confined to the mundane world of mere fact, which the Russian finds boring and fundamentally unreal. Where emotions, which a Russian considers the true stuff of life, are concerned, he delights in communicating his reactions. This theory, Hingley believes, could help to explain the psychological impasse which so often exists between a Russian and a typical Western citizen, who is more at home exchanging information than emotional responses, at least with comparative strangers. It is not that Russians are more or less tight-lipped or more or less communicative than non-Russians, but that the areas within which these qualities are displayed tend to be mutually exclusive.[95] If he is dealing with facts, the Russian is secretive; if he is dealing with emotions, expansive. Since Westerners, particularly Anglo-Saxons, tend toward the other extreme, much opportunity for misunderstanding and failure to communicate exists.

In his negotiating simulations, Robert Bathurst found that Soviet emigrés started negotiations with an overall picture. They asked what this negotiation meant for U.S.-Soviet relations. As Bathurst saw it, they were asking: "Does the U.S. love us?" They could not really engage in the details of the negotiations until this overall question was answered. U.S. negotiators, on the other hand, took a narrower view of the negotiations, tending to focus on particulars.[96] The American negotiating style, with its strongly legalistic background, seeks to make certain that both sides are working on the basis of the same facts, that any agreement is precisely worded and understood the same way by both sides, and that there are no loopholes to be a source of future disagreement or unequal exploitation—in cultural terms, an extremely low-context approach to negotiations. One of the most common admonitions in negotiating with the Soviets is to avoid general agreements, to pin down the details, because the Soviets will generally adhere to the strict letter of an agreement, but interpret any vagueness to the utmost in their favor. This is clearly good advice. The point I want to make here, however, is that the Soviet preference for generalized statements of principle is not necessarily simply a matter of deliberate, preplanned chicanery. The desire to negotiate on the basis of a set of mutually agreed principles arises from a gut-level sense that these are the truly important elements of the negotiation, not the mere factual details, which time will in any case quickly erode.[97] Write Wedge and Muromcew:

> Soviet representatives constantly demand settlement of general principles first, and will only then consider the specific instances, the technical and administrative details, and the practical issues. There is only one "right" way to solve problems, especially political ones, and that is to agree on the principle first, and having done that to proceed to the particulars. This absolutistic and deductive Soviet approach constantly clashes with the pragmatic and legalistic approach favored in the West.[98]

Andrei Gromyko, by a number of accounts, fits this pattern very closely. According to a U.S. diplomat who has been in numerous negotiating sessions that Gromyko headed on the Soviet side, Gromyko invariably began his presentation with an extensive *weltanschauung*, a lengthy presentation laying out his view of the world, how the present talks fit into it, and what principles he believed should guide them. This was not the kind of thing, my interlocutor thought, that American negotiators usually did very well, although he gave U.S. START negotiator Max Kampelman high marks as an exception in this regard. Another U.S. official described a Gromyko opening to a meeting with an American Secretary of State that, although succinct, displayed the same traits. "Now, Mr. Secretary," Gromyko asked, "tell me, is the U.S. for peace or is it for war?"

Soviet suspicion of foreigners and concern for secrecy certainly approached and perhaps surpassed historically high levels during the Stalin era. Even during the most difficult days of World War II, Stalin put the need to maintain secrecy above the need to obtain more effective Allied help. He refused to permit an Allied bomber group to base in the Caucasus where it could have helped fight the German siege of Stalingrad. He supplied a shopping list of lend-lease needs, but would not supply information to justify it. Nor would he permit U.S. military observers the kind of travel and observation that would have enabled more effective lend-lease assistance.[99]

A high water mark of sorts may have been reached during the Stalin era, but the succeeding ebbs and flows have left Soviet suspicion and secretiveness at levels that far exceed those readily comprehensible to a Westerner. The SALT I talks are notable not only for what they achieved, but also for the way information was exchanged. The United States provided data on its weapons systems. It also provided the data used in the negotiations on the Soviet weapons systems being discussed. The Soviet negotiators, at least those on the Foreign Ministry side, had no knowledge of Soviet force levels. On one frequently commented upon occasion, in fact, a Soviet military member of the delegation took his American counterparts to task for the amount of information they were providing to Soviet civilians, who did not need to know that sort of thing. This remained the basic Soviet stance until the signature of the INF Treaty in December 1987, when the Soviets did provide detailed data on the location, technical characteristics, and numbers of the weapons under discussion.[100]

Soviet borrowing, or stealing, from a technologically more advanced West has long antecedents in Russian history. So does the sense that the extent of the country's technological backwardness is a state secret. Soviet negotiations during the SALT talks assumed: "(1) that the security of the state depends on the maintenance of secrecy and territorial immunity from foreign observation, and (2) that opponents will use every possible means of penetration."[101] Western countries have been assumed throughout Russian history to have malevolent intentions, which knowledge of its backwardness could only excite. The Marxist-Leninist division of the world into mutually antagonistic socialist and capitalist camps provides strong reinforcement to one of the most often noted impulses in Russian history.

Knowledge, to a Soviet negotiator, is most definitely power. It is to be expected that each side will attempt to acquire it by whatever means it can. This is how professionals conduct their business. For either side to wax indignant or emotional about the means used may serve propaganda purposes, but actually to feel betrayed by the other side's activities in this area is incomprehensible. American negotiators, I believe, generally understand this intellectually, but by and large continue to have mixed feelings about it. In his simulations, Bathurst found that Soviet emigrés almost invariably assigned a member of their negotiating team the task of gathering intelligence about the other side's position and intentions. This never occurred to the Americans.[102] I interviewed a senior American diplomat who had served two tours in Moscow. On both occasions he found himself in the position of dealing with Foreign Ministry officials who knew considerably more about the state of U.S.–Soviet negotiations on the issues for which the American was responsible in the embassy than the American did. His counterparts reacted by using their superior knowledge actively as a weapon, dismissing him as a serious interlocutor and attempting to adopt a position of dominance. While there may be good reasons in particular instances for keeping information about the state of U.S.–Soviet negotiations on close hold, there are also costs. When American diplomats in Moscow do not know what is happening on an issue that they are responsible for covering, their ability to handle that issue is nil, and their ability to handle other issues can also be damaged.

VRANYO

> If you don't like it, don't listen; but don't interfere with the lying.
>
> —A Russian saying

At a dinner with his Soviet intelligence contacts in Moscow during World War II, General Deane described the wild ride he had just had through the streets of Moscow on the way to the dinner. Deane had been taken to the dinner in the car of one of his two Soviet hosts. The chauffeur had obviously been instructed to lose Deane's chauffeur, who was following in a much faster, American-made car. Deane's chauffeur liked nothing better than driving as fast as he could in the car, and Deane knew at the time, he told the Soviets, that the effort to lose his chauffeur would be to no avail. The Soviets chuckled at the story and let it go until, when the dinner was nearly over, the one in whose car Deane had been transported came back to the subject. He explained that Deane had been "taken to the meeting place in such a roundabout way because his chauffeur knew that he (i.e., the Soviet official) would be late for his appointment and did not want Deane to be embarrassed by arriving there first." Deane remarked that the ride had been at a tremendous rate of speed for an effort to arrive late and, entering into the spirit of the exchange, went on to ask why Soviet officials all had their cars fitted out with heavy black curtains. The Soviet official replied that the curtains prevented the occupants from being sunburned, at which, as Deane describes it, "I surrendered."[103]

Deane was being treated in this exchange to a delightful example of *vranyo* at its best. Ronald Hingley describes *vranyo* as the Russian national brand of leg-pulling, ribbing, or blarney. It is not, or should not be, an outright lie, for which the term *lozh* is reserved, but rather the dissemination of an untruth indicative of a lively imagination. As a classic example of *vranyo*, Hingley likes the story told in Turgenev's *Smoke* of the sportsman who, while beating an unfamiliar countryside for game, was directed by a helpful rustic to a nearby marsh offering a vast profusion of wild fowl helpfully waiting to be shot. The huntsman trudged on, only to discover that both marsh and birds were pure mirages.[104]

The distinction between *vranyo* and *lozh* can be subtle, but it is important. *Vranyo* in its pure form is an art, an exercise in imagination, a tall tale told for the joy of it, not in an effort to gain advantage at the expense of the listener. True, the hunter in Turgenev's story was inconvenienced at having to walk around looking fruitlessly for a swamp and game where neither existed, but he suffered no real harm. And in a sense, in the mind of the rustic who told the tale, the swamp and the game "should" have been there, in the same sense that Potemkin's villages "should" have existed on the banks of the river as the Empress Catherine floated by. That which should be, but is not, can be created by an act of imagination.

General Deane's memoirs show that he had a good ear for *vranyo,* whether or not he ever actually heard the term used. On another occasion, he had arranged to make a trip to the front to observe the Red Army in battle. He was told on July 10 that the Soviet Chief of Staff, Marshall Vasilievsky, on whom he would be calling, would have kidney trouble until July 20, and therefore Deane should not leave Moscow until after that date. As Deane puts it, "undoubtedly there was some excellent and logical reason for a delay in my departure—probably Marshall Vasilievsky's schedule. It was typically Russian . . . to have some fantastic reason put forth with a perfectly straight face in preference to the real one."[105]

Hingley, perhaps having a bit of fun himself with the concept, divides the Soviet era into three periods: the age of truth under Lenin, when the public believed that the leader believed what he was saying; the age of outright lies, or *lozh,* under Stalin; and the emergence of public *vranyo* under Khrushchev. Khrushchev, according to Hingley,

> reintroduced vranyo partly through personal example. Statements such as cultivating maize, catching up with America and the like often carried so strong a whiff of fantasy, and were obviously made partly for fun. But the spread of vranyo derived less from Khrushchev's own sterling example than from the relaxations over which he presided by enabling more communication to take place. Whereas your old time purveyor of vranyo enjoyed strictly amateur status, we have with Intourist guides, members of delegations and the like, officially licensed greeters or contact people who bear all the signs of having been drilled in the gentle art of manipulating foreigners at some highly secret central school of vranyo.[106]

Deane's experiences indicate that *vranyo* was far from being a lost art under Stalin, but perhaps its practice was confined to private communications. The emergence of "official" *vranyo* during and since the Khrushchev era has, to the ear of the connoisseur, produced substantial adulteration in the art form. The official version, designed particularly for the foreigner, injects substantial portions of truth into an essentially tall tale, producing a contrived verisimilitude devoid of the element of play characteristic of classic *vranyo.*[107]

The historical origins of *vranyo* are unknown, but if Charles J. Halperin's analysis of the Russian literary response to the Mongol conquest is correct, that response was essentially one of *vranyo*.

> The Russian response stands alone. Religious ideologues in other conquered medieval societies, Christian, Muslim, and pagan, all directly addressed the questions raised by their own defeat. Russia's ambiguous position in the Golden Horde, the lack of a continual Tatar presence, and the heritage of Kievan relations with steppe nomads combined to make the Russian response of leaving the relationship between Russia and the Mongols unexplored and unarticulated. The bookmen (Russia's chroniclers of the era) give the impression that the Mongols had no greater impact on Russian history and society than earlier steppe peoples, and historians have accepted this as true. Yet because of the ideology of silence, the Kievan posture did not reflect the reality even of the Kievan period, much less of the radically altered circumstances following the Mongol conquest.[108]

Halperin goes on to argue that any expressed familiarity with the Tatars and their customs in medieval Russia carried a suggestion of both blasphemy and treason because of the religious and political hatred with which they were viewed. But this denied reality, since "for three centuries the Mongols were an integral, unavoidable fact of Russian existence, and Russians, whether they wanted to or not, became intimately familiar with them, both as individuals and as a society."[109] The Russian chroniclers of the period, then, by an act of imagination, created an image of society as it should have been, not as it was. What is this, if not *vranyo* on a grand scale?

There is an element of self-aggrandizement in *vranyo*. The telling of the tale is intended to make the teller for at least a moment the center of attention, perhaps to make him feel better, more important, more worthy. But, classically at least, it did not carry with it an intent to demean the listener. In some cases, in fact, the listener might participate in and extend the *vranyo*. Leonid Andreyev imagines as a typical exercise in group *vranyo* a party held in honor of the tenth anniversary of the day the honoree received his first slap in the face. Not a soul at the party really believed that the event was worthy of celebration, but each attendee could look forward to a party commemorating his own "achievements." A speaker declares that until the honored guest received the slap ten years ago, the same understanding of a slap in the face simply did not exist. Each succeeding speaker felt the need to improve on his predecessor's story, until by the end of the party it was solemnly asserted that the honoree had alone received all of the world's slaps. And the man who excused himself from a social obligation on the pretext that his aunt had just died, when all knew perfectly well that she had not, did so because if she had died he would have deserved all the sympathy that his listeners could muster. The *vranyo* gave the speaker his own moment of attention when all were concerned with his aunt's health and, more importantly, with how the loss of his aunt affected the speaker.[110]

But self-aggrandizement is only part of the motivation for *vranyo,* and in accomplished hands not necessarily the most important part. It lifts the gloom, pushes back the darkness. Dostoevsky, many of whose fictional characters were accomplished purveyors of *vranyo,* felt that it flourished in his country because the truth was too banal, too wearisome to Russians. There was need to bring in some color, some hope, even if this required a substantial dose of deception, even self-deception.[111] Yet this deception is really only on the surface. While the purveyor of *vranyo* may be able to persuade himself for the moment of the truth of his tale, he knows at a deeper level, or at least will realize later, that it is all total nonsense. It is the attention of the listener that he wants, accompanied by a convincing semblance of belief.

Soviet duplicity in negotiations has been much commented upon. Bishop, for example, describes it as a characteristic of Soviet negotiators that observers have identified as recurring with noteworthy frequency.[112] A young Soviet foreign policy consultant told Hedrick Smith that to the Soviet Union, deceit is a compensation for weakness, for a feeling of inferiority before foreigners. "As a nation," he said, "we cannot deal with others equally. Either we are more powerful or they are. And if they are, and we feel it, we compensate for it by deceiving them."[113] Anyone sitting opposite a Soviet negotiator, however, should have clearly in mind the distinction between *lozh* and *vranyo,* both to protect himself from the former and not to miss the opportunity of enjoying a potentially delightful example of the latter. Mistakes are inevitable, but with a bit of practice a Western negotiator can begin to enjoy the *vranyo* without being victimized by the *lozh.* One criterion is clear. If the tale being told is designed to gain an unfair, unilateral advantage, it is *lozh,* or at best a highly corrupted form of *vranyo.*

A distinction must be made between the failure to carry out an agreement, which clearly involves duplicity, and the explanation for the failure, which may partake of *vranyo.* Deane, who was highly skeptical of Soviet trustworthiness in carrying out agreements, had the following to say about how Soviets view the matter:

> The Soviet leaders pride themselves on living up to their agreements. I really believe that they think they do. However, they are past masters at rationalizing and dissembling. . . . When Soviet leaders are unable to rationalize sufficiently to void an agreement which they regret, they are particularly adept at creating conditions which make it impossible of fulfillment. Anything can happen in such cases—key officials will get sick, others will be out of town, boats will sink, and so on and so on—with the result that the agreement might just as well not have been made.[114]

A decision not to carry out an agreement is clearly duplicitous by Western standards. It may, to a Soviet, be perfectly in accord with the historical dialectic, and therefore the right thing to do. The explanation thereof may be *lozh,* or it may be *vranyo.* The agreement is not going to be carried out in any case, and the story is made up to help the foreigner feel better about it, as well as to help the

Soviet official off the hook. The story's connection to the broken agreement carries with it a strong whiff of *lozh,* yet the inventiveness of the tale may qualify it as at least a corrupted form of *vranyo.*

You may be *"vranyoed"* when you least expect it. I was having lunch with some American friends at a hotel in Tallin one pleasant May afternoon. We had a train to catch and, knowing how slow service can be in Soviet restaurants, got there three hours ahead of the train's departure. We placed our order and, after about thirty minutes, began to inquire about it, receiving assurances that it would be along shortly. Time passed with more assurances, but no food. After about an hour, I decided to assert myself and went into the kitchen raising hell and demanding to see the manager. That got some attention, and he came fairly promptly to our table. "We've been waiting for an hour," we said. "Where is our lunch?" We had, it must be remembered, been assured repeatedly that the food was on its way. "I am terribly sorry," said the manager, "but your waiter got sick and went home—with your order." What really happened we will never know. Probably the order had simply been forgotten. We had to start all over again and finally did get lunch. We made the train, too, barely. But what a nice, classically *vranyo* touch the manager's final three words gave to his explanation for the lack of service. Imagine the waiter slipping out of the back door of the restaurant, too sick to work, but still clutching our order in his hand.

In his negotiating simulations, Robert Bathurst found that Soviet emigrés, in addition to complicating the negotiations with detail and peripheral questions, regularly created documents that "proved" their position. But they were astonished that the Americans believed the truth of the documents. They said things like "why do the Americans believe what we are telling them?"[115] This is an example of corrupted *vranyo,* in which the tale is not expected to be believed but is intended to convey a one-sided advantage if perchance it should be.

Classic *vranyo,* it must be remembered, is a tale told for the joy of telling. There is no intention of taking advantage of the listener, nor is there any hope of it, since there is no expectation that the listener will really believe the story. Yet there is, Hingley argues, a certain etiquette (or, in Hall's terms, a "situational dialect") involved in being a recipient of *vranyo.*

> Those who seek to demonstrate the falsehood of a given piece of vranyo may unwittingly hurt some harmless craftsman by implying that it was a piece of lozh all along. Does the vranyo artist expect to be believed? Certainly not. There could be no greater error than to conclude that these creative effusions are meant to be taken seriously. They are intended to be accepted with a serious and respectful countenance, but that is a different matter. By believing, literally, a piece of vranyo—a phenomenon surprisingly common among more gullible Western visitors to Russia—the recipient gravely insults his host's inventive powers, implying in effect that they have not been called into play at all. There is no fun in feeding vranyo to an innocent who happily accepts it with an expression of beatific silliness on his face.[116]

The skilled Soviet diplomat is capable of switching between *lozh* and *vranyo* without missing a beat. Robert Kennedy met with Ambassador Anatoliy Dobrynin in early September 1962, as concern was beginning to mount in the United States about the possibility that the Soviet Union was putting offensive weapons into Cuba. That, in fact, was exactly what the Soviet Union was doing. Dobrynin conveyed Khrushchev's assurances that the Soviet Union had no intention of putting offensive weapons into Cuba and added that the Soviet leader would do nothing to disrupt relations prior to the mid-term elections. He liked the president and did not wish to embarrass him.[117] The assurance of no offensive weapons was a blatant falsehood, which Dobrynin was clearly conveying under instructions. There is no way of knowing whether he was aware of the actual state of affairs, but there is also no reason to doubt that he would have carried out his instructions in any case. The final remark about Khrushchev's liking for Kennedy was a piece of *vranyo* which Dobrynin probably simply threw in as a nice touch, something that would provide further reassurance and please the president's brother. In fact, if Shevchenko's memoirs are to be believed, and no one in government with whom I have spoken has questioned their accuracy, Khrushchev actually thought Kennedy was weak-willed and ineffectual (and was taking steps that, if successful, would embarrass the hell out of him), and Dobrynin was certainly in a position to know this.

It is not always easy to know whether you are hearing *lozh, vranyo,* or corrupted *vranyo,* since the intention of the teller is so crucial to the determination. *Vranyo* as a pure art form does, unfortunately, appear to be relatively rare among Soviet diplomats. This may force you to expose a piece of *vranyo* that you would just as soon let pass, or find it used against you later. On one occasion, I headed an American delegation during a month-long round of talks in Moscow on consular and administrative matters. The chief Soviet delegate opened the round with a strong expression of his country's concern about the abysmal security situation its diplomatic personnel faced in the United States. Without giving any specifics, he said that the U.S. response to this concern would be a key determinant of the prospects for success in the talks. It happened that I had as a temporary member of my delegation an officer from our consulate in Leningrad. This officer had, the prior week, been attacked in a Soviet restaurant as he was leaving after having lunch with a Soviet dissident. He had been knocked down, punched, and kicked. This sort of incident does not occur by chance in the Soviet Union. He was obviously being delivered an emphatic message about meeting with the Soviet citizen in question. I replied to the Soviet delegate by pointing out the specific steps the United States had taken since the last round of talks to respond to Soviet complaints on security. I noted the generality of the present complaints and the difficulty of responding to them effectively. I then pointed out that, by contrast, there was a very specific incident involving the security of a member of my delegation on which we were still awaiting a reply from the Soviet government.

My counterpart responded that the Foreign Ministry had looked into the matter and determined that there had been no attack on the American consul, the incident had not happened. Knowing that my colleague did not want the matter to become a focal point of these negotiations, with some feelings of disquiet I let this astonishing denial pass with a simple query about how the Soviet government would react if the United States responded to its security complaints simply by flatly denying that any incidents occurred. About a week later, after my colleague had returned to Leningrad and during another fruitless discussion of security in which I had contrasted specific U.S. problems such as his with generalized Soviet complaints, my counterpart told me that he had previously stated that the incident to which I was referring had never occurred, that he had done this in the presence of the American diplomat who had allegedly been attacked, and that the diplomat's silence clearly indicated that he accepted the Soviet view. In deference to my colleague, I had treated the initial statement by the Soviet delegate as *vranyo* by not challenging it. His effort to take advantage of that was clearly out of bounds, however, a no-no in terms of classical *vranyo*-mongering, and I offered to bring the American consul back from Leningrad to correct any misimpression that might have arisen. There was no interest in this on the Soviet side.

During the two years that I headed the bilateral relations section of the Soviet desk at the State Department, we had periodic incidents in which employees of the Soviet embassy were nabbed for shoplifting. Since they had diplomatic immunity, they were released as soon as someone from the embassy verified their identity. But the embassy position was that all of these were incidents of pure harassment, mounted by the U.S. "special services," and further evidence of the security problems their people had in this country. Their invariable practice was to demand to see me as soon as they learned of an incident. Since it usually took at least a day for us to get the facts of the cases from the local police authorities, the Soviet embassy was able to register its complaint and put its version of the facts—at best corrupted *vranyo*, at worst *lozh*—on the table without our being able to do more than say we would look into the matter. They were never interested later in hearing what we had learned from the police.

I finally got sick of this, particularly since I knew from my service in Moscow that in the event of an embarrassing incident involving deliberate harassment of an American diplomat the Foreign Ministry was quite capable of simply refusing to see anyone from our embassy until it had put together its version of the facts. When I got the next call from the Soviet embassy on one of these cases, my schedule was too full to permit a meeting that day. There was great gnashing of teeth and complaints to my superiors about my unprecedented refusal to meet that very day with a Soviet diplomat, but I stuck to my guns. When I met with the Soviet embassy officers the next day, I was able to reply to their complaints by asking why the spouse of an embassy employee would go on a shopping expedition carrying a large, but completely empty purse—no identification, no money, no cosmetics, no comb, nothing but space, which as she exited from the store was occupied with goods bearing that store's labels. One can only imagine what might have been made of this empty purse in the hands of a skilled artisan of *vranyo*, but alas, my Soviet counterparts were able to assay nothing more than a weak assertion that carrying an empty purse was very common among Soviet women. The Soviet embassy admitted nothing, but the couple in question was quietly sent home shortly thereafter.

I had, on another occasion, the opportunity to purvey a bit of *vranyo* myself to my regular visitors from the Soviet embassy. Our office had just changed to a faster word-processing system, and the old screens were temporarily stacked in my office waiting to be moved elsewhere. I knew that the Soviet embassy was still using typewriters and could not resist the opportunity to point out the state of American technology in this area. As my visitors were leaving, I apologized for all of the "junk" stacked up in my office, saying that it was out of date and waiting to be thrown out. Their faces slipped into momentary expressions of disbelief, but they recovered quickly and offered solemnly to take the junk off my hands, an offer I parried by referring to non-existent union regulations on moving obsolete office equipment.

When a Russian resorts to *vranyo,* it is, Dostoevsky writes, obvious to other Russians. The situation to another Russian is so obviously strained that he immediately recognizes the fabrication.[118] But it may elude a foreigner, particularly in a negotiating situation. Developing an ear for *vranyo,* however, is worth the effort. It will enable you to successfully challenge a *lozh,* to avoid being ensnared by a corrupted form of *vranyo,* and to enjoy to its fullest a finely crafted example of the genre.

CHAPTER 3

THE BIRD IN THE HAND AND OTHER SOVIET NEGOTIATING TACTICS

A bird is seen by its flight.

—Russian proverb

BY NEGOTIATING TACTICS, I MEAN THE BEHAVIORS THAT ONE chooses in the negotiating process to achieve one's objectives. Both behavior and choice are relevant. Your perceptions of the other side's intentions may be important, but they are not part of your tactics. Your tactics are what you do as a result of your perceptions. I assume that, generally speaking, an effective negotiator's tactics will be chosen consciously and with forethought. There may be negotiators who are so instinctively attuned to the process that they achieve brilliant results without thinking about their tactics beforehand. For most of us, however, the results are not likely to be impressive. Tactics come more from the head; style more from the gut. The set of tactics chosen repeatedly may be an expression of negotiating style. But while the tactics are chosen, or justified on an intellectual level, the negotiator's believing in their effectiveness and being comfortable with them arise from a deeper level, the level that has to do with the negotiating style. Style, since it arises from these deeper, unquestioned levels of belief, is not usually deliberately chosen. But conscious awareness of your own and the other side's negotiating styles may enable you to choose tactics, or adjust elements of your own style in advantageous ways.

Joseph Whelan describes Stalin's behavior in his negotiations with Harriman and Beaverbrook as the "tactic of abuse." He considers it a particularly effective example of the historic Russian negotiating ability, through diplomacy, to create a position of strength out of one of weakness.[1] As we tried to show in the previous chapter, the tactic, although perhaps deliberately chosen, had its roots in some more fundamental elements of the Soviet negotiating style, including a belief in the importance of resolving dominance/submission issues and an ability to switch moods dramatically, quickly, and easily. The books and articles available on Soviet negotiating tactics, often referred to as Soviet negotiating behavior, are legion. This brief chapter will not attempt to duplicate or exhaust the available literature. Rather, our intent is to look at some of the more frequently commented upon Soviet negotiating tactics and to examine the utility of interpreting them as manifestations of the Soviet negotiating style, drawing on the ideas previously presented.

The range of tactics available to negotiators, whether Soviet, American, or other, while theoretically as unlimited as the fertile human imagination, in practice is finite. The tactics used by Soviet negotiators will not be unknown to their American counterparts, and vice-versa. As an American arms control negotiator put it to me, Soviet negotiators have at their disposal the entire range of negotiating tactics, as do we. His conclusion was that the two sides did not differ greatly in their approaches to negotiations. The objective of negotiators on both sides is to advance their countries' respective interests. Their negotiating tactics are the means to that end, and each side uses whatever set of tactics is most effective. This view is another variant of the "we are all human beings together" theme. While it can be a useful corrective to an outlook based on primitive, knee-jerk anticommunism, I do not think it is a very helpful guide to American negotiators. Soviet negotiators, as previously discussed, differ greatly from their American counterparts in the historical, cultural, and political background they bring to the table, as well as in the institutional framework within which they operate and the constraints that framework imposes on them. This affects not only their negotiating style, but also their tactical approach to negotiations.

The issue of whether there is a growing convergence in approaches to negotiating is, however, one that merits consideration. In his detailed study of Soviet negotiating behavior, Whelan concludes that the Soviet diplomat of today is well trained, in a prestigious occupation, and a great improvement over earlier generations of Soviet diplomats.[2] To the extent Soviet negotiators have been acculturated in Western diplomatic practice, their own behavior may begin to converge with it, and we may come to see a less distinctive Soviet negotiating style. This is an issue that will have to be considered as we look at continuity and change in Mikhail Gorbachev's Soviet Union. For now, let us look at a variety of behaviors that numerous negotiators and observers have described as "typical" of what we might call classic Soviet negotiating behavior.

In his best-seller, *You Can Negotiate Anything*, Herb Cohen maintains that Soviet negotiating tactics place them at the competitive end of a competitive/collaborative continuum of negotiating styles and, incidentally, at the opposite end of his own recommended style. A Soviet-style negotiator, whether from Moscow or from Peoria, shows the same six negotiating traits:

1. Extreme initial positions.
2. Limited authority.
3. Emotional tactics.
4. Adversary concessions perceived as weakness.
5. Stingy in their concessions.
6. Ignore deadlines.[3]

Among the conditions necessary for the success of these tactics, Cohen argues, is a lack of awareness by the victim that the other side is employing them. Forewarned is forearmed.

Christer Jönsson did an extensive review of the literature on Soviet negotiating behavior and its typical characteristics. His objective was to develop a set of hypotheses about Soviet negotiating behavior that he could "test" in a specific case study—the nuclear test ban negotiations. He found that the following typical characteristics of Soviet negotiating behavior recurred in the literature:

1. Suspicion of the U.S. and expectation that the U.S. will be hostile to the Soviet Union;
2. Reluctance to compromise;
3. Perception that concessions by the other side are an indication of weakness and should be followed by the Soviet Union sticking to its original proposal or even taking a harder line;
4. Use of the "red herring" technique, i.e., to make startling and extravagant demands; then, when these have stirred up sufficient anxiety, to withdraw some of them, and to demand a concession in return;
5. Extensive use of publicity as a means of negotiation;
6. Reliance on a cycle of commitment to positions which are repeated numerous times and for an extended period of time, eventually to be abandoned and taken up by a new commitment which is just as stubbornly pursued;
7. Willingness to suddenly abandon its position or commitment without particular concern for continuity or credibility;
8. Reluctance to use informal meetings as a negotiating tool;
9. Seeking "agreements in principle";
10. Frequent use of propaganda in negotiations, sometimes as a primary objective of the negotiations, sometimes as a means of achieving agreement;
11. A tendency for increases in international tension to affect Soviet bargaining behavior in a variety of specific negotiations (i.e., Soviet bargaining in specific negotiations more affected by the overall level of the relationship than by the specific process of the negotiation or the issues involved).[4]

Jönsson's list seems fairly exhaustive and includes behaviors that I believe are more usefully considered as aspects of the Soviet negotiating style than as tactics. My own list of the tactics about which I would want American negotiators to be aware contains considerable overlap with those of Cohen and Jönsson. Anyone going into negotiations with the Soviets should have a clear idea of how they perceive and use:

1. time;
2. generalized language;
3. detail;
4. the bird in the hand;
5. silence;
6. extreme positions;
7. appeal to a higher power.

TIME

My personal experience and what I know of U.S. negotiations with the Soviet Union convince me that Soviet negotiators are trained to believe that they can use time to their advantage in negotiations with Western, or at least American, representatives. They are also concerned to ensure that time will not be used against them. As one long-time observer and practitioner puts it, Soviet negotiators "show a keen understanding of the importance of timing, and frequently try to exploit situations to show that they are not susceptible to time pressure."[5] Let me say at the outset that the perception that time is used more effectively by Soviet than by Western negotiators may have been more true some years ago than it is now. This is an area in which we have become much more effective negotiators. We seldom now let ourselves be backed up against time deadlines, particularly self-imposed ones. On occasion, we have even been able to take advantage of Soviet mistakes in this area.[6] The decade-long MBFR talks in Vienna, the lengthy CSCE negotiations in Madrid, and the START talks demonstrate, on the positive side, patience, determination, and staying power. But Soviet use of the tactic of time must be considered because I believe that they still use it and that there are some very basic institutional reasons, which they understand, why they believe they can still turn time to their advantage on occasion, albeit perhaps not as often.

The American approach to negotiating with the Soviet Union is affected on the grand scale by the four-year rhythm of presidential politics. On a smaller scale it is affected by the two- to three-year rhythm of diplomatic and negotiating assignments. Achievement-oriented Americans who devote two or more years of their lives to a subject are often struck by the desire to leave behind some memento of their work, something they have done to mark their passage. American presidents, assured of a place in history, have correspondingly greater, but not dissimilar goals. To both, an agreement with the other nuclear superpower, some step that can be thought of as improving relations, putting them on a more sensible and secure footing, or perhaps even contributing to world peace, can be that memento, that mark.

I am convinced that Soviet negotiators, from the bottom to the top, are consciously aware of these cycles and these impulses and consciously try to employ time as a tactic to benefit from them. One of the clear patterns that Bathurst found in his negotiating simulations was the U.S. side's desire for quick results and the Soviet side's awareness and use of this desire.[7] In my own experience, I have had my Soviet counterpart, trying to eke out some further concession toward the end of a negotiation, talk about the opportunity we had to achieve something of benefit to our countries, if only the U.S. side could _____ (you can fill in the blanks).

A number of commentators have used the analogies of chess and poker to illustrate differences in how Soviets and Americans approach negotiations. Readers who consider the analogies overworked, if not completely misleading, may groan, but I suggest we take another look at them. The skilled American poker player is aware of time proceeding along two continua: one comprises the entire session of the game, or contest; the other is a series of discrete events marked by the individual hands. Each discrete event is complete unto itself, but the results, behavior, and observation from it form part of the overall continuum and contribute to the end result. The better poker players understand the process and incorporate it into their game. The poorer ones simply stagger from hand to hand. Chess is a single continuum of time, but for planning strategy can be usefully divided into beginning, middle, and end games.

The American negotiator should, I believe, assume that the Soviet side is operating as though it were playing three chess games simultaneously, although not necessarily at the same rate of play. One involves the negotiation at hand. The second has to do with the American negotiator. The third concerns the overall U.S.-Soviet relationship. Each of the contests may be at any one of the beginning, middle, or end game points on the time continuum.

The beginning game for the Soviets with a new American negotiator is, on the conscious level, to attempt to exploit the American's naiveté and achievement-orientation while at the same time laying the groundwork for the longer-term relationship. The two may be at cross-purposes. Early exploitation may produce disillusionment and anger, which will harm the longer-term relationship, but, as we have previously discussed, the Soviets are generally unwilling to let concern for hypothetical future costs stand in the way of a tangible immediate gain. The underlying agenda for the Soviets is to establish whether the long-term relationship with the individual concerned is to be one of dominance/submission or equality. A period of testing is likely. If the American allows himself to be cowed, the Soviets will move into a middle game in which he will be bullied, exploited, and treated with contempt. Since most Americans react instinctively against efforts to push them around, the middle game is more likely to be marked by a relationship of assumed equality and professional, sometimes personal, camaraderie. Soviet behavior during this middle game phase closely resembles Western negotiating behavior and may contribute to the impression that it is, in fact, indistinguishable from that of Western negotiators. This impression may be particularly strong if the opening game efforts at exploitation or testing have been attenuated or perfunctory. The arms control negotiations, for example, have become sufficiently institutionalized, and the freedom of action of American negotiators is so limited that Soviet negotiators may move almost immediately into middle game interactions with their American counterparts. The length and ferocity of the Soviet opening game is likely to be greatest when they are dealing on their own turf with a newly arrived embassy officer who has no previous experience in Soviet affairs. The end game again becomes one of more specific effort at exploitation, this time not of the American's naiveté, but of his achievement-orientation, his desire to accomplish something tangible. The Soviets may be desperately anxious to pin down something concrete before a particular individual departs, while feigning indifference as the remaining days tick off.

There are two characteristic ways for the Soviets to handle the opening phase of a specific negotiation. One is to place an extreme position on the table. The other is to try to draw out the other side's opening position without revealing their own. They are variations on the same theme. Reveal nothing, or as little as possible, about your real position and learn as much as you can about the other side's. Begin things with a very positive generalized opening statement about the great things the two sides are going to accomplish, but then react negatively to whatever the other side initially proposes. Counterpunch. This is very much in keeping with Stalin's treatment of Harriman and Beaverbrook. It is a tactic that was not interred with him.

The best tactic for handling this may not necessarily be to respond along the same lines. Your counterpart may have to demonstrate to Moscow that the Western side is prepared to offer up something interesting in return for Soviet quids before he is authorized to engage in give-and-take. I found this personally in Consular Review Talks with the Soviets. In that instance they clearly had to await a Moscow decision to engage after extracting as much as I was prepared to tell them about what the United States was prepared to throw into the pot. They obtained enough to whet Soviet appetites, got permission to engage, and we ultimately signed an agreement. If I had stonewalled, they might never have received the go-ahead, and this round of talks would have dissolved into fruitless bickering, as several previous rounds had. Interestingly, Raymond Garthoff drew similar conclusions about the initial Soviet approach to the SALT I talks:

> We did not realize at the time that the SALT preparatory talks opened in Helsinki in November 1969 that Soviet commitment to SALT was tentative, but by the time that first session closed a month later it became clear that the talks had been approved in Moscow—they believed that the United States had shown it was indeed interested in serious negotiations. If that had not been the case, Moscow would probably have ended the talks or turned them into familiar disarmament propaganda exchanges.[8]

The middle game is again one of more traditional bargaining tactics of give-and take, although the Soviets remain more likely than most negotiators to stonewall, to put off any concessions until the eleventh hour.

It is in the end game that the Soviets feel they excel, and it is here that they believe they have the greatest relative advantage over American negotiators. The Soviets love the end game, the distention of time, the brinksmanship. It is here that their almost instinctive tendency to respond to a concession by going on the attack manifests itself most distinctively. At the point that Americans see the agreement as virtually completed and are already beginning to imagine their place in history, accept congratulations, and consider their next task, the Soviets come into their own as end game players. Previously dropped positions will begin to resurface. Russian-language texts will begin to show anomalies. Complications or new issues will arise. One more American step will be needed to bring this to a successful conclusion. The prize will seem within your grasp but will remain tantalizingly just out of reach. And the days will pass.

If you are an American negotiator visiting the country, living in a Moscow hotel, and missing your family, this can seem like it is going on forever. If you have placed yourself up against a time deadline, whether by an ill-advised public statement anticipating an arms agreement by Christmas or a phone call to your spouse promising that you will be home in time for your child's birthday, you can be certain that the Soviets will do everything possible to use the bind in which you have put yourself to extract something additional from you. Soviet negotiators are constantly on the lookout for signs during the end game that reaching an agreement has become an end in itself. They expect this to happen during the final phases of a given negotiation, during the final days of a given American negotiator's tenure in the job, and during the mid-election or closing phases of a particular presidency. And they will exploit it mercilessly when they see it.

There are two ways of responding effectively to these end game tactics. One is to sit them out. Patience is not a Soviet monopoly. As indicated above, the United States has learned a lot about the need for patience in negotiating with the Soviets. We have even learned to sit through our own publicly self-imposed time frames for reaching agreement. The other is to be prepared to walk away without an agreement. The other side's advantage in knowing you have promised to be home in time for your child's birthday is an advantage to them only as long as they believe you are committed to reaching an agreement before leaving. If they know you are prepared to depart without an agreement, the deadline begins to work against them. Some practitioners believe that their Soviet counterparts, more accustomed to pressing the other side against time deadlines than to themselves being pressed against them, are more likely to make substantial concessions or to overlook significant details when their side feels the time pressure than Americans would be in similar circumstances. Howard J. Stoertz, for example, suggests that when the top Soviet leadership wants an agreement, Soviet negotiators may be prepared to meet numerous American demands in order to get one quickly.[9]

GENERALIZED LANGUAGE

There is perhaps no more oft-repeated maxim for negotiating with the Soviets than to avoid generalized statements of intent or agreements that are not explicit in specifying exactly what the obligations of each side are. In his negotiating guide, Tony Bishop says that Soviet negotiators tend to prefer broad agreements couched in vague and often ambiguous language, and frequently press for very general agreements that presuppose, often falsely, a community or continuity of aims between the parties, or for agreements in principle which, when it comes to implementation, they use as a convenient escape hatch.[10] Lenin referred, apparently approvingly, to Bismarck's dictum that acceptance "in principle" meant, in the language of diplomacy, rejection in actuality.[11] Anticipating our discussion in the next chapter on the dialectic, an agreement may be perfectly valid, or true at the time it is made; but circumstances change and the agreement inevitably becomes less and less a valid reflection of reality. The more specific it is, the more quickly it becomes invalid. A more broadly worded agreement may be susceptible to interpretation that will permit it to remain relevant for far longer. The principles are likely to remain valid far longer than the concrete details. It is crucial, therefore, that they be expressed correctly. A reinterpretation that reflects changing reality but remains in accord with still valid principles does not do violence to an agreement, but rather enriches it. In cynical hands this can be nothing more than a rather high-blown rationalization for deliberate chicanery. Bishop's view keeps something of the sense of dialectical movement, while bringing in the reality of power.

> Soviet representatives are not persuaded by eloquence or reasoned arguments, but rely on a calculation of forces. They see any agreement as an arrangement codifying the momentary relationship of forces, a snap-shot of a power equation or of the relative positions of the parties at a particular moment. Since these relationships are not static but ever changing reality, an agreement has no intrinsic moral binding force. The Soviets tend to respect its letter, as long as it is sufficiently detailed and precise. But when conditions change, they expect to be free to renegotiate, modify, ignore, abrogate or apply it selectively as the new circumstances dictate. There is for them no such thing as a permanent or absolute "settlement."[12]

The Soviet desire for agreement on principles, which we have previously discussed, is not identical to agreement "in principle." Nor is it necessarily a bad idea, or necessarily motivated simply by a desire ultimately to reach an agreement with loopholes wide enough to drive a truck through. Agreement on the basic concepts that govern an agreement can be useful. But referring back to those basic concepts or principles if the agreement itself does not spell out specific behavior is likely to prove fruitless. As Leon Sloss and M. Scott Davis put it in their summary of Soviet negotiating style and tactics: "The concept of 'the spirit of the agreement' has no place in the Soviet approach to arms control."[13] They should have generalized even further. It has no place in the Soviet approach to negotiations. We prefer to negotiate agreements that spell out obligations in detail and, in the implementation phase, assuming the good faith of both parties, to lay stress on the spirit of the agreements. The Soviets prefer more broadly worded agreements but expect in implementation to be required to do no more than what is precisely laid out in the written document. I share the view of many of those who have negotiated with the Soviets. They will generally carry out the letter of their obligations, but they will exploit any imprecision and lack of clarity to and beyond the limits of a Western conception of reasonableness. Oral agreements that supplement or expand upon obligations undertaken in a written document are likely to have a half life of about as long as it takes to walk out of the room in which they were negotiated.

DETAIL

The other side of the Soviet preference for generalized statements of principle is a capability for negotiations of the most painstaking and detailed kind. When the performance of the other side is of importance to them, they want to know exactly what to expect. Or, as Bishop puts it: "When the object of negotiation is a practical agreement where precise execution is required, Soviet negotiators can be persnickety and legalistic. They will argue endlessly over minor matters."[14] Bathurst's simulation finding that the Soviet emigrés tended to overwhelm their American counterparts with detail, with complications,[15] certainly has its parallels in government to government negotiations, although I am not certain how often the Americans are overwhelmed. Wedge and Muromcew found during the SALT I talks a characteristic Soviet pattern of asking specific questions and demanding detailed answers.[16] This pattern may be particularly noticeable during the earlier phases of a negotiation. It dovetails nicely with the Soviet preference for counterpunching. In the Consular Review Talks that I headed, I found it was critical to keep a constant eye on the Russian-language texts that we were handed. Old language kept finding its way back into them, or phrases were used that, when pursued across the table, turned out to have not exactly the meaning they appeared to on first glance.

Americans are often fond of making a distinction between form and substance and of showing their democratic inclinations by not insisting upon, or ignoring, elements of form. There is a belief among Soviet negotiators that form affects substance, or at least that it can affect it. I was told about a Soviet negotiator who kept careful track of the size of the American delegation. If it was smaller than the Soviet, he made sure that both sides were fully represented at the table, with his delegation spilling around the ends. If his delegation was smaller, the Soviet would try to reach agreement before the meeting to limit the number of attendees. Did this give his side an advantage? I do not know, but he evidently thought it might.

This attention to form can be carried to what may seem to an American as absurd lengths, but should not necessarily be treated as absurd. A Soviet negotiator, toward the end of a complicated negotiation that has involved concessions on both sides and produced a package that appears to meet both sides' needs, may, in keeping with the previously discussed Soviet negotiating style as concerns compromise, tally up the number of items on which each side has made concessions. If he finds that more items have been conceded by his side than by the American, he is likely to ask the U.S. side to do more. One response to this would be to argue the balanced nature of the package as thus far agreed to—the quantitatively greater number of Soviet concessions matched by the qualitatively greater U.S. concessions. It is an approach I have used in the past, with notable lack of impact. The argument may be perfectly true, but it is not likely to meet the Soviet negotiator's needs. He has to sell the agreement to his superiors and wants to look good in the process. Some language that he can present to them as a concession, even if it is purely hortatory and non-binding, may be sufficient to wrap up the negotiation. In other words, in some circumstances a Soviet negotiator may be perfectly prepared to accept an "agreement in principle" or other language which, if he offered it himself, he would know would be of no practical effect. Form can not only affect substance, it can also triumph over it, and not only to the benefit of the other side.

THE BIRD IN THE HAND

American negotiators are sometimes concerned to create the right atmosphere for a negotiation, believing that the context within which it occurs can impact significantly on the prospects for a satisfactory outcome. I am certainly prepared to concede that it is more desirable to conduct a negotiation in a good atmosphere than in a poisonous one. At a minimum, it is a more pleasant experience. The question is: What do you have to do to get the desired atmosphere? Bishop notes that Soviet negotiators often promise vague future gains in return for immediate and firm commitments. [17] Granting a favor to the Soviet side in the hope that this will later pay negotiating dividends is almost always an exercise in futility. I would be even more categorical. Never grant a tangible immediate benefit in return for a promised future one. You will wind up negotiating again for the promised Soviet action and will more likely have to give up something else to get it. I have seen it happen time and again. You may even find, as we discussed in chapter 2, that your magnanimous gesture, intended to create a better atmosphere, may instead have contributed to a worse one.

Some years ago, we agreed to allow the Soviets to occupy an apartment complex they had built in Washington (we were also building one in Moscow, but its completion was several years off) in return for an agreement to provide our embassy a new school building, a warehouse, and some additional, badly needed apartments for its staff. The Soviets moved into their apartment building. We had not yet even been shown any prospective apartments and had not reached agreement on either the cost or location of the school building or warehouse. Finally, we were shown some apartments, which were totally unsatisfactory. Months passed, and ultimately we were offered some apartments that would do after extensive remodeling. But the rent the Soviets wanted for them was exorbitant, as was the rent for the warehouse. The issues of who would do the remodeling and where the materials would come from had never been decided and also required extensive negotiating. Problems and delays dogged us every step of the way. What incentive did the Soviets have to cooperate except to be nice guys? They were comfortably ensconced in their apartments in Washington.

Shortly before I departed Moscow on reassignment in 1979, we reached agreement with the Soviet government on provision of land for a new embassy *dacha*, or recreational facility. We promptly delivered whatever our part of the bargain was. Plans were made with a Finnish firm to construct a prefabricated *dacha*. The embassy hoped to occupy it within six months. When I returned to Washington to head the bilateral section of the Soviet desk in 1982, after three years at a pleasant African post where I did not have to be concerned with these issues, we still did not have the land on which the *dacha* was to be constructed. We had been shown a series of unsatisfactory sites. Finally, a site was agreed upon, but it had no utilities. Getting them took years, literally. We finally got the utilities, and the *dacha*, toward the end of my two years on the Soviet desk. We held up a city zoning variance at the new Soviet embassy construction site and tied it to resolution of the *dacha* issue. Many and frequent were the moans and groans from the Soviet side about this linkage of "apples and peaches." And ultimately the linkage only worked when construction activity at the embassy site reached the point at which the variance was critical to further progress.

Our *dacha* troubles are worth one more anecdote, told to me by a State Department interpreter who was there. Our side was meeting in Moscow with the Soviet agency charged with dealing with the administrative problems of diplomatic missions. The newly arrived U.S. negotiator had not been making much progress. He told his Soviet counterpart that the U.S. side had been told by the Soviet embassy in Washington that if we gave them permission to acquire a *dacha* in the United States things would go smoothly in Moscow in discussions for our new *dacha*. We had done so. They had the *dacha*. The Soviet replied: "You should not have done that. You should have tied them together."

A favorite Soviet tactic when they are faced with a stubborn U.S. negotiator on "housekeeping" issues like those discussed above—probably someone who has served at our embassy in Moscow—is to appeal to a higher level. The American in question, they intimate, is unreasonable, perhaps immature or reflexively anti-Soviet. This is such a small issue, not the kind of thing that should stand in the way of improving our relationship. Let us get rid of these small annoyances. It works all too often. Former Secretary of State Henry Kissinger was a great target for this approach. He was dealing with issues of grand policy, as a secretary of state should. Housekeeping issues, like the sites for the new U.S. and Soviet embassies, were throwaways, stage-setters. Whether he ever received anything on the larger policy level in return for his agreeableness on housekeeping issues I do not know. But everything I do know about negotiating with the Soviets leads me to doubt it. The correct response, of course, in most cases (every rule has its exceptions), is to refer these appeals back down to the level at which they are normally handled, but this runs against the American can-do grain, particularly when that trait is laced with a bit of ego involvement. I know. Even at my relatively modest level on the Soviet desk, I was also occasionally on that end of the process.

General Deane's World War II experiences in Moscow led him to conclude that "there is no such thing as banking good will in Russia. Each proposition is negotiated on its merits without regard to past favors."[18] Writing several decades later, Tony Bishop made similar observations. "They [Soviet negotiators] tend to see negotiations as a form of horse-trading or a series of unrelated individual bargains. Soviet counter-concessions must therefore be obtained on the spot, not with delay, as a condition of concessions, otherwise they will probably not be obtained at all.''[19] If you give your Soviet counterpart a bird in the hand, you are going to wind up beating the bush for a long time.

SILENCE

Does silence signify consent? American negotiators have repeatedly found that their Soviet counterparts will interpret American silence as consent. Jönsson found in his study of the nuclear test ban negotiations that Soviet negotiators consistently interpreted the absence of U.S. objections to an idea or principle as agreement to it.[20] Max Kampelman has pointed out that stating your position eleven times is not enough. If you do not state it the twelfth time, the Soviet side will conclude it is no longer important to you.[21] Another U.S. arms control negotiator pointed out to me the importance of responding to Soviet assertions concerning the U.S. negotiating position. The Soviets, he said, will interpret the failure to respond as evidence that they have succeeded in sowing some doubt in the American's mind and will attempt to take advantage of it. My own experience confirms this, a striking example being the Soviet negotiator who denied that the American consul in Leningrad had been attacked and several days later asserted that the failure to respond to his assertion demonstrated that we accepted it as the truth.

But do the Soviets view their own silence as signifying consent? At the end of the Yalta Conference, the Soviets said that Russian silence on issues should not be taken as consent, but rather as disapproval.[22] American negotiators rarely hear such unequivocal statements from their Soviet counterparts. Secretary of State Kissinger often adopted the practice of issuing a public statement of how the United States interpreted language in an agreement with the Soviets. Since the Soviets were informed in advance of what he was going to say, the implication was that their silence meant consent. But subsequent experience casts doubt on the efficacy of this practice. In fact, Soviet silence in such circumstances leaves them with their options completely open. They can either say nothing, implying acquiescence and approval, or later express disapproval and state that they had never agreed to any such thing. Or they can do both at different times depending on their interests at the moment.

The rationale for such unilateral statements of interpretation, as I understand it, is that they provided a way of bridging differences that had not been resolved at the table and finalizing agreements that might otherwise not have been reached. In other words, this was another way of enabling form to triumph over substance. Well, as I have previously indicated, that can be done in negotiations with the Soviets, but only in a fairly narrow range of instances. On substantive issues of importance, this means of bridging differences that could not be resolved at the table is not likely to work. You cannot take Soviet silence for consent in such cases. "The Soviets will not feel in any way bound by unilateral statements of interpretation by others, even when made in formal negotiating sessions."[23]

What is to be done if the alternative is no agreement at all? That is a difficult question to answer in the abstract. There may be cases when a flawed agreement is better than none at all. But such agreements carry within them the seeds of future problems, future American accusations of Soviet noncompliance and bad faith and Soviet accusations of American arrogance and self-righteousness. The longer-term interests of developing more workable relationships between the two superpowers are more likely to be served by not announcing an agreement until the two sides have reached a mutual understanding on all issues. The difficulty is that these longer-term interests may run counter to the shorter-range interests of particular American administrations, and domestic political needs often take precedence over rational foreign policy choices. The Soviets are well aware of this, a point elaborated on in our discussion of their use of the tactic of time.

EXTREME POSITIONS

As we have previously discussed, the Soviets are inclined both institutionally and temperamentally to plop down extreme demands and then to defend them doggedly over an extended period of time. They have no institutional pressures for "reasonableness" in negotiating with a foreign power. In addition, their negotiators are able with apparent ease to defend a position vehemently and at length and then to switch overnight to equally vehement defense of a substantially changed position. Cohen considers extreme demands a prominent characteristic of the Soviet-style negotiator.[24] Jönsson and others have termed this the "red herring" technique. Jönsson did not find it characteristic of Soviet behavior in his case study,[25] but so many others who have negotiated with the Soviet Union have remarked on it that I think Jönsson's case must be considered the exception. A couple of my respondents pointed out not only that Soviet negotiators will take an extreme or hard line, but also that when they do eventually move from it they will seek a counter-concession from the other side. As one put it, it is "nonsense" for them to seek a concession in return for moving away from a stupid position that they have stuck to for a long time. But the Soviet belief that time is on their side, both in the specific negotiation and in the more general sense of the competition between capitalism and socialism, contributes to a willingness to engage in what often seems to American negotiators to be endless and pointless repetition of an argument that is going nowhere. Also, when they do begin to move, they will want to go over immediately to the attack—for example, by stressing the importance of their concession and demanding equal responsiveness from the other side—so as to avoid conveying an impression of weakness, which in their view would stimulate further demands from the other side.

APPEAL TO A HIGHER POWER

The Soviets appear to use publicity both as a means of negotiating and as an alternative to it. Jönsson's hypothesis stresses the former. Bishop puts more emphasis on the latter.

A particular negotiation may have an opening phase which Moscow sees as essentially "demonstrative"; the negotiation may then become more confidential and serious; but if external circumstances change, Moscow may at any moment wish it to become "demonstrative" once more. A Soviet request that a given negotiation be conducted in confidence and without publicity generally indicates an intention to begin negotiating in earnest; it is not a commitment to complete the negotiation or preserve confidentiality indefinitely. [26]

Most negotiations with the Soviets do not involve publicity simply because the subject matter is not such as to be of great public interest. The many Americans engaged in commercial transactions or in private exchanges are unlikely to find their negotiations the subject of public scrutiny. Most government-to-government negotiations of the everyday, nuts and bolts variety are also unlikely to be candidates for public attention. In fact, one of the objectives in such negotiations is to handle them at a technical level. Stalemate at the technical level invites publicity, which immediately kicks the negotiation up to the political level, where a totally different set of issues is involved.

The Soviet resort to publicity in negotiations is a specific example of the more general tendency, referred to above, to appeal over the head of their negotiating counterpart, to appeal to a higher power. At best, the higher level may give them the agreement they want. Alternatively, it is a way of applying pressure, of keeping the negotiator off balance and looking over his or her shoulder. But belief in the efficacy of the tactic has its roots in the Soviet negotiator's experience in his own society. The Soviet Union is not a society where the rule of law prevails. The arbitrariness of power this implies has another side. Almost anything can be done, if the right person can be persuaded to do it. You must find out who that person is, gain access to him, get his ear, and enlist his sympathy. You must try to make the transaction between the two of you a human one, not one of authority. A Soviet negotiator, with no experince of operating in a system of rule of law, has no understanding of how it works, of its constraints. At a basic level, he does not really believe in its existence. Decisions are made by people. If you are not cooperating, or cannot, he must find the person who can and will.

CHAPTER 4

TRUTH, REALITY, AND POWER
The World through Soviet Eyes

> It is the Russian attitude to Truth that is, of all things, the most baffling. For the Russians, this attitude to Truth is at once a source of strength and an inspiration: for us it usually seems mere confusion.
>
> —Geoffrey Gorer and John Rickman,
> *The People of Great Russia*

IF, AS WE HAVE PREVIOUSLY SUGGESTED, SOVIET CULTURE IS much further toward the high-context end of the scale than is American, it becomes all the more important for U.S. negotiators not only to be expert in the particular substantive issue at hand, but also to be sufficiently sensitized to pick up the contextual clues to Soviet positions. Such clues will not be explicitly stated but are nevertheless likely to be far more important for understanding the Soviet approach and goals in the negotiation at hand than equivalent information about the lower-context U.S. approach.

Soviet expectations of negotiations derive from their view of the world, a view that passes through two distinctively important filters—Marxist-Leninist ideology and Russian political culture. Knowing something about the salient characteristics of these filters is the starting point for understanding Soviet negotiating behavior.[1] We also need to try to develop some sense of which aspects of these filters operate as "front of the mind" concepts and which generally operate at a deeper, unconscious level. The distinction can be important, since the likely success of a particular negotiating approach—in general terms, for example, intellectual argument versus emotional appeal—may well depend on whether it corresponds to the type of belief system held by the other side. Moreover, the susceptibility of a belief system to change will vary. Those aspects that are accepted intellectually are likely to be much more susceptible to change through acquiring new knowledge and awareness of changed circumstances than those held at a more fundamental level. Corresponding attributes of negotiating behavior would also be more or less susceptible to ease and rapidity of change.[2]

IDEOLOGY

The role that Marxism-Leninism plays in Soviet international conduct has been endlessly debated, often with more heat than light shed on the subject. Are the Soviets godless communists with a blueprint for taking over the world? Or are they modern-day Russian nationalists, essentially status quo in orientation and with the historic Russian fear of attack from abroad? The persistence of the debate reflects the durability of our own ideological stereotypes and the need to transcend them. A widely held view that attempts to bridge these differences is that the most important thing to understand about Marxism-Leninism is the function it performs, which is the perpetuation in power of the Communist Party of the Soviet Union, or more specifically of its ruling component, the *nomenklatura*.[3] The operative parts of the ideology, then, are those that contribute to *nomenklatura* rule.

Unfortunately, this concept does not help us to understand what Soviet negotiators believe, since it is compatible with the view that they are complete cynics, using the ideology to perpetuate themselves in power, or that they believe it, partly because it perpetuates them in power. The first formulation suggests, in effect, that ideology does not matter in negotiations with the Soviets—it is necessary and sufficient to understand their behavior in pure self-interest terms. It is only the function of the ideology that matters, not the particular form it has taken. But it seems to me that R. N. Carew Hunt had a good point in telling us that we should hesitate before concluding that the Soviet leadership cannot possibly believe in the myths it propounds: "we should remind ourselves that no class or party ever finds it difficult to persuade itself of the soundness of the principles on which it bases its claim to rule."[4]

During the three years that I spent at the American embassy in Moscow, I sensed a general consensus among my colleagues that ideology does matter in Soviet behavior, but a difficulty in articulating exactly how it comes into play. Adam B. Ulam's distinction between the prescriptive, the analytical, and the symbolic, or quasi-religious, functions of ideology captures some of this sense. I share Ulam's view that the prescriptive, or blueprint, element of Marxism-Leninism no longer plays a significant role in foreign policy, but that the analytical (an approach to understanding both domestic and international politics) and the symbolic (the sense that the adherents are moving forward with the forces of history and that the success of their state is predicated upon the truth of the doctrine) remain important for understanding Soviet international behavior.[5] Two concepts that I have come to believe are important to understanding Soviet negotiating behavior are the dialectical nature of reality and the correlation of forces.

The first, it seems to me, while having both analytic and symbolic components, operates at the level of basic, unquestioned belief, while the second is a consciously applied tool.[6]

Dialectics, Reality and Truth

Wrapping the American mind around the Soviet "isms"—Marxism-Leninism and dialectical materialism—was no easy task for those of us at the U.S. embassy in Moscow, and we were living there with some claim either to being or to becoming Soviet specialists. Little wonder, then, that the "isms" are impenetrable to most Americans. But they do not necessarily come easy to Soviet citizens either, as the following Moscow anecdote illustrates.

> A Russian peasant once went to the priest and asked him for a definition of dialectics. Said the priest: "If two men come to your house, one with dirty hands, one with clean hands, and you have only enough water for one of them to wash, to whom would you give the water?" To which the peasant replied: "To the one with the dirty hands!" "No," said the priest, "you'd give it to the man who cares most about his cleanliness. Now the next day, if the same two come to you and you have enough water for only one, would you give it to the man with the clean hands or the man with the dirty hands?" The peasant replied confidently, "To the one with clean hands." "No," said the priest, "you would give it to the one with the dirty hands because his hands are dirty. Do you understand?" "No," said the peasant, thoroughly confused. "Well," said the priest, "that's dialectics."[7]

Viewing the world through a dialectical or a Marxist-Leninist framework does not come easily to most Americans. In fact, it is so alien that there is a tendency, in a kind of realpolitik offshoot of the "they are humans just like us" school to consider the use of Marxist-Leninist terminology in the international arena simply a politically useful cover for an approach to world politics that boils down to simple, traditional pursuit of national interest. Raymond L. Garthoff, who believes that approach misses some essential factors, says:

> We have not even begun to analyze critically the underlying postulates of either the American or the Soviet conceptions. For example, consider the Soviet proposition that "the class struggle" and "national liberation struggle" are not and cannot be affected by detente. . . . Most Americans see that proposition as communist mumbo-jumbo being used as a transparently self-serving argument to excuse pursuit of Soviet interests. In fact, a Soviet leader considers that proposition to be a self-evident truth: detente is a policy, while the class struggle is an objective phenomenon in the historical process that cannot be abolished by policy decision, even if the Soviet leaders wanted to do so.[8]

Americans generally find it easier to view Soviet leaders and officials as cynics, spouting nonsensical doctrine while pursuing personal aggrandizement because, while we may condemn the behavior, we find it comprehensible. It is easier for us to understand cynics than true believers, except for those among us inclined toward the latter themselves. But we have a responsibility to dig more deeply, a responsibility that comes with superpower status in the nuclear era. As Garthoff puts it: "The consistent failure of each side to sense and recognize the different perspectives and perceptions of the other has been strongly detrimental to the development of their relations, compounding their real differences. . . . Rather than recognize a differing perception, judging it to be a valid alternative perception or misperception, both sides typically ascribe a different and usually malevolent purpose to each other."[9]

Alfred G. Meyer sees ideology functioning as the frame of reference for individuals in a society, their set of concepts for perceiving the world and its problems, hence their means of orienting themselves in the universe.[10] Ideology, then, has to do with what we perceive as reality, as truth. It also has to do with the process of reasoning or thought by which we apprehend reality. There is considerable reason to believe that this process operates differently in the Russian mind than in the American mind.

Hegelianism, which produced minimal impact on the American intellect, by most accounts exercised enormous influence in nineteenth-century Russia. James H. Billington considers that Hegel, more than any other single man, changed the course of Russian intellectual history during the remarkable decade from 1838 to 1848.[11] What was there about Hegelianism to which the Russian mind responded with such enthusiasm? Philosophy, Billington argues, as understood in the Russia of the time was closer to the occult idea of "divine wisdom" than to the understanding of philosophy as rational and analytical investigation in the manner of Descartes, Hume, or Kant.[12] Its objective was to discover and reveal Truth rather than to consider man's capability for doing so. Consider in this context Gorer and Rickman's description of the Russian apprehension of Truth.

> Although Truth is a coherent system it is not consistent according to the usual standards of Occidental logic. Truth embraces contradictions both in space and time; the fact that the truth revealed to-day, or the application of the truth demanded to-day, is not the same as the truth (or application) of yesterday, does not mean that one or the other ceases to be part of Truth. Truth is so great that it contains all contradictions; Russians do not reject these contradictions, nor is it certain that they perceive them as contradictions, in the way non-Russians would do. . . . It is this conviction that they live in the Truth and pursue it as do the people of no other nation which gives the mystical overtones to the phrase "Holy Russia" and the newer form "Soviet Motherland."[13]

Hegel presented an all-encompassing world vision, an interpretation of the whole of history and an intellectual tool for comprehending it—the dialectic. The dialectic both described the process of historical movement and provided a means of understanding it. Most educated Americans, when confronted with the term "dialectic," say to themselves "oh yes, thesis-antithesis-synthesis" and promptly forget about it. We approach problem-solving differently, and it is difficult for us to conceive of an approach to problem-solving that differs radically from our own. But suppose, as Garthoff argues, there is more to it. How can we get a handle on it, and how would it affect Soviet negotiating behavior?

Khrushchev's October 26, 1962 letter to President Kennedy during the height of the Cuban missile crisis is one of the most well-known documents of modern-day international politics, despite the fact that only small excerpts from it have been published. It is, by the accounts of those who have seen it, a remarkable document to have been written by one chief of state to another. Robert Kennedy described it as long and emotional, but not incoherent, marked chiefly by Khrushchev's horror of the effects of nuclear war.[14] Khrushchev attempted to assure President Kennedy that the missiles were in Cuba strictly for defensive purposes and would never be used to attack the United States. "You can be calm in this regard," he wrote, "that we are of sound mind and understand perfectly well that if we attack you, you will respond the same way. But you too will receive the same that you hurl against us. And I think that you also understand this. . . . This indicates that we are normal people, *that we correctly understand and correctly evaluate the situation*."[15]

What, in this highly dangerous and emotional situation, did Khrushchev mean when he referred to "normal people" who "correctly understand and correctly evaluate the situation"? Evidently, on the surface he meant that both leaders comprehended the catastrophe that nuclear war would bring. But I believe that Khrushchev's use of this particular terminology reveals more than that. An essential component of the claim to legitimacy of the Soviet Communist Party, and of its leaders, is that their understanding of the forces of history and their ability to act in accordance with them give them the right to rule. The self-serving aspects of this claim are obvious, but there is more to it than that. The Soviet ruling class is taught from a very early age both a philosophy of history and a way of understanding reality that differ dramatically from ours. If we are to understand them, we must develop some ability to see the world through their eyes.

Russian intellectual history has proved infertile ground for any philosophy arguing skepticism or mankind's limited ability to comprehend reality fully. In religion, orthodoxy dominated thought. Major pre-nineteenth-century movements of resistance to authority came not from modernizers, but from believers who considered any change in religious practice or social mores a deviation from God's ordained order. The nineteenth-century Russian intellectual, exposed to Western thought, could easily be brought to reject Russian Orthodoxy as a hopelessly retrogressive religion. But their rejection was of a particular creed, not of the underlying belief that an all-encompassing understanding of the meaning of life or the nature of reality was possible. They had a "penchant for translating every practical problem into an abstract point of doctrine, for raising specific concrete issues to the level of universal laws [and] compounded a lovable, unselfish impracticality with a rigidly doctrinaire and uncritical approach to questions of dogma."[16]

Hegel's sweeping philosophy of history provided an intellectually and emotionally congenial substitute for the rejected faith of Orthodoxy. As Nicholas Berdyaev puts it, the religious make-up of the Russian people contributes to an inclination in Russian thinking "towards totalitarian doctrines and a totalitarian way of looking at life as a whole."[17] Later generations of Russian intellectuals found in Marx's materialist dialectic the same assurance that the course of history could be known and that they could gauge the rightness of their behavior accordingly. The Russian Marxist could thereby "live in Truth." It was not only the manifest injustices of tsardom that cried out for revolution; history demanded it.

Dialectical materialism performs for educated Soviets what Meyer sees as one of the fundamental functions of an ideology: it provides their set of concepts for perceiving the world and its problems, their means of orienting themselves in the universe. The foundation for this understanding is dialectical materialism's theory of knowledge.[18] It is important to reiterate that we are not making any claim here that the principles of this theory of knowledge operate on the conscious level, or even that most Soviets could, if asked, easily describe or interpret them. Neither do most Americans consciously adduce, for example, the "scientific method" when they engage in problem solving. And, if asked to describe it, they could probably give only the most general description. Nevertheless, their approach to problem solving is not random. The system they use may be unconscious and non-verbalized, but it is a system. Each culture has its own rules for learning; if we are to understand a different culture, we must be prepared to set aside the learning models handed down in our culture.[19]

There are three fundamental components to dialectical materialism's theory of knowledge. The first asserts that reality exists independently of the observer's perception of it. There is a real, material world out there that exists whether or not we can see it, or understand it, or even believe in it. In Lenin's words:

> The sole 'property' of matter with whose recognition philosophical materialism is bound up is the property of being an objective reality, of existing outside our mind. . . . Dialectical materialism insists on the approximate, relative character of every scientific theory of the structure of matter and its properties . . . nature is infinite, but it infinitely exists. And it is this sole categorical, this sole unconditional recognition of nature's existence outside the mind and perceptions of man that distinguishes dialectical materialism from relativist agnosticism and idealism.[20]

We do not intend here to try to place dialectical materialism in the context of Western philosophy, a job that in any case, Thomas J. Blakeley, among others, has done very nicely.[21] But perhaps a couple of roadmarks may be of help. The materialist affirmation of the primacy of matter differs in essence from the idealist philosopher's assertion of the primacy of soul, idea, consciousness, the subjective. Plato, for example, insists that the material world as we perceive it with our senses differs from the unchanging world of Forms, which is in principle intellectually knowable. The quality of redness exists for Plato independently of our perception of the color red, which may change over time.[22] Reality consists in these (paradoxically) ideal Forms, not in our imperfect perception of them. With wisdom, with intellectual understanding, could come a fuller comprehension of this "real," nonmaterial world. At an even further remove from a materialist conception of reality is, for example, Berkeley's assertion that the material world exists only by virtue of our perception, or, in the absence of any human being's perception, as ideas in the mind of God.[23]

The second assertion of dialectical materialism's theory of knowledge is that reality operates in accordance with the laws of the dialectic. Thus, absent some understanding of dialectical processes, our ability to comprehend reality is inevitably limited. All the more so since, according to the third component, thought is a reflection of reality. Kant, on the other hand, does not fully accept the theory of reflection. While conceding that things may exist "out there" independently of our knowledge of them, he contends that the world that we can know is inevitably limited by the categories we impose on it. The world that we know is not only a material one, but also one we have partly created, and we cannot stand outside it.

Dialectical materialism's theory of knowledge asserts the ultimate knowability of the real world. Thought undertaken in conscious knowledge of the laws of the dialectic is naturally capable of being a considerably more accurate reflection of reality than thought that is ignorant of it. There is both a subjective dialectic and an objective dialectic. Our knowledge of reality is the subjective dialectic. Reality itself is the objective dialectic. It is dynamic, never at rest, always changing. It follows, then, that the subjective dialectic must also be in continual movement if it is to attain, and retain, correspondence with reality, the objective dialectic. In fact, Absolute Truth is the full correspondence of the subjective to the objective dialectic, of our thoughts to reality. "For us, Marxists, truth is that which corresponds to reality."[24] It is both a state of being and a process, a description of the state of correspondence, but a dynamic also, since reality is always changing, and unchanging Truth would be a contradiction in terms. Relative truth is knowledge that is a basically true reflection of reality, but is limited and valid only under certain conditions and relations.

The problem in making decisions, in acting, is to ensure that the reality one perceives is a true reflection of objective reality. This is accomplished by successfully making the leap from sense-knowledge (immediate, practical contact with the objective dialectic) to intellectual knowledge (an abstract and schematic reflection of the objective dialectic). The key to making the leap successfully is practice. In Lenin's words, "From living perception to abstract thought, and from this to practice, such is the dialectical path of the cognition of truth."[25] Employing your knowledge of history, of the dialectic, you act in the world. The outcome of your action is the criterion for judging how well you understood reality, and helps you to understand it more fully. "Life itself," the Soviets say repeatedly, "teaches." We lose touch with reality either by refusing to learn from life, from practice, or by lacking the intellectual tools to do so because we are incapable of thinking with either spontaneous or conscious awareness of the objective dialectic.

Any educated Soviet, particularly any Soviet leader, must approach problems with an understanding of the dialectic or be unfit for leadership. A major foreign policy reversal, or for that matter a major domestic failure, has in the Soviet system been taken to mean either that the person in charge has incorrectly applied Marxism-Leninism to the situation at hand, or, particularly under Stalin, that he deliberately acted treasonously.[26] Thus, when Khrushchev, in an evidently emotional state, wrote to Kennedy that "we are normal people" who "correctly understand and correctly evaluate the situation," he was saying far more than that the situation was dangerous. The Soviet leader had, in fact, made a profound mistake in his understanding and evaluation of the situation. He was in the process of agonizing reappraisal necessitated by the intractability of reality, by the fact that events had shown his analysis of the situation to have been fundamentally flawed.

The key point to be kept in mind in this context is that, if the Soviet leadership had made a fundamentally incorrect analysis of the situation, its primary responsibility was to bring its actions back into closer accord with reality. This responsibility devolved on them not only as Soviet leaders, or as communists, but also as human beings. Responsible people, acting in knowledge of the historical dialectic, would not take actions that would start a nuclear war. Madmen might, or persons out of touch with reality (and therefore unfit to rule), but not "normal people" who "correctly understand and correctly evaluate the situation." Moreover, considerations of face are decidedly secondary in this kind of situation. You may put the best face you can on a change in course, but it is less important how your change in direction looks to the outside world than that you bring your policy into closer correspondence with reality.

It is quite possible for Soviet decision-makers to be cynical about some aspects of Marxism-Leninism, perhaps particularly of its use as a means of justifying their own positions, and at the same time employ, not even at a conscious level, the analytical tools we have been discussing as a means of solving problems. Peter Reddaway suggests that middle rank Party officials probably accept the Party ideology more fully than any other, since they have little information to interfere with their ability to rationalize. He believes the top leadership may be more cynical. Uri Ra'anan, however, argues that this cynicism has its limits:

> Whatever cynicism vis-à-vis the tenets of its revolutionary creed the Soviet elite may display . . . there remains a residual ideological factor, unmatched by any phenomenon of the tsarist period, that plays a crucial role both in the Soviet analysis of the international situation and in the imperatives that motivate Soviet actions. The reference, of course, is to the dialectic.[27]

There is considerable evidence that force-feeding dialectical materialism to adults has little, or perhaps even negative, impact. Required classes in the subject at the university level are, by all accounts, attended only if there is no way out and marked by polite indifference at best, often by unconcealed inattention. Steven White has found that more than two-thirds of those who attended Party education classes in Rostov-on-Don admitted that they rarely made use of the Marxist-Leninist classics, and a further 15 percent confessed that they made no use of them at all. In Uzbekistan, as many as 61 percent made minimal or no preparation at all for their Party education classes.[28]

No one who has spent time in the Soviet Union would argue that there is not profound cynicism in the society as a whole. The ubiquitous posters proclaiming the triumph of one or another aspect of socialism/communism, glorifying the Party, or calling on the people for still greater achievements are remarkable both for the extent to which newly arrived Westerners see them and the extent to which Soviets fail to. The preoccupation of the Soviet people with material possessions as a symbol of status is as profound as that of any other people in the world. Many, perhaps most, of those who join the Party do so to get ahead in the world—to get a better job, to improve their chances of getting into the university of their choice, to get better housing. The leadership certainly manipulates ideological symbols as a tool for maintaining power. As we have previously seen, this has led some Westerners to argue that in contemporary Soviet society ideology is no more than an instrument for maintaining the dominance of the ruling class. Daniel Bell, for example, argues that "while dogma such as dialectical materialism, historical materialism, the superiority of collective property, and the nature of scientific communism remain on a formal level, the doctrinal core, the central fact is not any specific theoretical formulation, but the basic demand for belief in the Party itself."[29] It is, however, a long step from saying that the Party uses ideology to perpetuate itself in power to saying that the Party has no ideology other than the perpetuation of its power. The perpetuation of its rule is an interest of the Party, or of the ruling class, not an ideology.

Just as class interest must be distinguished from ideology, so also must Party doctrine. The same debate about whether the ideology is believed or simply used as a tool for perpetuating the position of the ruling class exists about doctrine. The fact that the Party leadership has at different times espoused contradictory doctrinal tenets (the inevitability of war versus peaceful coexistence, for example) has been taken to demonstrate that doctrine is used for *post hoc* rationalizations of policy decisions taken on strictly practical grounds rather than believed. But this is not as clear as it may seem. Doctrine has to do not with Absolute Truth, but with partial truth. It is taken to be a basically correct reflection of reality, but one that may be bounded by time and circumstance. As reality changes, doctrine will have to as well. Thus, two contradictory tenets of doctrine may both be accurate reflections of a reality that over time has undergone qualitative change. It is not cynical for someone whose view of reality has been filtered through dialectical materialism to espouse seemingly contradictory positions at different points in time. If reality has changed, so must doctrine.

Nevertheless, if we take doctrine to refer to pronouncements that are verifiable, but unverified (such as peaceful coexistence), and ideology to comprise both doctrine and the unverifiable concepts from which it is derived (the dialectical nature of reality, for example), it appears that the more empirical nature of doctrine, the fact that it is more "front of the mind," renders it more susceptible to conscious manipulation. We could, then, define doctrine as that set of intellectual constructs that the Party uses to legitimize the advancement of its interests. The Party leadership no doubt does consciously manipulate some of the ideological symbols that justify and legitimize its rule. Can we consider that the set of such symbols constitutes the doctrine of the Party—ideas to which public obeisance must be paid, which most likely play little or no role in actual decision-making, but against which all decisions must be capable of justification? Soviet leaders may understand Party doctrine only dimly, or may even be completely cynical about it, but because it is a primary instrument of rule they will never consider it unimportant. The role of keeper of the doctrine is critical and is treated as such. It has been held in the Politburo in recent years by Suslov, Andropov, Chernenko, and Gorbachev—all either king-makers or future kings or both. But is there a remainder? Is some of it believed and not simply manipulated? The point here, after all, is not how we define doctrine, but what Soviets think of it. I suspect that after self-interest and deliberate manipulation are removed, an element of belief remains, at least among some Soviets some of the time, but the rampant cynicism that Soviet emigrés attribute to their former leaders suggests that the component of actual belief in elements of the doctrine may be small.

In any case, Party doctrine generally plays little explicit role in international negotiations. Even if they believed it whole-heartedly, contemporary Soviet negotiators would not expect it to make any impression on representatives of the West. The language of Soviet negotiators may, therefore, be remarkably free of the cant that pervades the Soviet media. It would be a mistake, however, to conclude from the absence of recitations of doctrinal cant that Soviet negotiators do not bring with them to the table a set of ideological expectations and predispositions. Ideology is more subtle, more deep-seated, and more difficult to summarize in a few words than doctrine, but it is also a more important determinant of Soviet negotiating behavior. Adomeit's study of the 1948 and 1961 Berlin crises led him to conclude that ideology "furnished important portions of the analytical and perceptual framework, operational principles and legitimation of Soviet behavior in both crises."[30]

At some level, educated Soviets must absorb a system of understanding and interpreting the world around them, just as Americans learn something we call "the scientific method." Seweryn Bialer believes that ideology is best "understood as a part of culture, a slowly changing combination of doctrinal inputs and the historical experience and predispositions that run parallel to doctrine. This ideology, these beliefs, are operational for Soviet foreign policy-making." In this sense, "the study of Soviet ideology provides a key to understanding the changing Soviet definition of its national interest."[31]

The rote study of dialectical materialism may be no more interesting to a young Soviet than the memorization of catechism questions to a young American

Catholic,[32] but basic concepts and outlooks may nevertheless be internalized. A Soviet official told his son some years ago that the Americans had put a man on the moon. His son refused to believe it, saying that it was not possible, the Americans were not communists and therefore could not have done such a thing.[33] Dialectics is a fundamental concept in Soviet schooling, introduced at a very early stage in a simplified form. Does it become a part of people's thought processes? A Soviet emigré puts it this way:

> Dialectics is incorporated everywhere, even in science courses, as a way of solving problems. People do acquire a dialectical way of thinking. You may not see it when you are talking about something like building a dacha, but whenever you see two people arguing you will see them using the dialectical method. They are using things such as the context, the need to understand circumstances. Even people who are not well educated will use dialectics. It becomes part of the back of the mind. In the camps, I have seen prisoners with very simple education using dialectics. Everything is permeated with it—the radio, etc.—so people learn it as a way of thinking.[34]

A Soviet negotiator who has internalized a dialectical approach to understanding reality is likely to differ in some important respects in his approach to negotiations from someone who has not. For one thing, he will not see things in either/or categories. Reality encompasses both conflict and cooperation.[35] The Soviet will see negotiations as a process, not as an event. Emigré Vladimir Bukovsky comments, "To a Soviet negotiator, negotiations are all process. Dialectics gives them another dimension which others lack. It is a strategy, even if it is not conceived in concrete terms by a negotiator in a particular negotiation."[36]

There is a tendency among American negotiators to view negotiations as an exercise in problem-solving. If a problem exists, you sit down at the table, hammer out an agreed solution, presumably with each side compromising from its original position, then you shake hands and part. That problem has been solved, bring on the next. A Soviet negotiator, on the other hand, will not view the signing of an agreement as the end of a negotiation, but as a stage in the process. Jonathan Dean describes the difference in the following way:

> Americans tend to consider that an agreement, once achieved, marks the end of the problem under discussion, and that the solution will administer itself. With a more accurate view of the ongoing character of East-West relations, the Soviets see implementation of an agreement as a continuing negotiation.[37]

This suggests that Soviet negotiators simply have a more accurate sense of *realpolitik* than do Americans. The almost innate sense of negotiations as a process stems, however, not from a *realpolitik* appreciation of East-West relations, but from a fundamentally different conception of reality. Someone who has been raised with a dialectical understanding of reality *knows* that as long as the issue about which a negotiation is concerned continues to exist, the negotiation will continue. It may be useful at various points in the negotiation to give current understandings between the parties concrete form in a written agreement. A carefully negotiated agreement will have validity because it will correspond to reality. But reality changes. The dialectic continues. Any agreement, because cast in concrete form, in writing, and therefore static, must over time bear less and less correspondence to reality. At some point, in order to bring it back into closer correspondence with reality, it will have to be either reinterpreted or renegotiated.

The preference of Soviet negotiators for agreements that use generalized wording has often been remarked, generally to the accompaniment of warnings to U.S. negotiators to beware of this, since the Soviets will interpret any ambiguity in their favor. We discussed this as an aspect of Soviet negotiating tactics. The point to be made here is that one of the explanations for Soviet preference for broadly worded agreements may well involve dialectics. A dialectical negotiator is likely to have a preference in most situations for a broadly worded agreement, since it will lend itself to reinterpretation, rather than requiring the generally more difficult process of renegotiation.

To take a hypothetical example, suppose during the early stages of World War II the United States and Great Britain had negotiated with the Soviet Union an understanding on the post-war political framework for Eastern Europe. Suppose further that this agreement precluded a Soviet military presence in the countries concerned and required genuinely free elections to determine their form of government. Would the Soviet Union have adhered to this agreement? Not likely. It might be sufficient to explain its violation to point to the fact that Stalin was personally treacherous, or that communists are inherently perfidious, or that overriding national interests were at stake. Any of these is possible, and any of them may be relevant to a particular situation, but I suggest that it adds a dimension to our understanding to consider that for someone who sees negotiations as part of a dialectical process, changes in objective reality would have been so overwhelming that the earlier agreement could no longer be considered valid. It would have been so totally out of correspondence with reality that a Soviet leader who adhered to it would have been in fundamental error. The agreement would have to be changed to reflect reality.

To an American, this is likely to be indistinguishable from sheer treachery. What about the principle of adhering to the agreements you have signed? There is no such thing as an abstract principle to a dialectical materialist. Nothing exists "out there" except reality. Correct behavior is that which corresponds to reality. This is different from saying that dialectical materialists have no principles. In fact, "principled positions" figure prominently in the Soviet negotiating lexicon. A principled position, if it is genuinely based on principle and not being floated as a negotiating ploy, accords with the historical dialectic and therefore partakes of historical truth. Abandoning a principled position, therefore, requires a Soviet negotiator to commit an untruth: "To the Soviet negotiator a compromise is not a practical adjustment of principles by partial concession, since principles are unviolable. Furthermore, there is only one 'right' way to proceed."[38] It may also be impossible if it requires him to deny the historical dialectic, since that operates independently of the wishes of men. Of course, one's understanding of the historical dialectic can always be clarified, or improved. It is constantly changing, and the principled positions of one set of circumstances may be the negotiating concessions of another. In the hands of a cynic, the possibilities for manipulation of such an outlook are inevitably vast, but we should not assume that those who hold such an outlook are inevitably cynics. Sophistry has antecedents, both philosophical and historical, which long predate Marxism, or the Soviet government.

It may be objected that this begs the question of whether it is pointless to try to negotiate with the Soviets. Whether cynics or believers, if the Soviet authorities consider their international obligations subject to reinterpretation at times and places of their own choosing, what reliance can be placed on them? In fact, this question poses the alternatives more starkly than is generally the case in the real world, as we understand it. In the first place, they will adhere to agreements that bear a reasonable correspondence to reality as they understand it. And reality is sufficiently intractable that despite all our differences we and they are not likely in most situations to have greatly variant interpretations of one another's immediate interests. In the second, they are aware that others believe in abstract principles—and those beliefs are a part of reality. Therefore, a reputation for living up to agreements may be in their interest.

Lenin commented on the relevance of "petit bourgeois" notions of morality in his typically pungent fashion.

> The 'legal and moral consciousness' of the broad masses of philistines will condemn, let us say, a blow struck at a blackleg [scab], when it was struck in the heat of defending a strike called for an increase of a starvation wage. We shall not advocate violence in such cases because it is inexpedient from the point of view of our struggle. But we shall not 'respect' this philistine 'consciousness'."[39]

Adomeit's analysis of Soviet risk-taking behavior led him to conclude that Lenin's dictum remains relevant. The Soviet leadership is guided by the belief that it should "never lose sight of the political objectives to be achieved, and in pursuing them [should not] be diverted by false notions of bourgeois morality." This does not, in Adomeit's view, mean that "Soviet leaders are insensitive to moral issues but their morality is different from ours."[40]

It should, moreover, be recognized that we, too, recognize the motive force of changed circumstances and rarely enter an agreement affecting important national interests without providing mechanisms for withdrawal. But it will always be difficult for a person operating from this framework to sacrifice a tangible, immediate gain in favor of an intangible such as reputation, or world opinion. The direction of influence runs primarily from the material world to the world of ideas, rather than the reverse. Stalin expressed this outlook with characteristic bluntness when he asked how many tanks the Pope had. Another implication of this outlook is, as one perceptive observer of Soviet negotiating behavior noted, you cannot bank good will with them.[41] Nor, it should be added, do they expect to be able to bank it with you.

This is the theory. Does it, in fact, correspond to reality? A British Foreign Office expert, who has for years been a chief interpreter at top-level meetings, considers that ideological conditioning gives the Soviet leadership a dynamic view of world relations. They tend to see negotiation and agreements not as final or self-contained settlements of problems. A negotiation is a snapshot of a point in time; an agreement is an arrangement codifying the momentary relationship of forces or the relative positions of the parties at a particular moment. Since these relationships represent not static but ever-changing reality, an agreement has no intrinsic moral binding force. Life itself changes the outcome.[42] Malcolm McIntosh, who recently retired from the British Cabinet Office after forty years of working on Soviet affairs, believes the Soviets see a relationship as a non-stop trade. From time to time, events occur that make it essential to sit down across the table, or at the summit, to design a stepping stone for the process; then the process goes on.[43]

After years of high-level negotiations with the Soviets, Ambassador Max Kampelman is convinced that dialectics is an integral part of their thought system. He admits that he expected to find "a more pragmatic view, maybe a more cynical view."[44] An American diplomat, who has served at our embassy in Moscow and been involved in negotiating with the Soviets in both the CSCE and START contexts, believes that dialectics may get at a fundamental difference between us and them, particularly as concerns the implementation phase of an agreement. While the Soviets, he argues, do not usually commit outright violations of their agreements, they do try to take every possible advantage of any loopholes or vagueness of wording or interpretation.[45]

If there is a single leitmotif of advice to Americans in dealing with Soviet negotiators that has come down through the years, it is to be wary of imprecise agreements. Sloss and Davis call the "general formulation" approach "an integral part of their negotiating strategy, primarily designed to give the Soviets ample latitude for interpreting an agreement later." "This penchant for liberally interpreting treaty language," they continue, "has, throughout the history of U.S.-Soviet diplomacy, raised major questions about the credibility of Soviet compliance."[46]

The Soviet preference for general formulations in agreements and their penchant for interpreting them liberally derive from their dialectical understanding of the nature of negotiations. Wedge and Muromcew found in analyzing the SALT I talks that "the subordination of detail to principle appears to represent the reasoning pattern of Soviet negotiators quite genuinely; they are as puzzled by the West's procedures as the West is by theirs, and as suspicious. This contrast of epistemological principles is a serious impediment to understanding, but does not appear to be dictated by any wish to avoid agreement."[47] For Soviets to see negotiations as a process that continues beyond the signing of an agreement is as "natural" as for an American to view an agreement as a contract.

The importance of this has once again been demonstrated in the INF Treaty implementation process. Implementing discussions, originally viewed by the U.S. side as purely technical, began with the Soviets several months after the treaty was signed. The Soviets, predictably, used them to see whether in the implementation phase they might through interpretation of treaty language walk back some of their late concessions. I took part in those talks and doubt that the Soviets expected their efforts either to succeed in any major way or to cause a major fuss. But they failed to understand the probable American reaction, particularly during the ratification period. Word of the problems soon leaked to the press, the Senate ratification process came to an abrupt halt, and the "technical" issues quickly became political ones, requiring an additional agreement between Secretary of State Shultz and Foreign Minister Shevardnadze to resolve. Could these issues have been resolved at the technical level? Probably, if either the Americans who went public had understood the Soviet negotiating process better or the Soviets had understood the American political process better.

We are not talking about right or wrong here. We are talking about understanding and effectiveness. Understanding negotiation as a process and alertness to the necessity for implementation have been commended to Americans as useful negotiating tools even within their own society.[48] They are crucial in negotiating with Soviets. Conscious of the fact that his Soviet counterpart approaches negotiations from a different perspective, the American negotiator can develop a strategy that maximizes his chances of achieving a favorable outcome.

The Correlation of Forces

Dialectics may, as Vladimir Bukovsky suggests, be a "back of the mind" concept, an analytic tool used routinely for interpreting the world, but rarely itself examined analytically. The correlation of forces appears, by contrast, to be decidedly front of the mind. A correct analysis of the correlation of forces in any situation is essential if the Party is to act correctly. The Party's right to rule rests on its assertion that its understanding of the forces of history permits it to do what is best not only for the Soviet Union but for all of mankind. In a world of unceasing conflict and change, the concept of the correlation of forces provides both a rock of stability and a compass of direction.

The discussion below is based primarily on Julian Lider's full-length study of the concept.[49] In keeping with dialectical materialism's theory of knowledge, the correlation of forces is a concept that purports to describe objectively existing reality. It exists "out there" independently of man's perception or interpretation of it. As an element of the real world, it is subject to the same dialectical laws as all other reality. The operation of these laws can be summarized in the following way. Any phenomenon that exists in the world is composed of both "old" and "new" parts, which exist simultaneously within it and which are in permanent conflict, or contradiction, with one another. The quantitative strength of the "new" increases gradually, as the strength of the "old" decreases. At some point, these changes lead to qualitative changes in the correlation of their forces and, through the clashes between them, to "radical changes in the essence of the phenomenon in question. . . . The final and most radical change consists in a revolutionary replacement (called 'negation') of the old essence of the phenomenon by a new essence, which means a transformation of this phenomenon into another one. In turn, the 'new' gradually becomes 'old' and weak and it is doomed to give way to yet another new phenomenon ('negation of the negation')."[50] The shape of the struggle between "old" and "new" is determined by the correlation of forces between them, a dynamic and constantly changing factor.

Policy must correctly reflect this objectively existing reality. When, for example, the struggle between the socialist and capitalist forces leads to a qualitative shift in the correlation of forces between them, policy must be changed to correspond to this new situation. The change from the doctrine of the inevitability of war to that of peaceful coexistence, to which we have previously referred, was required by a changed correlation of forces. The doctrine of the inevitability of war between the socialist and capitalist camps correctly reflected reality during an era when the socialist camp was encircled and fascism was the most dynamic force in the capitalist camp. The end of capitalist encirclement following World War II, the defeat of fascism, the growing strength of the socialist forces, and the advent of nuclear weapons produced a qualitative shift in the correlation of forces in favor of socialism. War, therefore, was no longer inevitable. The policy that corresponded to this new reality was peaceful coexistence. Robert V. Daniels cites the change under Khrushchev to the doctrine of peaceful coexistence as evidence for his view that doctrine is purely instrumental in the foreign policy area, that the objective of the Soviet leadership is "to retain a free hand for any opportune move, unrestricted by possible theoretical inhibitions."[51] This view assumes that underneath all of the ideological trappings the Soviet leadership's conceptual approach to international politics is essentially identical to ours, a view with which it is hopefully clear by now I am in considerable disagreement. Naturally Khrushchev perceived opportunities for himself and the Soviet Union under the new doctrine. A correct analysis of any situation always reveals opportunities. But the opportunities one perceives flow from one's intellectual constructs for understanding and interpreting reality. Those constructs are not identical to ours.

Your average Soviet negotiator is, of course, not likely to be thinking at this level of abstraction. But if we consider the phenomenon in question to be social forces, or social classes, we come quickly to a more concrete application of the concept. In analyzing the correlation of social forces, the analyst must include both their material and nonmaterial components. The former include economic assets, means of coercion, access to the mass media, and other means of information and ideological influence. The principal nonmaterial components are class consciousness, organization, and a rational and proper combat strategy.[52] The material components determine what the possibilities for struggle are. You must correctly assess them, but you cannot directly affect them. They exist independently of you. Strategy, on the other hand, is your responsibility. As Lider puts it, "the proper choice of the strategy and means used permits a successful exploitation of the [material] correlation of forces. Moreover, an appropriate strategy may lead to further advantageous changes in the correlation of forces," leading to even greater possibilities for action in the future. And in the final analysis, of course, one can only determine the accuracy of one's understanding of the correlation of forces by acting. Knowledge is by necessity incomplete; action increases knowledge. Wrote Lenin, "You cannot learn to swim unless you go into the water. There can be no contest in which all the chances are known beforehand."[53]

Turning to the international arena, Lider continues:

> The determining Marxist-Leninist category, which permeates the analysis of all three levels of international political relations . . . is the correlation of the two forces of the two socio-economic systems. This correlation cannot be reduced to a comparison of the parameters of military power. . . . It is a broad and complex class sociopolitical category. It should be viewed as a correlation of the class, social, economic, political, ideological, military, ethical and other forces in the two socio-economic systems of our times.[54]

Like the correlation of social forces, the correlation of international forces reflects objectively existing conditions in the international sphere and objective historical tendencies. But just as a proper strategy can affect the evolution of the correlation, so the actions of states affect the development of the correlation of international forces. In the current international system, Soviet theorists claim, the "impact of the military component of the correlation has diminished, while the importance of the economic, sociopolitical and moral-ideological components has increased."[55] Since the forces of history are on the side of the socialist camp, the greater influence of the nonmilitary components is yet another of that camp's assets.

One may question whether Soviet leaders or negotiators really believe this in light of abundant evidence that they, in fact, give inordinate attention to the military component of the correlation. This appears to be an area in which deep-seated elements of the political culture—to be discussed in the following section—clash with contemporary theory. As Lider notes, when we turn "from general concepts to the actual assessment, we see another picture. In both approaches the superpowers and their military power continue to be the main protagonists and the main items in the correlation."[56] In their behavior on the world scene, Soviet leaders appear often to rely heavily on those aspects of the correlation that concern military forces. " 'Forces' mean here both what a given protagonist possesses and what he is prepared to do in the non-material sense; the latter includes the will to act, the organizational abilities and, as mentioned above, the strategy prepared."[57] Lider's description of the importance of the nonmaterial components of the correlation during a war appears equally applicable to nonwar situations.

> It is considered that an active policy may profoundly affect the correlation of forces during a war. The outcome of war depends not only on the correlation of the military might of the countries or coalitions of countries, but also on a protagonist's ability to change the international situation to his own advantage and to create a military superiority at a given place and take advantage of it. Here the political strategy is closely linked to the military one.[58]

We must presume that the Soviets, like us, precede any negotiation with a policy review which produces guidelines for the conduct of the negotiations. An American foreign policy review will focus on U.S. interests: What are they? How can we advance/defend them? The equivalent Soviet policy review will use the correlation of forces as its organizing concept. But the questions that flow from it are likely to differ somewhat from those an American would ask. American interests are generally considered to be stable and consistent. If they change, it is only slowly and over an extended period of time. Thus, any analysis of the current situation will be presented against a background of constant U.S. interests. The Soviet, it is true, will also want to correctly analyze the current situation, the existing correlation of forces. But since the correlation is in constant movement, he will want to analyze very specifically the nature of the dynamic, the forces at play producing change and the direction of change. He will recommend a strategy or a course of action that will shift the correlation in favor of the Soviet Union, or create conditions favorable to such a shift. The organizing concept of his analysis requires such recommendations. An American asks: How can we defend U.S. interests? A Soviet asks: How can we shift the correlation in our favor? Even an unfavorable correlation can be made less unfavorable; losses can be minimized. And any agreement reached must be defendable in similar terms. As Thomas Wolfe put it, in reflecting on the SALT experience: "SALT and detente, as well as Soviet military power itself, are all seen as instruments of policy useful in one way or another to keep the United States from trying to arrest what, from the Soviet viewpoint, constitutes an inevitable, though admittedly uneven, process of transition to a new 'correlation of forces' in the world favorable to the Soviet Union and other 'fraternal' countries."[59]

American understanding both of the concept of the correlation of forces and how it is brought to bear on negotiations in which we are involved remains limited. Paul Nitze believes that it is an area to which we should be paying much greater attention in our strategic arms talks with the Soviets. Major Soviet foreign policy moves are preceded by a policy review, presumably reduced at some point to written form and given Politburo approval. A better understanding of how their perception of the correlation of forces affects the policy review—not just the military, but also the political, economic, and moral aspects—might, in Nitze's view, help us to get a better sense of where their policy review is going to come out and, thereby, to plan our own strategy more effectively.[60]

POLITICAL CULTURE

Behind the ubiquitous Communist Party slogans lies the other face of the Soviet Union, the older, more Russian face. It shows itself most visibly in the churches—Moscow, the city of a thousand churches, the Third Rome, now the capital of world atheism. The churches that remain open, many fewer than dot the skyline, are crowded. True, the attendees are mostly elderly women. But so have they reportedly been throughout the history of the Soviet regime, one generation after another taking its place before the iconostasis to celebrate the resurrection of Christ and the triumph of Christianity. They are, in effect, witnessing not only their faith, but also the stubbornness with which old Russia lives on despite a Soviet regime that has shown itself to be utterly ruthless in its efforts to impose its will upon the country. This is not to say that the present regime finds all aspects of old Russia uncongenial. To the contrary, as we shall see, it has drawn, both consciously and unconsciously, on Russian political culture for elements of support.

Much ink has been spilled in the perennial debate over the relative influence of Marxist-Leninist ideology and Russian political culture on Soviet foreign policy. Are the Soviets impelled by ideology or guided by traditional Russian national interests? It is hard to disagree with Teresa Rakowska-Harmstone's observation that the Soviet Union is neither Communist nor Russian; it is both.[61] The October Revolution did not abolish Russia, but neither has Russia been left unchanged by the Soviet regime. E. H. Carr nicely caught the dynamics of the process, while suggesting that ultimately old patterns exert more influence on new than the reverse.

> Revolutions do not, however, resolve the tension between change and continuity, but rather heighten it; . . . thus in the development of the revolution, the elements of change and continuity fight side by side, now conflicting and now coalescing, until a new and stable synthesis is established. The process may be a matter of a few years or a few generations. But, broadly speaking, the greater the distance in time from the initial impact of the revolution, the more decisively does the principle of continuity reassert itself against the principle of change.[62]

But what does this mean for Soviet negotiating behavior? We have already suggested that ideology enters the picture via thought processes deeply imbued with a dialectical approach to understanding reality and an analytical concept—the correlation of forces—that expects conflict and emphasizes the dynamic aspects of the negotiation process. What, then, of Russian political culture? How does it manifest itself in contemporary Soviet life and, more relevantly for our purposes, in Soviet negotiating behavior?

It is beyond the scope of this study to attempt a detailed analysis of Russian history and culture, a subject on which volumes have already been written. But we can at least make an effort to understand the principal shaping influences.

While there may be no unanimity among scholars on what those influences were, there is considerable overlap. James Billington writes that three forces in particular, "the natural surroundings, the Christian heritage, and the Western contacts of Russia hover bigger than life" over the history of Russian culture. Steven White sees the "equation between belief, nationality and citizenship—expressed in the celebrated formula autocracy, orthodoxy, nationality"—as the "most distinctive contribution of the old regime to the political culture of the Soviet regime which succeeded it."[63] In his uniquely insightful way, E. H. Carr traced the lasting impact of geographic imperatives:

> The great distances over which authority had to be organized made state-building in Russia an unusually slow and cumbrous process; and, in the unpropitious environment of the Russian steppe, forms of production and the social relations arising from them lagged far behind those of the more favoured west. And this time-lag, continuing throughout Russian history, created disparities which colored and determined all Russian relations with the west. . . . This historical pattern of the development of the Russian State had three important consequences. In the first place, it produced that chronically ambivalent attitude to Western Europe which ran through all subsequent Russian thought and policy. It was indispensable to imitate and "catch up with" the west as a means of self-defence against the west; the west was admired and envied as a model, as well as feared and hated as the potential enemy. Secondly, the pattern of development rested on the conception of "revolution from above". . . . Reform . . . came through pressure of external crisis, resulting in a belated demand within the ruling group for an efficient authority and for a strong leader to exercise it. Hence reform meant in Russia a strengthening concentration of [State] power. Thirdly, the pattern imposed by these conditions was one, not of orderly progress, but of spasmodic advance by fits and starts—a pattern not of evolution but of intermittent revolution.[64]

Authoritarian political structures have dominated the landscape of Russian history. Many observers, both Russian and Western, have traced their strength and durability to the more than two centuries of Russian subjection to Tatar rule. Tucker sees Stalinism as at least in part a throwback to a revolutionary process seen earlier in Russian history, when the princes and tsars of Muscovy sought to resist Mongol domination by building a strong military-national state, which required one or another form of compulsory service from all classes. Tibor Szamuely treats the subject in more detail and is fairly representative in his stress upon the absolute, unlimited power of the Khan and the gradual acceptance by the emerging state of Muscovy of the basic Mongol principles of unqualified submission to the State and universal, compulsory, and permanent state service of all individuals and classes of society. Szamuely adds, however, that these principles were reinforced and fixed by three additional centuries of unremitting struggle against Tatar raiders from the south, seeking slaves and plunder. "The closing of the southern frontier and the establishment of security from Tatar incursion became, and remained until the end of the eighteenth century, the all-important, overriding object of the Russian State. This task demanded a total, unremitting and ruthless concentration of all national resources, both human and material, that for scope and intensity is probably unparalleled, over a comparable period of time, by any other nation.'' George Vernadsky traced in some detail the evolution in Muscovy of the authoritarian institutions imposed by the Mongols, while contrasting them with the freedom he sees as characteristic of the Kievan period of Russian history.[65] In a recent book, Charles J. Halperin argues against this view, asserting that Byzantium had bequeathed to Russia even before the arrival of the Mongols not only its form of Christianity, but also its political authoritarianism. Edward Keenan, however, considers that evidence is lacking for the assertion that Muscovite political culture was significantly influenced by either the form or the practice of Byzantine political culture or ideology.[66]

We will leave to others the resolution of these differences. The essential fact for our purposes is that authoritarian politics in Russia has deep roots and great durability. Over the past half millennium, while concepts of individual rights and limitations on political authority were slowly and painfully gaining a place in Western politics, authoritarianism remained deeply entrenched in Russia. It can be argued, in fact, as we look back from our current vantage point, that if there has been a trend in Russian history it has been toward increasing concentration of power in the State, and at least equally arbitrary use of that power. Tsars might be more or less capricious in their exercise of power. They might be reactionary or reformist. But all were dedicated to maintaining their hold on power, on the right to rule as they saw fit. Their Soviet successors fit comfortably into this tradition. The effect of this essential political fact on the Soviet style of negotiating has been vast.

In a significant article on Muscovite political folkways, Edward Keenan distinguishes between court, bureaucratic, and peasant political cultures and traces their development and ultimate melding in this century into a single Soviet political culture. The article defies easy summarization, but some attempt must be made to trace its main lines. Keenan suggests that in peasant society the imperatives of simple survival—against slave raiders, disease, and a harsh climate—made the village unit the most significant autonomous actor in peasant life. The village was far more important than the individual or even the family unit, neither of which had sufficiently assured viability in this environment. The village itself was so vulnerable that minimization of risk was the primary objective of collective decisions. Individual interests were subordinated to group viability and individual activity seen as potentially destructive of the group. Such destructive activity was to be avoided, not by the internalization of taboos, as in much of northern Europe, but by greater reliance on institutionalized subordination of the individual to the group. Within the household, its head was an autocrat, but both his power and that of the household were constrained by the larger interests of the village. This peasant political culture changed little before the advent of the twentieth century.

Court culture revolved around the tsar, who acted as a kind of referee in court politics, which essentially concerned clan maneuvering to arrange desirable marriages. Decision-making was collegial and the process was informal. Within the court, the tsar was not all-powerful, although that might be the impression conveyed to outsiders. Individuals were expected to adhere to group decisions and their interests were subordinated to those of the group. There were many similarities between court and bureaucratic cultures, but also some significant differences. While family connections were important, as in court society, there were no bureaucratic clans, and upward mobility, within this stratum, was not limited by heredity or family. Decision-making was not collegial, but vertical, via an institutionalized chain of command.

Keenan finds common features among the three cultures that he sees as the basic attributes of the Russian political culture.

1. Political status and social function were determined by a combination of birth, personal affiliation and the balance of interests of the other players, rather than by the rules of a political structure.
2. Membership in these closed and informal systems conferred significant rewards and an assured role in collective decision-making, but also required acquiescence in the decisions of the system's governing mechanism. Excessively aggressive attempts to increase individual power or status were seen as potentially threatening to the system and ran the risk of severe group sanctions.
3. Policy in all three cultures tended to opt for stability and risk-avoidance over change or "progress."
4. The sytems were reluctant to allow nonparticipants access to the generalized principles of their operation, either by promulgating laws or articulating ideologies. In other words, participants followed the rule of neglasnost, not telling outsiders how the system really works.[67]

In discussing the effect of ideology on the Soviet outlook, we tried to point out that the Russian dissident tradition shared some important basic elements of the Russian outlook on the world with the system it sought to replace. Keenan reinforces this point. The dissident counter-culture, like the dominant Russian political culture, was not particularly interested in systematic political theory, in juridical or constitutional structures that would impact on the forms and limits of power. Rather, it sought to ensure the just and moral use of power. Power and the institutions of the state should be used, not to insure the rights of the individual, but his perfection.[68] Yet Russia's dissidents, particularly as the country moved through the nineteenth century, were also profoundly alienated from the numerically dominant, but politically quiescent, peasant society. They arose from the upper classes, the merged court and bureaucratic cultures, which looked to the West for intellectual stimulus. This ambivalence had a profound impact on the Russian revolutionary movement, and on the Soviet state which developed out of the ultimate merger of the peasant and upper class political cultures. We will turn to this shortly, as we consider Lenin and the Bolshevik party which he founded and led to victory in 1917.

First, however, we need to consider the effect of this tradition on the Soviet view of the world. The Soviet rulers, like their Russian predecessors, face the West with, as Carr put it, a mixture of admiration, envy, and fear. Russia's ruling class has always looked to the West for models, albeit sometimes models to be emulated, other times models to be despised. This chronic ambivalence also lies deep in Russian history. As Halperin puts it:

> During the Mongol period, Medieval Russia chanced to be at the interface of two vast and irreconcilable worlds. Considered from the West, Russia lay at the distant rim of European Christendom, on the most remote reaches of the frontier. Contemplated from the East, Russia was the westernmost of the huge Mongol dominions stretching all the way from the China Sea. It is part of the conundrum of medieval Russia that it was part and yet not a part of both realms. Tied culturally to Byzantium and the West, politically to the pagan and later Muslim East, Russia under the Golden Horde was from either perspective an anomaly.[69]

And so it has remained, its combination of European and Oriental traits and traditions a source of mystery to outsiders and confusion to its own inhabitants. As described by Seweryn Bialer: "Geographically, and to some extent culturally, Russia is both a European and Asian country. This geographic circumstance, however, instead of being a source of strength, led instead to its alienation from both Europe and Asia."[70]

But as the Soviet Union looks out on the world, its reaction to the view to the West differs greatly from its reaction to the view to the East. Its basic view of the West, I believe, is as technologically advanced, corrupt, and threatening. Its view of the East is as powerful, capricious, and threatening. The traditional, much-discussed Russian sense of insecurity is a component of both views, but manifests itself quite differently. During three years in the Soviet Union, I sensed a visceral component to the Soviet fear of China that is largely missing from its reaction to the United States. Sovietologist Bialer has written about his own similar impressions:

> Anyone who has traveled in the Soviet Union and has talked about China with Soviet citizens is struck by both the primitiveness and the intensity of their views. Such conversations leave the inescapable impression that in the Russian popular mind, China looms as a danger of overwhelming proportions. The citizen will give some lip service to the danger from the 'Western imperialists'. . . . But when it comes to the Chinese, his deepest feelings are unconcealed fear, distrust, aversion, even hatred. . . . There is a clear association between China and Genghis Khan and the Russian suffering under the Tatar-Mongol yoke.[71]

Age-old memories of the "Tatar yoke" may indeed play a part in this, but Russian history since the end of Tatar domination has reinforced those memories.

In coping with military threats from the West, Russia has traditionally compensated for its technological inferiority with patience and numbers. It might take huge losses and surrender vast territories, but much more often than not it eventually prevails, regaining what it has lost and then some. The Soviet Union's posture toward the West today is that traditional one. For that reason, I believe, it is known and relatively comfortable. But as it looks East, Moscow faces a neighbor that not only stirs ancient fears, but is also in a military position analogous to Moscow's vis-à-vis the West. Clearly inferior technologically, China has vast reserves of manpower, a sense of time and history, and appears to have the will to use both effectively. Thus, the theme that dominates the Soviet Union's relations with the West is inferiority; the theme that dominates its relations with China is insecurity.

The Russian political culture cannot be understood without reference to orthodoxy. The Church early became subservient to, and a pillar of support for, the State. But the influence of religious orthodoxy goes far beyond that. Keenan is only one among a number of students of Russian history who have argued that following the era of Peter the Great, there were really two Russian histories—a history of the small, sophisticated urban upper classes, and that of the immense rural mass which essentially dropped into a historical backwater and did not emerge again until the time of the revolution, or perhaps of the emancipation of the serfs.[72] The upper classes, alternately repelled by and attracted to the West, gave birth to a remarkable cultural flowering in the nineteenth century. For the Slavophiles among them, Russia was the Third Rome, a repository of values long lost in a Western world that could corrupt, but not teach. Even the Westernizers considered that Russia had a mission, or a Word; it could bring something to the West, as well as learn from it. In their own thought processes, the Westernizers belonged to the classic Russian tradition. They might reject Orthodoxy, but they accepted Hegel or Marx with the same fervor and with the same expectation that herein lay the answer, herein lay the Truth which they could follow and live by.

None of this, however, found any resonance among the great masses of the population, "among whom the old religious beliefs and hopes were still preserved. The Western influences which led on to the remarkable Russian culture of the nineteenth century found no welcome among the bulk of the people."[73] The Russian people of the Petrine era, and their descendants, showed themselves to be both deeply and traditionally religious. As Billington puts it: "For the historian of culture, however, the real drama of the seventeenth century follows from the determination of many Russians to remain—through all the changes and challenges of the age—blagochestivye: ardently loyal to a sacred past."[74] This determination led, on the one hand, to the passive resistance of the Old Believers and, on the other, to peasant insurrections. These rebellions "were animated by one recurring political ideal: belief in a 'true tsar'," who would "come to their aid if only the intervening wall of administrators and bureaucrats could be torn down."[75] Tsardom was not in question, only the identity of the ruler.

Against this background we need to consider the impact of Lenin on the Soviet Union, of Russia on Lenin, and of the Bolshevik synthesis of Marxism and Russian political culture.

THE RUSSIAN PAST, THE SOVIET PRESENT

Writing as X in *Foreign Affairs* forty years ago, George Kennan posed the difficulties of understanding Soviet behavior in classic terms:

> The political personality of Soviet power as we know it today is the product of ideology and circumstances: ideology inherited by the present Soviet leaders from the movement in which they had their political origin, and circumstances of the power which they now have exercised for nearly three decades in Russia. There can be few tasks of psychological analysis more difficult than to try to trace the interaction of these two forces and the relative role of each in the determination of official Soviet conduct. Yet the attempt must be made if that conduct is to be understood and effectively countered.[76]

An additional four decades of knowledge and experience have only emphasized the difficulty of the task.

Tracing the interaction of these forces must begin with Lenin. Over the years, Lenin has taken on the attributes of a combination of Jesus Christ, George Washington, and Abraham Lincoln in Soviet eyes. With the disgrace of Trotsky, the ambivalent status of Stalin, and the nonperson status of most of the other purged and murdered heroes of the Revolution, Lenin stands not simply as *primus inter pares*, but alone in the pantheon of the Soviet Union's leaders. Viewed from the Soviet context, this status in not undeserved. By dint of single-minded determination and intellectual and political genius, Lenin brought a small group of exiles and outcasts with a history of ineffectuality and infighting to the leadership of the largest country on earth. His genius was in the adaptation of Marxism to the Russian political culture.[77] His single-mindedness was in the pursuit of power.

Lenin is a complex and contradictory figure. Descended from one Kalmuk and two German grandparents, he remained quintessentially Russian while in constant revolt against both his country's socioeconomic and political system and the pernicious effects of that system on the ideals and morals of his countrymen. Berdyaev saw Lenin as combining in himself two traditions: "the tradition of the Russian revolutionary intelligentsia in its most maximalist tendency, and the tradition of the Russian government in its most despotic aspect." Billington, on the other hand, stresses how Lenin differed from almost all of his intellectual predecessors in nineteenth-century Russia: "It was his profound alienation from the dominant intellectual trends of the late imperial period which enabled him to appear as the bearer of a genuinely new order of things. . . . Lenin focused his attention on one all-consuming objective that had not traditionally been uppermost in the thinking of the intelligentsia: the attainment of power." J. N. Bochenski believed that it is not possible to understand dialectical materialism correctly without knowing Lenin's character. "He was," wrote Bochenski, "a man of outstanding ability, and an engineer on a vast scale—a technician of power and of revolution."[78]

For Lenin, the quintessential political question was "*kto kovo*," who rules whom, or who has power over whom. He did not consider power divisible, nor did he consider that it could be shared in any but the very short term. In any situation of power-sharing, one side or the other would sooner or later, and probably sooner, rule. In his own political struggles, Lenin showed himself ready to sacrifice size, whether of adherents or of geography, in return for retaining full control over his organization. In "On the Eve of October 1917," Lenin wrote: "At the conference, we must immediately consolidate the Bolshevik faction without worrying about numbers, without being afraid about leaving the vacillators in the camp of the vacillating: they are more useful to the cause of the revolution there than in the stronghold of the resolute and courageous fighters."[79] He insisted upon rigid control of the trade unions by the party elite, even at the price of some narrowing of the labor movement.[80] The Bolshevik/Menshevik split at the 1903 Party congress concerned both power and doctrine about it. Again, Lenin showed himself prepared to split the Party rather than share power or compromise on Party organization. The issue began with a division over whether the party should stick to its Western model or adapt itself to specifically Russian conditions and quickly broadened into fundamental questions of Marxist doctrine. The Mensheviks, Carr argues, were unconsciously from the very first, Westernizers and the Bolsheviks the Easterners.[81] Lenin was determined to have a party that corresponded with his sense of political reality, a very home-grown, Russian sense. "Classes," he said in 1918, "are led by parties and parties are led by individuals who are called leaders. . . . What is necessary is individual rule, the recognition of the dictatorial powers of one man. All phrases about equal rights are nonsense."[82] For Lenin, the Treaty of Brest-Litovsk was about keeping power. The Germans might acquire some territory, but the Bolsheviks would remain in power. History would show whether Germany could keep control of the territory it had gained.

Nathan Leites's ambitious and controversial *A Study of Bolshevism*[83] attempts, by drawing primarily though not exclusively on the work of Lenin, to show how the ideas of Marx and Engels were transmuted into a code of Bolshevik behavior for acquiring and maintaining power. At the psychological level, Leites sees the Bolsheviks as driven by a reaction against the perceived weaknesses in the Russian character, by a conviction that all relations between people turn on the question of who controls whom (another variant of Lenin's *kto-kovo*), and by a deepseated fear of being controlled by an outside force. In fact, of course, at the same time the Bolsheviks were at one level reacting against some elements of the Russian tradition, they were at another level embracing other aspects of it. Lenin's success was not simply a matter of having burned away from his own character the impurities of the Russian outlook. It was, as discussed above, at least equally a matter of having embodied within himself an acute awareness of what Russia needed and would permit in a revolutionary movement.

"Russian" traits that Bolshevism opposes include carelessness in making decisions, procrastination, lack of mental alertness, vagueness, a tendency to be divorced from reality.[84] Leites drew together the axioms of behavior that he believed Bolsheviks developed to counter these and other undesirable Russian characteristics into what he termed an "operational code." The implications in this terminology of an ideological blueprint for behavior have led many, who see such an approach as simplistic, simply to dismiss Leites's effort, even to view it as bizarre. Without explicitly mentioning Leites, though presumably having him, as well as others, in mind, Samuel L. Sharp called it "dubious scholarship to collect quotations . . . from Lenin and Stalin without regard to the time, place, circumstances, composition of the audience, and, whenever ascertainable, immediate purposes of such utterances." Robert Jervis suggests that several aspects of the operational code are not unique to Bolshevism, but rather are commonly held by a state that believes that it is confronted by an implacably hostile adversary.[85] (But if two men exhibit the symptoms of paranoia, is it irrelevant that one really is being pursued by an implacably hostile adversary and one is not? The path toward eliminating the symptoms, or at least dealing effectively with the person exhibiting them, would seem to be considerably different in the two cases. Why does the Soviet Union see itself as confronted by an implacably hostile adversary? Because it is? Because its view of the world convinces it that it is? If the latter, what are the respective roles of ideology and political culture in producing that world view? And what are the implications for negotiating with it?)

In fact, though Leites's work must be handled with care, it is as full of insights about Soviet negotiating behavior as it is provocative. Alex George has drawn on it for a convincing analysis of Soviet "optimizing" behavior in the international arena, which he contrasts with a Western tendency toward "satisficing." George likens the beliefs and premises Leites discussed to a prism that influences perceptions of political events and estimates of particular situations. They also provide standards and guidelines that influence the choice of strategy and tactics, the structuring and weighing of alternative courses of action. They are an important, but not the only, variable in decision-making.[86]

The Bolshevik outlook on political action rejects strategies that confine goals to those that are highly feasible. It argues instead for attempting to maximize the gains sought in a particular situation, reasoning that: (a) action must often be taken on the basis of incomplete knowledge; only action itself can increase knowledge; (b) what can be achieved cannot be predicted in advance—it can only become known in the process of struggle, by attempting to get the most out of a situation; (c) in choosing goals in a particular situation, one should, therefore, limit them only by assessing what is objectively possible in the situation—that is, not impossible to achieve by intelligent use of resources at one's disposal.[87] In a particular situation, a person espousing this outlook will have not a single objective, but a set of graduated objectives, how many of which can be achieved will be determined in the course of the struggle.

Hannes Adomeit, who contrasts his inductive approach to understanding Soviet behavior with the deductive approach used by Leites and George, concludes that the approaches coincide in their finding that operational principles and recurring patterns of behavior exist that are specifically Soviet. He believes they must be explained in significant part by Soviet ideology.[88]

Lenin's bequest to Russia was not only the approach to the analysis of political action we have been discussing, but also an organization, the Communist Party of the Soviet Union, which has shown itself to be an exceptionally adept instrument for the maintenance of political power. Like Lenin himself, the Party is rooted deeply in Russian culture and has over the decades adapted itself to Russian realities. While it can be argued with some justice that it has expressed those realities in forms so perverted as to be virtually unrecognizable, it is far closer to the truth to see the durability of Communist Party rule in the Soviet Union as reflective of its adaptation to Russian realities than to see it solely as an alien influence imposed by force on an innocent and unwilling Russian people. The Bolshevik Party, Lenin's carefully forged instrument of revolution, whose creed of centralism, elitism, and conspiratorial rule was most compatible with traditional patterns, became, of all the "organizations and trends that had competed for hegemony in the revolutionary period . . . the principal agent and beneficiary of the reestablishment of political stability."[89]

Those who study political culture find it useful to distinguish between official, dominant, and elite political cultures. Archie Brown defines dominant political culture as "subjective perceptions of history and politics, fundamental political beliefs and values, foci of identification and loyalty, and political knowledge and expectations."[90] Ideology, in Bialer's understanding of it as "a part of culture, a slowly changing combination of doctrinal inputs and the historical experience and predispositions that run parallel to doctrine,"[91] forms a part of the dominant political culture of the Soviet Union. Marxist-Leninist doctrine, on the other hand, is its official political culture.

The Soviet Union of today differs from tsarist Russia less in the contrast between its dominant and its official cultures than in the fact that the great gap in Russia between the elite and dominant political cultures has been considerably narrowed in Soviet society. The Bolshevik revolution was a product of the dissident strain of Russia's elite political culture, intellectually influenced by the West, but fundamentally more deeply attached to older Russian values than its members themselves knew. So deeply, in fact, that the Revolution itself can be seen as essentially a revitalization and restoration of long dominant patterns of the political culture rather than as a break with them. But the intelligentsia that led this Revolution had yet to come to terms with Russia's peasant culture and were, in fact, alienated from it.[92]

During the first several decades of Soviet rule, the Communist Party was a vehicle of social mobility. Lenin and his cohorts may have been from the Russian intelligentsia, but their successors were not. It has been argued, in fact, that Stalin's accession to power initiated a revolution within the revolution, the second at least as significant for Russian history as the first. The murder of massive numbers of the intelligentsia, combined with the education and accession to positions of influence of former peasants at last brought to a substantial end the centuries-old split in Russia between the urban upper classes and the rural masses. Vakar sees in this the triumph in Soviet society of the peasant point of view, which instead of yielding to "Marxist enlightenment," supplanted it, or at least forced an amalgam owing more to the traditions of the village than to the writings of Marx. The immediate historical background of Soviet society, in his view, is the Muscovite state up to the time of Peter the Great, when the split in Russian society occurred. Billington also sees the Stalin era as having some of its deepest roots in pre-Petrine Moscow. Stalin, in his view, "was able to succeed Lenin as supreme dictator not only because he was a deft intriguer and organizer but also because he was closer than his rivals to the crude mentality of the average Russian. Unlike most other Bolshevik leaders—many of whom were of Jewish, Polish, or Baltic origin—Stalin had been deeply schooled in the catechistic theology of Orthodoxy."[93]

Tucker considers that the Stalinist period resurrected some patterns of thought, values, and institutional forms characteristic of tsarism at certain times. Bialer's view is similar:

> Another factor promoting stability is the predominantly lower-class origin of the upper political strata in the Soviet Union. Since the working class and the political elite share the same tradition and come from similar socioeconomic backgrounds, there results a symmetry of cultural attitudes and tastes cutting across the rulers and the working classes. This is reflected in the official culture and language of the society. The Soviet Union is one of the few societies where the cultures of the mass and the elite are almost inseparable. . . . The institutional framework that emerged in the Stalin era fitted rather well with the antecedent political culture of Tsarist Russia at the most critical points, and to all appearances the contemporary Soviet political culture still 'fits' this relatively unchanged institutional pattern quite well.[94]

This "fit" between contemporary Soviet political culture and its Russian antecedents is critical to an understanding of the Soviet negotiating style. The stable political culture that began to emerge toward the end of the Stalin era was characterized by: the establishment of a new political elite, drawn predominantly from the peasant class, but increasingly self-perpetuating; the reestablishment of extreme centralization; loss of military, bureaucratic, and party autonomy, except in the innermost party circles; the replacement of ideological revolutionism by the traditional combination of pragmatism and distrust of innovation; reassertion of old patterns of caution and risk-avoidance.[95] Areas in which contemporary ideology reinforces traditional institutional patterns and outlooks of political culture should be particularly important drivers of Soviet negotiating style and behavior. Conversely, in areas where the traditions are in conflict, we should expect far greater ambivalence, uncertainty, and mixed signals in how the Soviets negotiate.

Lenin's authoritarianism was securely rooted in the Russian political culture. The Party he bequeathed to Soviet society institutionalized that authoritarianism. But Lenin and, although perhaps to a somewhat lesser extent, most of his fellow Bolsheviks were revolutionaries, risk-takers on a grand scale. Their influence dwindled and was eventually lost in Stalin's Soviet Union, as they were murdered and replaced by leaders with peasant roots, who brought with them the Russian peasant's traditional risk-aversion. The murderous excesses of the Stalin era only reinforced this risk-aversion until, under Brezhnev, it became the dominant leitmotif of an era. Cohen sees this social and political conservatism expressing itself "daily in all areas of life as a preference for tradition and order and a fear of innovation and disorder."[96]

But Stalin also brought something qualitatively new to the political culture of his country. His crucial operative aim was *control*, and the system he left behind was an "elaborate, completely centralized bureaucratic mechanism for the command and control of society."[97] Lenin's authoritarian party was transformed into a mechanism for a degree of social control of unprecedented scope. From what we know of Stalin, control was probably in large part an end in itself. But there was another objective, perhaps partly rationalization, but also partly real. The Party was to be the instrument for achieving progress, for transforming the material basis of Soviet society. And by exercising an unprecedented degree of control over Soviet society, it could achieve progress, while avoiding risk. Thus, Stalin's "new Soviet man" could incorporate within himself traditional Russian authoritarianism and risk-aversion, while persuading himself that the control mechanisms in place were instruments of progress.

Before summarizing the elements of ideology and political culture that affect Soviet negotiating behavior, a couple of general points should be made about the present impact of long-established patterns in Russian society. The first concerns the relationship between power and status. The Soviet Union has throughout its history been a society of scarcity, both of material items and of the other things people find desirable. Obtaining them has not been a function of wealth, as in Western society, but rather of access. Power, or position, or access to persons with one or the other, is the key to getting things done, or getting what you want. Wealth, in the United States, provides access to power. In Soviet society, power produces access to wealth, or to whatever other good—influence, status, etc.—is desired. The Soviet Union and tsarist Russia are more alike than different in this regard. Bialer puts the relationship in the following way:

> Two traditional Russian characteristics are noteworthy for their imprint on the Soviet mind-set. First, there is the relationship between status, class, and political power in Russian history: traditionally, political power has been more of a source of high status or class than vice versa. Second, there is the lack of status and class

autonomy vis-à-vis the state. Accordingly, even the highest status has always required service to the state and is reaffirmed by that service. The Soviet theory and practice of politics, wherein relations to the Party-state serve as the wellspring of class and social status, falls well within the Russian tradition.[98]

Soviet negotiators are enormously privileged members of their society. While they are not well paid in monetary terms, they have access to housing and other material goods which enable a life-style about which most of their countrymen can only dream. And they have access to the rarest good of all in Soviet society: the opportunity to travel abroad. All of this depends entirely upon the positions they hold. It is a rare Soviet negotiator who has an important Party position or any other source of power that would provide a basis for independent maneuvering. The positions they hold give them access; loss of the position carries with it many more implications than loss of an equivalent position in the United States. The age of mass communications has produced a loss of independence for diplomats the world over, but perhaps no negotiators feel more constrained by their instructions, or more compelled to play to the home audience, than the Soviets. This can be frustrating for American negotiators, but it can also provide opportunities.

Finally, as students of Lenin and as individuals acculturated in their own society, Soviet negotiators will be keenly attuned to power relationships, both as they affect the negotiations at hand generally and as they operate on the other side of the table. The American negotiator who, anxious to put his Soviet counterpart into an understandable frame of reference, identifies this focus on power as essentially the same as a Western negotiator's pursuit of his country's interests makes an oversimplification that in the long run will hurt his effectiveness.

Russian political culture, then, manifests itself in Soviet negotiating behavior via: (a) authoritarian political traditions; (b) ambivalence toward the West—insecurity tinged with inferiority, but also accompanied by a sense of moral superiority; (c) a cast of mind that welcomes the traditional rather than the new, but that at the same time seeks to understand life in its entirety; and (d) aversion to risk-taking. The impact of ideology on these traits is mixed. Marxism-Leninism is fully compatible with Russia's authoritarian political traditions. It reinforces the old Russian sense of mission or destiny. The West is corrupt and doomed, but also dangerous; the Soviet Union is history's handmaiden and must remain pure in order to fulfill her destiny. Reality, truth can be understood, and men can act in accordance with it. Excessive risk, or adventurism, must be avoided, but one must push to the limits of the achievable. This can be accomplished by exercising firm and complete control over one's own behavior and over the process in which one is involved. What we observe of Soviet negotiating behavior—its style and tactics—has its origins in these deeply engrained traits of ideology and political culture.

CHAPTER 5

BALALAIKA, BROWNIAN MOTION, AND MOVEMENT:
Gorbachev and Soviet Negotiating Behavior

Truth is always positive, real.

—Reportedly Mikhail Gorbachev's favorite
Marxist-Leninist phrase

AUTHORITARIANISM, RISK-AVOIDANCE, AND CONTROL, PERHAPS the three most important characteristics of the Soviet political culture, exercise an enormous influence on Soviet negotiating conduct. To the extent that these characteristics change, Soviet negotiating conduct will also, sooner or later, undergo change. And to the extent that Gorbachev truly seeks reform in Soviet society, he must seek change in these deep-seated elements of his country's political culture. Reform and negotiating conduct are thus inextricably linked, and we must examine the former if we hope to say anything meaningful about the future of the latter.

Everything changes. The question is how fast, and with what relevance to our concerns. There is today much that is new at the top in the Soviet Union. In Mikhail Gorbachev, the country has a new leader, with a new style of leadership. Soviet Foreign Ministry officials with whom I have met have referred to the changes he has inaugurated as a "revolution." An American correspondent with years of experience in Moscow calls him smarter and more imaginative than any Western leader around.[1] Moreover, with his accession, the torch passed to a new leadership generation whose experiences in its politically formative years were greatly different from those of its predecessors.

No one argues that the changes introduced in Soviet society under Gorbachev have not been real. But their long-range significance will depend on how fundamentally they challenge the authoritarianism, risk-avoidance, and control that have characterized Soviet society. Discussing changes in Soviet society in the 1960s, Daniel Bell posed the following questions:

Do the current debates in science, philosophy, economics, sociology, and literature portend a revision of Marxist-Leninist dogma to bring it in line with the mainstream of Western rationalist thought (as so much of Marxism actually was, in its pre-Stalinist phase)? Will there be a more open forum of intellectual discussion and literary and philosophical "experimentation" so that some new doctrinal commitments will emerge? Or is the current ferment simply an "accommodation" on the part of the regime to momentary pressures, an accommodation that might be revoked by the ruling elite when it feels that changes have gone too far?[2]

Addressing the Soviet foreign policy outlook in 1975, Morton Schwartz speculated that:

The weltanschauung of previous Kremlin leaders was largely a function of two major characteristics of Russia's international situation: a near-permanent threat of invasion and danger of war and an historic sense of inferiority before a technologically more advanced Western culture. On both counts, important changes have recently taken place . . . which eventually may produce significant modifications in Russia's traditional world outlook. . . . Western willingness to recognize the USSR's great power role has helped reassure the Kremlin authorities of the legitimacy of their place in world affairs. Such reassurance, regarding both security and reputation, has already given rise to an increasingly sophisticated and self-confident Soviet diplomacy. It may, in time, nurture a spirit of reasonableness and cooperation.[3]

Bell's questions about Soviet domestic developments, though posed about another leader and another leadership generation, are no less relevant today. They warn us to be careful in evaluating both the nature and the durability of change in Soviet society. Schwartz's hopes for Soviet foreign policy reasonableness and cooperation were expressed at a time when detente was coming unraveled, in large part because of a Soviet weapons build-up that went beyond anything we could understand as equality and a Third World posture that appeared to presume not equality, but a dominant Soviet role. As we look at the possibility for changes in Soviet foreign policy behavior, we need to keep in mind not only the time frame involved but also what might happen in the meantime.

DOMESTIC DEVELOPMENTS UNDER GORBACHEV

There are some things happening in the Soviet Union today that are unprecedented (or at least without precedent over the past six decades), but we must be clear about what is unusual and what is not. For the Soviet Union to allow Andrei Sakharov to return to Moscow after years of forced exile in Gorky was neither unusual nor surprising. There is ample precedent. Only his prominence, the same prominence that for so long protected him against the harsh treatment accorded other Soviet human rights activists, made the step noteworthy. Gorbachev's call to Sakharov in Gorky presaging the end of his exile was unusual. What I personally found most surprising was the offer by Soviet radio and television of the use of their facilities for an uncensored interview of Sakharov by the Western press. Throughout Soviet history, the regime's insistence on controlling information flow, both into and out of the country, has been a constant. For it not only to allow, but to assist an uncontrolled interview with the country's most prominent dissident was a startling change.[4] Since then, similar treatment has been afforded Roy Medvedev, the prominent and independent-minded Soviet historian who was treated as a nonperson during the Brezhnev era. With Sakharov's travel to the United States late in 1988, the Gorbachev regime breached yet another theretofore sacrosanct barrier. It released from its control not only the country's most promiment dissident, but also the possessor of some of its most sensitive, albeit increasingly dated, nuclear secrets.

The candor of discussions about the country's problems in the Soviet media recalls the 1920s—and no period since.[5] *Glasnost*, publicity (but usually translated in the West by a term with a more positive cast—openness), has become the catchword in the West for this aspect of Gorbachev's policies. Soviet intellectuals may wonder how far it will go and how long it will last, but they do not doubt that it is there. It is a time for bringing to light works "written for the drawer." Pasternak has been rehabilitated, even posthumously reinstated in the Soviet Writers' Union, and his long-forbidden *Doctor Zhivago* was published in 1988 in *Novy Mir*. The editor of *Novy Mir* has publicly called Solzhenitsyn's *Cancer Ward* a serious work and talked about publishing it in the Soviet Union. In film and the theatre, as in literature, the bounds of the permissible are being pushed outward. The film producers' and writers' associations held elections that were reportedly democratic. Subsequently, a number of previously banned films were released, including two starring the late, much-beloved poet and songwriter, Vladimir Vysotsky. *Repentance*, a powerful Georgian film which indicts not only Stalin and his generation, but the generation that followed them, was released to enormous audiences, both in the Soviet Union and abroad.

Yet in some ways it is the regime's greater willingness to allow its citizens information from the outside world that is the most interesting and perhaps the most revealing. Jamming of the BBC and the VOA has ended. Prime Minister Thatcher and Secretary of State Shultz have been allowed to address Soviet television audiences live. Shultz told them how many troops their country had in Afghanistan and that they are not wanted there, sentiments that in 1980 earned Sakharov his lengthy exile to Gorky.

But this increasing openness to the outside world is not confined to government-to-government contacts. Indeed, some of the most interesting may be going on in the private arena. A San Francisco businessman has set up a computer and videophone link-up with the Soviet Union. He runs an electronic mail service and has used the phone link for several impromptu exchanges. One, between a group of American and Soviet students, illustrates some of the changes that have occurred. While in Moscow on a visit, he realized that a fortuitous location of the phones in the United States and the Soviet Union would allow a link-up between a student meeting at a California university and one at a Soviet university. When he approached the Soviet with whom he dealt on questions involving use of the phones, the latter asked the standard questions: Who would speak on the American side? What subjects would be discussed? The American replied that on the American side whoever wanted to would speak, and they would speak about whatever they wanted to. The Soviet not only agreed, he did it without, as far as the American could tell, consulting anyone else.[6]

The generally accepted explanation for these changes is that Gorbachev considers them necessary to end the stagnation of the Soviet economy. An optimistic interpretation holds that the Soviet leaders are aware of the explosion in scientific research and information exchange occurring in the rest of the world. They have accepted the fact that their country must inevitably be left further and further behind the cutting edge of scientific advance unless it takes drastic steps to integrate itself more effectively into the scientific world. This requires opening up of the dissemination of information—into the country, out of it, and within it. And they realize that they will not be able to restrict this information flow simply to areas of scientific research of military or economic priority. This implies a major decrease in the Party's control over the flow of information and, effectively, over the intellectual life of the country, a development of potentially far-reaching consequences.

In the economic sphere, Gorbachev's overall aim has been to encourage personal responsibility, initiative, and innovation. He has urged his countrymen in the provinces not to wait for instructions from Moscow. "You know the Party's view," he tells them, "now go ahead and make decisions." He has endeavored to create opportunities for initiative by allowing private cooperatives to function in the service sector of the economy. A November 1986 law authorized limited private enterprise in services such as shoe repair, taxi driving, small-scale construction, and agriculture. Moscow's first private, cooperative restaurant opened in 1987, even before the new law formally went into effect. The novelty, and its combination of high prices and good food and service, the reverse of the situation in the country's state-run restaurants, made reservations long in advance a necessity. Its popularity quickly spawned an ever-growing number of imitators and greatly decreased the problem of getting reservations. By the end of 1988, there were thousands of cooperatives in existence, offering everything from translation services to off-shift production of manufactured goods. Rubles have traditionally been in far greater supply in Soviet society than quality goods and services and have chased them in the black market. This limited experiment suggests that they would readily enough pursue them in the legal market, if the goods and services were available there. Money, rather than access, would then become the most fungible valuable, a fundamental change in a long-established pattern.

The debate on the significance of these changes is complicated. It concerns, first, whether Gorbachev intends changes that would affect any fundamental aspects of the nature of the Soviet system. Second, if he does, whether the Soviet power structure will permit any changes that appear to threaten its interests. Finally, whether changes pushed through from the top will have any long-term effect on fundamental aspects of the society's long-established political culture. Archie Brown, the author/editor of several respected works on the Soviet political culture, sees *glasnost* not just as a change in policy, but as an attempt to change the prevailing political culture by Party intellectuals who see it as an obstacle to reform.[7] Whether political culture is susceptible to substantial change over a relatively brief period of time is questionable. As Brown himself earlier noted: "If there is anything on which scholars who use the concept of political culture actually agree, it is that this is a concept which is of long-term, rather than short-term, significance, and that the basic political beliefs and values which are vital components of a political culture tend to change slowly."[8] But there is also considerable question about whether the leadership generation to which Gorbachev belongs really intends any fundamental change.

Robert Jervis has argued convincingly that leadership generations share common experiences which affect their perceptual predispositions. The impact any given event has on the individual and on the common outlook of the generation depends on whether or not the individual experienced the event firsthand, whether it occurred early in his adult life or career, whether it had important consequences for him or his nation, and whether he is familiar with a range of international events that facilitate alternative perceptions. Since people absorb many of the values and beliefs that dominate the climate of opinion at the time when they first begin to think about politics, all those who come of age at the time are affected similarly. The general lack of information young Soviets have about developments and opinions in the rest of the world has led some observers to expect greater continuity from one generation to the next than would occur in more open, pluralistic societies. Alex George, for example, believes that radically oriented elites, such as the Marxists, who claim to have a special understanding of history and historical development, will take special care to transmit key elements of their belief system, their "sacred political culture," to new leaders. "Change in such an elite's belief system, then, does not follow simply from the fact that the composition of the top leadership changes."[9]

The central organizing concept of the Stalinist political system is control. The Party controls the society; the *nomenklatura* controls the Party. Authority is not divided. There are no autonomous institutions. Each level follows the orders of the level above it and looks to that higher level for guidance and legitimacy. A good factory worker in a small provincial town is offered the job of foreman, if he joins the Party. Although he will only be supervising a few workers, he will be in a position of authority, and he should therefore be in the Party. A group of jazz lovers organizes a concert, but it must be under the sponsorship of the local Komsomol because it is a public, organized group activity. Avant-garde artists organize an exhibition—under the sponsorship of the Graphic Artists' Union.

This is how it has been in Soviet society for most of its history. It is a system of rule rooted in the Russian political culture and reinforced by the dominant ideology. What is tantalizing about Gorbachev's reforms is that at minimum they nibble around the edges of control and, if carried to their logical conclusion, could gobble great chunks out of it. In his speech marking the seventieth anniversary of Soviet rule, Gorbachev called for a new culture of socialist democracy, the lack of which, he said, gives rise to such defects as bureaucracy, abuse of power, undue reverence for rank, bad management, and irresponsibility.[10] *Glasnost* suggests that information is no longer going to be an instrument of rule, but rather an instrument of knowledge. *Perestroika* (restructuring, or, sometimes, reform) calls into question some of the Soviet system's key economic and political institutions. Opening the economy to private initiative strikes potentially at the very heart of the material system of rewards enjoyed by the *nomenklatura*, the ruling class. And Gorbachev's proposal for competitive elections strikes even more fundamentally at their right to rule. A Soviet emigré, formerly imprisoned for his human rights activities, considers the impact of such a step, were it truly to be implemented, historic, since the holders of positions of authority would, over time, begin to answer to their constituents as their sources of power rather than to their superiors.[11]

Does the new leadership generation differ sufficiently from those that preceded it that it would actually be prepared to give up some elements of control, to share authority? The early professional experiences that the leaders of Gorbachev's generation share do differ dramatically from those shared by Brezhnev and his cohort. The Brezhnev generation rose into positions of authority in the late 1930s to replace those who died in Stalin's purges. They led the country to victory against Hitler and, with this to legitimate their rule, survived Stalin, deposed Khrushchev when he appeared to threaten them, and held on to power until, finally and belatedly, an enfeebled Chernenko, who personified their loss of capabilities, died. Gorbachev's accession to power really did mark a generational change. Most of the remaining members of Brezhnev's cohort soon retired or moved into ceremonial positions. The new leaders were men who were either too young to have seen service against Hitler's armies at all or fought in the last years of the war in the lower enlisted or officer ranks. They knew Stalin as the leader of their youth, but moved into professional life after his death. Their early professional experiences were predominantly during the brief, erratic Khrushchev era. What should be expected of them?

Bialer, an astute observer of the Soviet scene, sees the new generation as less ideological and more interested in efficiency in domestic policies. Its members believe that discipline is required, rather than fundamental changes. On foreign policy, they are nationalistic and hard-line: "One should remember that these are also the people who gave a standing ovation when Gorbachev mentioned Stalin's name in his speech at the May 1985 celebration marking the fortieth anniversary of the victory in World War II." Partial economic reforms, harsh domestic discipline, and a nationalistic, ambitious, and hard-line foreign policy may be this group's preferred future orientation for the Soviet Union.[12] As for the top leadership, "there is no evidence whatsoever that the new leadership has a critical attitude toward the classical, that is Stalinist, economic system and the post-Stalinist political system. As a matter of fact, Gorbachev and his lieutenants are quite optimistic that the economy can be made to work well and that the political system is basically sound. . . . All the system really needs is better leadership and more effective policies.'' Soviet emigré Zhores Medvedev, reviewing developments after Gorbachev's first year in office, essentially shared this analysis. He found that few social and political changes had been introduced and that Gorbachev's measures resembled those undertaken under previous leadership.[13]

One of the intriguing aspects of Gorbachev's leadership, however, is that the steps he has proposed have consistently outdistanced those expected by most professional Soviet-watchers. Developments in the economic arena since Bialer and Medvedev wrote have made clear that some key components of the Stalinist economic system are being attacked. A mid-1987 article in *Novy Mir* traced the economy's problems back to the 1920s, to Stalin's post-NEP steps to create a command economy. Gorbachev, responding to an evidently planted question while casting his vote in the June 1987 election for Supreme Soviet deputies, approved the analysis, while distancing himself from such prescriptive elements in it as accepting the necessity for large-scale unemployment. Even a Soviet leader is not likely to speak in favor of unemployment on election day. And yet, the steps approved at the Party's Central Committee meeting immediately thereafter—the key one a reform of the enormous central planning apparatus which would eliminate or radically reduce its control over production quotas and prices—would, most outside observers believe, produce both unemployment and higher prices. The limited goals and objectives earlier attributed to Gorbachev are now more generally considered those of the go-slow faction within the Politburo, led by Yegor Ligachev.

This faction retains enormous power and influence in Soviet society. It espouses traditional Russian and/or Soviet values and appeals to the deep-seated conservative impulses of the populace. Its members may be a minority on the Politburo, but they appear to have at least a potential majority on the Central Committee. In October and November 1987, they apparently dealt Gorbachev several significant defeats: the disgrace and political destruction of candidate Politburo member Boris Yeltsin, the point man of Soviet reform; the departure of Secretary of State Shultz from Moscow with no progress on the INF Treaty, planned as the centerpiece of Gorbachev's visit to the United States in December; and the imposition of an obviously committee-drafted speech interpreting Soviet history which Gorbachev read on November 2 to mark the seventieth anniversary celebration of the communist revolution.

While some observers have argued that Yeltsin essentially self-destructed, the fact remains that his fall from power could only have been, and was seen in Soviet society as, a defeat both for Gorbachev personally and for reform. Yet, as general secretary, Gorbachev has enormous capabilities for shaking off these setbacks and pressing ahead with the essential elements of his program. He has distanced himself personally from Yeltsin, encouraging the impression that personal failings and not policy issues were the cause of Yeltsin's disgrace. Within days after Shultz's departure, he despatched Foreign Minister Shevardnadze to

Washington to salvage both the INF Treaty and the summit. And after his November 2 speech, with its jarring reference to Stalin as the leader of the defense of Leninism in the 1920s, its minimalization of the number of Soviet victims of the purges ("many thousands"), and its equation of Stalin's Molotov/Ribbentrop pact with Lenin's Brest/Litovsk Treaty, he pressed ahead with his plans for a June 1988 Party Conference to give renewed impetus to his reform program. Five months later, counterattacking against a reportedly Ligachev-inspired antireform letter in *Sovetskaya Rossiya*, he gave new courage to supporters of change.

At the June 1988 Party Conference, the first since 1941, Gorbachev secured approval of major elements of his reform program. If the measures are carried out, there will be transfer of some of the power now exercised by the Party to popularly elected legislatures; party officials will have to compete for election to office, and they and government officials will be limited to two terms totaling ten years. An expanded national legislature will be created, and a powerful new post of president (or chairman) of the Soviet Union established. Party involvement in economic management would be further limited. Several months later, Gorbachev summoned the Central Committee and in peremptory fashion directed the retirement of all but one of the remaining Brezhnev-era Politburo members, a step that some observers believed, perhaps prematurely, broke the back of Party resistance to his program.

So dramatic have these developments been that professional Soviet watchers, once determinedly skeptical about the significance of Gorbachev's reforms, now risk being mesmerized by the bravura performance of this unusual Soviet leader. No sooner have they concluded that the Stalinist command economy will not be restructured than Gorbachev proposes to do exactly that. Burkharin's rehabilitation would be too bold a step—and it happens. Trotsky will remain a nonperson—and *Komsomolskaya Pravda* reports a respected Soviet's view that he was not a criminal and that his works, though wrong, should be published and studied in the Soviet Union.[14] Lenin will never be criticized—and an article suggests that some of his views were mistaken. It has become so risky to predict what will happen next in Soviet reform that a U.S. correspondent, writing fancifully about an unimaginably open Party Conference, had it televising a fistfight between Ligachev and Yeltsin—and watched on Soviet television, less than a week later, the political equivalent of just such a battle between them.

We can only keep these day-to-day developments in perspective if we see them in the context of the fundamental attributes of the Soviet political culture—how they affect, and are affected by, Soviet authoritarianism, risk-avoidance, and control. For now, the ultimate significance of the leadership-imposed changes occurring in Soviet society remains a question mark. Greater knowledge of the outside world, if it occurs, could eventually have profound impact on the Soviet Union, but in a time frame measured in decades, not years. The new leadership generation has also inherited a socioeconomic Soviet Union profoundly changed from the one their elders took command of four decades ago. Industrialization, urbanization, and education are not necessarily liberalizing forces, but they are certainly forces for social change. The enormous social mobility that characterized the early decades of the Soviet Union appears to be decreasing. The rise to power and prominence under Stalin of peasants and their sons has, as we have seen,[15] been characterized by some students of Russian history as a revolution within the revolution. The values of pre-Petrine Muscovy, in their view, came to dominate Soviet political life, transmitted by a peasantry that had for centuries been cut off from awareness of the outside world and that was unaffected by the Western intellectual currents that stimulated the Russian intelligentsia. Stalin appealed to their conservative and authoritarian impulses.

These impulses remain strong in Soviet society today. Cohen sees this profound conservatism, which dominates almost all levels of Soviet society, "from the family to the Politburo, from the local authorities to the state *nachalstvo*, as the principal obstacle to reform."[16] But must these impulses not inevitably weaken as succeeding generations lose contact with traditional, rural Russia? Vakar, who laid great stress on the effects of the authoritarian peasant mentality, believed that they must. In 1961 he wrote, "the generation now chafing against controls designed for a nation of peasants, when it comes to power must at least relax the system enough to accommodate its own greater variety of interests and tastes, occupations and perspectives." And yet, one cannot help but wonder, again, about at least the short-term significance of such relaxation. There was good reason for Brzezinski to conclude in 1976 that Soviet adaptability "appears to be narrowly circumscribed by the institutional weight and vested interests of the existing system, by its ideological legacies, and by the cumulative effects of political tradition on behavior and thought."[17]

The reaction in the Soviet Union to Nikita Khrushchev, the system's last major reformist leader, led to more than two decades of Brezhnevian rule, a period that looked initially like one of healing stability, but eventually came to be seen as stultifying stagnation. Keenan sees the Brezhnev period as one in which a number of underlying features of the traditional political culture reasserted themselves after several decades of turmoil and rapid change. The bulk of the population, he wrote, "shares with its leaders a conviction that only a powerfully centralized and oligarchic government can provide the order which they all crave" and relies "more confidently upon informal and personal relationships than upon those defined by the legalistic niceties so admired elsewhere."[18] As a reformer, Khrushchev is generally considered a failure, done in by his own erratic behavior, by his inability to master deeply imbedded elements of the political culture, and by the self-interest of the *nomenklatura*. His legacy to Soviet political life—an end to Stalinist terror—was of immense importance, but it also was consonant with the country's political traditions and served the interests of its elite. Khrushchev has loosely been termed a populist; his educational reforms and his "meat and milk" slogan did speak to popular needs and against the privileges of an increasingly stratified society. But his erratic attempts to encourage more liberal discussion of both political and consumer matters violated what Keenan calls the fundamental principle of *neglasnost*, or internal discussion, and aroused popular, as well as elite, concern that he was unleashing forces that could not be controlled. His efforts to decentralize political and economic structures challenged elite interests, while being seen by broad sections of the populace as possibly harmful to them personally and without any believable positive outcomes that would offset the risks.[19]

Gorbachev, by contrast, may be a reformer, but he is no populist. Some of his reforms might challenge the perquisites of the political elite, but others would widen the gap between the haves and the have-nots. He makes no apologies for this. If he has his way, Soviet society for the foreseeable future is to see more application of the adage: "From each according to his ability; to each according to his work." It is far from clear that the average Soviet worker, accustomed to a low risk, low reward economic system, will leap at the opportunity to change to a higher risk, higher reward system, particularly if the risks come now and the rewards are promissory notes on the future. By May 1987, 40 percent of Kazakh workers queried in a survey were prepared to say they did not want any changes in the wage system, and 62 percent of the workers in a Moscow plumbing factory asserted that *perestroika* simply meant more work for them.[20] The peasant mentality seems still to predominate in the bulk of the population. In his seventieth anniversary speech, Gorbachev recognized the continuing appeal of those who would resist reform by pretending to be concerned about its costs. Naturally, he said, nobody says he opposes restructuring. Rather, they play the role of fighting against its costs. But how long can they go on frightening us with all sorts of costs? How long, indeed? Gorbachev's popular nickname, Balalaika, because he keeps repeating the same melody,[21] seems to reflect some of the same widespread skepticism that dogged Khrushchev.

What of the intelligentsia? While Gorbachev evidently looks to it as a major support for his reform program, it is questionable whether there is a thirst for freedom, as Westerners understand it, among educated Soviets, let alone among the populace at large. There is too little in their knowledge and tradition to allow them easily to internalize its values. Even among many of those who oppose the regime, or have left the country, authoritarianism is deeply rooted. They see the West as weak; unable to recognize the supple strength of disparity, they confuse it with decadence and anarchy. They would strengthen us by imposing their version of order, of discipline. Sakharov represents the best of the Soviet intelligentsia, not the norm.

The principle of coercion, one Western observer believes, is assumed by the Soviets themselves to operate in all areas of Soviet life, even those where it, in fact, does not.[22] But there is an enormous thirst for knowledge of and contact with the outside world. This is the direction of the pressures that younger generations will exert and are exerting now. Some will embrace what they learn; others will recoil from it. This also is part of the Russian tradition. We cannot predict the outcome of an opening of Soviet society to the outside world, but we can expect it to be profound. Exposure of the Russian officer corps to Paris after Napoleon's defeat produced the Decembrists, and the Decembrists fathered the

Russian revolutionary movement, which finally had its 1917. But the process took a century, and the outcome was certainly not what most nineteenth-century Russian revolutionaries had in mind.

Time has been telescoped and the long-delayed impact of Soviet infrastructural changes may be sudden and profound. For the moment, however, traditional, authoritarian forces seem still to predominate. As one observer has cleverly noted, many things may change in Gorbachev's Soviet Union, but not how change is initiated and who is in charge. Decisions will still come from the central authorities. Until the way things change begins to change, the reforms in vision are tenuous, subject to reversal by opponents within the ruling Politburo or to subversion by the Soviet bureaucracy.[23] On the one hand, Gorbachev's reform programs would leave him as both Party general secretary and president of the Soviet Union, an accumulation of institutional if not personal, power, unsurpassed since Stalin. And the system will be recapitulated on the local level, with Party leaders automatically nominated to lead the corresponding government body (albeit theoretically, at least, subject to rejection by secret ballot). On the other hand, Gorbachev could go the way of Khrushchev; his reforms, threatening too many vested interests and coalescing opposition, could be rejected as "hare-brained" schemes.

Even if he personally survives politically, his reforms could ultimately suffer the fate of Kosygin's, which were swallowed without a trace in the swamp of the Soviet bureaucracy. Several brief visits to the Soviet Union between the time of the June 1987 Central Committee meeting and early 1988 highlighted for me the possibility of the latter fate. *Perestroika*, as handled by the Soviet media, seemed generally indistinguishable from the slogans that always dot the Soviet landscape. The system had geared itself up to proselytize *perestroika*, as the preceding year it had called for overfulfilling the plan, and the year before that, shock labor. I was left with the impression that if any bureaucracy, anywhere, could take a slogan concerning reform or restructuring, empty it of content, and feed it to the public as more of the same pablum, it would be the Soviet bureaucracy.

The sudden, dramatic Politburo and Supreme Soviet changes that Gorbachev engineered on September 30 and October 1, 1988—most notably the retirement of Gromyko and almost all of the Brezhnev-era holdovers in the top leadership—appeared intended not only to strengthen his hand at the top, but also to send an unmistakable signal to the apparatus to get with the reform program. The effect will probably be to drive resistance further underground, but not to end it.

Glasnost—publicity, public discussion, openness—is evidently intended to provide the tension that will keep *perestroika* from being reduced to meaningless phrase-mongering. Gorbachev himself has said that democracy is the principal guarantee of the irreversibility of *perestroika*, and that there is no democracy without *glasnost*.[24] As long as there is disagreement about the content of *perestroika* there is life to it. But what does this do to control from the top, to democratic centralism? At what point do the content and extent of *perestroika* become defined on high, after which discussion must end? Gorbachev himself has already said that *glasnost* ends where socialism begins. My own guess is that, after the dust has settled, in the short run the authoritarian elements of the Soviet system will remain intact. Tradition and vested interests will be too great to overcome. But perhaps some elements of reduced control and greater willingness to accept risk will have been put in place which, over the longer run, will produce the kind of opening to the outside world that can produce more basic changes in Soviet society. In the meantime, as we deal with the current Soviet leadership, we should remember that for all his determination and apparent vision Gorbachev, the father of *glasnost*, is himself of peasant stock. He is a product of his culture, as well as a reformer.

FOREIGN POLICY DEVELOPMENTS UNDER GORBACHEV

There is no doubt that Soviet foreign policy has developed a new and more persuasive public posture under Gorbachev. At issue, once again, is whether anything of substance has really changed. The distinction is important. As Dimitri Simes noted: "America should welcome a more effective Soviet foreign policy only to the extent that it simultaneously becomes more moderate. Otherwise the United States and the West as a whole may find themselves mesmerized by an impressive Kremlin performance, forgetting that its final act is supposed to be their own demise."[25] Personnel changes by themselves would account for some of the regime's increased effectiveness in public relations. Gorbachev did not initially focus on the Soviet foreign policy establishment, but when he did turn his attention to it he began a series of personnel changes that have been as extensive as those that have occurred in the top Party leadership.

The first, and most essential step was the elevation of Andrei Gromyko to the post of Chairman of the Presidium of the Supreme Soviet, the titular head of state. The ceremonial aspects of the job—the meeting and greeting of foreign dignitaries—made it a natural for Gromyko. Despite his dour mien, Gromyko had unsurpassed foreign policy experience and more personal acquaintance by far with foreign leaders than any other member of the Politburo. His lengthy full Politburo tenure and unsurpassed foreign policy experience eventually brought him, during the Chernenko interregnum, to a position of paramount importance in foreign policy decisions. If Gorbachev was going to take control of foreign policy, Gromyko had to be moved out of the Foreign Ministry. Western observers are in disagreement about whether Gromyko was one of the Brezhnev generation members who supported or opposed Gorbachev's succession to Chernenko as general secretary. In either event, he played his cards well enough that early forced retirement, à la Romanov, Grishin, and Kunayev, was not in the cards.

Gromyko may have willingly accepted the move to the more prestigious and, many would argue despite its ceremonial aspects, more powerful position of titular chief of state. The position assured Gromyko of membership on the Politburo for as long as he held it, and in the past it often carried with it tenure for life.

Gromyko received the number two protocol position in the Soviet media and spoke out publicly on foreign policy issues. Thus, of all the members of the Brezhnev generation, he came through the initial transition of power to the younger generation in the best shape. And yet, despite his full Politburo status, his highly prestigious position, and his unequaled foreign policy experience, how quickly one gained the impression that the shape and direction of Soviet foreign policy were now in other hands. (On September 30 and October 1, 1988, Gromyko retired with honor from his Party and government posts, perhaps the most prominent Soviet leader ever to do so.)

Gromyko's successor at the Foreign Ministry in June 1985, Eduard Shevardnadze, began with no known credentials for the job except for long-term ties to Gorbachev but has impressed observers with his manner and ability. In spring 1986 two key appointments as Central Committee department heads dealing with foreign policy matters went to ambassadors with long experience in North America—Anatoliy Dobrynin, former ambassador to the United States, and Aleksandr Yakovlev, former ambassador to Canada. Dobrynin took over the International Department and Yakovlev, who has more experience as a Party official than as a diplomat, became head of Soviet propaganda activities, both domestic and external. Yakovlev has since continued his upward climb, achieving full Politburo status and, according to Soviet sources, replacing Ligachev in 1988 in the powerful position of ideological overseer. Aleksandr Bessmertnykh, a former deputy to Dobrynin in Washington, moved up from his post as head of the American division initially to Deputy Foreign Minister and in November 1988 to First Deputy Foreign Minister. Another elderly Brezhnev holdover, Igor Ilichev, was replaced as Deputy Foreign Minister by Anatoliy Adamishin, a younger foreign affairs professional who had headed one of the Western European divisions in the Foreign Ministry.

By the end of 1988 Gorbachev had in place a foreign policy apparatus that was demonstrably younger—although hardly wet behind the ears; many were in their sixties—and presumably more congenial to him. He apparently listens to their advice and often takes it. The view of the older generation toward Shevardnadze's appointment is illustrated by the toast a high-ranking Foreign Ministry official offered during a visit to a Western country: "To my Foreign Minister, and I mean Foreign Minister Gromyko." This was some eighteen months after Shevardnadze had assumed the post. *Glasnost* or not, the official in question was soon thereafter posted to the Soviet overseas equivalent of Siberia, though whether knowledge of the posting was father to the toast or the reverse is unclear.

One area of change that has been noted in Soviet negotiating behavior under Gorbachev is a decrease in Stalinesque "tactics of abuse." We will consider Soviet negotiating style and tactics in some detail in the following section. The point I wish to make here is that confrontational tactics need to be distinguished from toughness in negotiating. Gorbachev has, in fact, shown himself to be a tough, as well as an innovative, negotiator. The contrast between Soviet handling of the British expulsion of large numbers of their diplomats in 1971 and 1986 is instructive. In 1971, acting on the basis of information obtained from a high-ranking defector, Britain expelled ninety Soviet diplomats and refused to permit another fifteen to return to their posts. Under Brezhnev, the Soviets responded by threatening major expulsions in retaliation but ultimately expelled only a token number of British embassy personnel. In 1986, Britain also expelled a large number of Soviet diplomats as spies. Under Gorbachev, the Soviets responded by expelling an equal number of British diplomats. The British responded with further expulsions and saw an equal number of their diplomats expelled in retaliation. At this point, the British, facing total decimation of their embassy in Moscow, called off the expulsion war. The Iron Lady was forced to bow to the steelier will of Mr. Glasnost. The impression in the British Foreign Office was that, based on the level of confidence with which Soviet Foreign Ministry officials were operating and the hints they dropped, their policy of tit-for-tat came right from the top and strict reciprocity would be followed straight down the line.[26] France, New Zealand, and Canada have since had similar exchanges with the Soviet Union under Gorbachev, with similar results which also contrasted sharply with Soviet behavior in similar instances under Brezhnev.

The U.S. experience with the Soviets on cases involving spying by Soviet officials and mutual expulsions confirms the impression that under Gorbachev the Soviet Union is not going to shrink from diplomatic confrontations. In 1978, we arrested three Soviet citizens for espionage. One, a diplomat, had immunity. He was released and returned to the Soviet Union. The other two, Rudolf Chernayev and Vadik Enger, were employees of the United Nations and did not have diplomatic immunity. While they were in custody, the Soviets arrested an American businessman in Moscow on what were obviously trumped-up charges of currency violations. He was chosen, apparently, because he was the fiancé of an American secretary at the embassy, which was the closest the Soviets could come to a U.S. official. The Soviets and the American were released to the custody of their respective embassies pending trial. The American was tried three months later, convicted (despite his own strong defense, which included demonstrating that he was out of the country at the time one of the prosecution witnesses testified he had engaged in illegal currency transactions), given a suspended five-year sentence, and permitted to leave the country. Over a month later, the two Soviets were tried, convicted, and sentenced to fifty-year prison terms. The following April, they were exchanged for five imprisoned Soviet human rights activists. The United States had held firm to the principle that Soviet employees of the United Nations were subject to U.S. law and would not be treated as having *de facto* diplomatic immunity if they engaged in espionage. The subsequent exchange was both politically realistic and humanitarian.

The U.S. experience in 1986 was much different, although events began similarly, with the arrest of Gennadi Zakharov, a Soviet employee of the United Nations, for espionage. The Soviet Union responded in predictable fashion, by fabricating grounds for the arrest of an American in Moscow who did not have diplomatic immunity—in this case a correspondent, Nicholas Daniloff. If the scenario had thereafter unfolded as in previous instances, the U.S. government would have reacted stiffly to the Daniloff arrest, followed by discussions that would have led to the release of him and the Soviets to the custody of their respective embassies. The Soviets would have been tried and, if found guilty, would have been exchanged for imprisoned Soviet human rights activists. Daniloff might or might not have been tried, but in any case he would have been out of the Soviet Union before the exchange occurred. This would have met minimum Soviet objectives—to get the release of their KGB agents. It would also have met U.S. objectives of demonstrating that Soviet citizens without diplomatic immunity were subject to U.S. law, secured Daniloff's release without setting the precedent of exchanging what in effect was a Soviet hostage for spies, and performed a humanitarian act that required the Soviets to pay at least a small price for using their U.N. citizen employees for espionage.

The initial U.S. government reaction was equivocal, a reaction that, as our earlier discussion has indicated, is likely to produce a digging in by the Soviets on their position. An "informed White House official," speaking from the Western White House in Santa Barbara, said that the United States had not ruled out the possibility of a swap for Daniloff and that the United States wanted to avoid having this incident disrupt either the arms control talks or summit preparations.[27] Hearing this, the Soviets did exactly as one would have predicted. They took a very tough stance. The upshot was that Zakharov was given a pro forma trial, sentenced to five years' probation and expelled—in effect, he was allowed to leave the United States in exchange for Daniloff. Some days later a Soviet human rights activist and his spouse were allowed to depart the Soviet Union, allowing the United States to maintain that this was the exchange, and not Daniloff. Out of this the Soviets got implicit acknowledgement of their assertion of *de facto* diplomatic immunity for their U.N. employees and reinforcement for their hostage-taking policy in such cases. This outcome will come back to haunt us, particularly given current concern about Soviet espionage. It has left an entire category of Soviet citizens in the United States—their U.N. employees—the ability to take greater risks in their espionage activities, secure in their *de facto* immunity from U.S. law.

It is difficult to know whether the Soviets were tougher and more successful in this interaction than in similar ones in the past because it was handled poorly by the United States, particularly initially, or because the Soviet leadership was much more prepared than in the past to refuse to back off. Perhaps there was an interaction between the two. But our effort to take a tough line subsequently on expulsions also produced a stiff Soviet reaction. We expelled 55 Soviet employees to bring the number at their bilateral missions down to a ceiling of 225 in Washington and 26 in San Francisco. The Soviets did not respond as they had in recent similar cases involving British, French, and New Zealand expulsions. Rather than get into a tit-for-tat numbers game with us, they responded by withdrawing all Soviet employees at the U.S. embassy and consulate general, asserting that if the United States wanted equivalence, it could have it—exact equivalence. Any U.S. employees brought in to replace Soviet chauffeurs, janitors, and so forth above the ceilings of 225 and 26 in Moscow and Leningrad would have to replace Americans already at post. The effect of this was to require us in some cases to move persons doing substantive political and economic work to maintenance work and in other cases to require them to do double duty. To those whose chief concern is to avoid allowing the Soviets to learn more about us, the exchange was well worthwhile. Subsequent reports that U.S. Marine guards had sexual relationships with Soviet female employees of the embassy and were thereafter induced to allow KGB personnel access to its secure areas (although evidence to prove the latter allegation was not discovered) lend legitimacy to the concerns. But we have paid costs in terms of our ability to know and understand what is happening in Soviet society. First-hand knowledge of that still predominantly closed society is irreplacable and should be considered vital to decision-making about how to deal with our superpower adversary.

At least on these kinds of issues, then, Soviet negotiating behavior under Gorbachev has been both tougher and more effective than under his predecessors, though perhaps also free of the elements of bombast and threat that were previously prominent. A possible interpretation of this is that Gorbachev may feel the need to demonstrate that his willingness to make concessions in the arms control area, to try to move toward agreements on such issues so vital to national security, does not mean that he is not prepared to defend Soviet interests. A tough line on expulsions and similar issues may enable him to fend off charges from domestic critics that he is soft on capitalism.[28] Whereas Kissinger tended to demonstrate flexibility on strictly bilateral issues to set the stage properly with the Soviets for negotiations on larger foreign policy issues, this suggests that Gorbachev may tend to be uncompromising on them so as to set the stage within his own political establishment for negotiations on other foreign policy issues. It is an interesting hypothesis, worth watching, on which the data are as yet insufficient.

Whether Soviet behavior on espionage and expulsion issues has any implications for their approach to other issues on the U.S.-Soviet agenda may be questioned. At a minimum, these confrontations show a side of Gorbachev that differs from the image he usually projects, the steel teeth that Andrei Gromyko told his colleagues accompany his nice smile. U.S.-Soviet negotiations are normally organized around four issue areas. Bilateral issues, such as those discussed above and many others concerning the nuts and bolts of everyday diplomacy, are often handled below the political level and without publicity. Human rights issues are always on the U.S. agenda, usually to the intense annoyance of the Soviets. Regional disputes, including the Middle East, Afghanistan, Central America, and southern Africa are discussed at summit meetings, in periodic experts' meetings at the assistant secretary level, and regularly at the working level. Arms control negotiations are conducted primarily during high-level meetings and by the START (formerly SALT) delegations in Geneva.

Even if one assumes that the top Soviet leader is exempt from the general Soviet hesitancy about taking the initiative in negotiations, Gorbachev's activities in the arms control area have been notable. Dimitri Simes, hardly an unalloyed admirer, credits Gorbachev with a dynamic and imaginative arms control policy which has helped him determine the focus of the East-West dialogue. START negotiator Max Kampelman contrasts the general Soviet pattern of not coming up with initiatives, with the initiatives they have shown in the current negotiations. He cautions, however, that it will be necessary to put together the final package before it will be possible to answer whether this new pattern is meaningful.[29] Paul Nitze is even more cautious about how to interpret Soviet arms control negotiating under Gorbachev. The heads of their START, INF, and space negotiating teams, he believes, have no leeway to take the initiative. This represents no change from the previous pattern. (In fact, U.S. START negotiators are also tightly bound by their instructions, as they will freely admit.) Nitze considers the significant difference under Gorbachev to be a greater emphasis on propaganda in the process. Actual negotiating on these issues, and the military considerations that were previously predominant in Soviet negotiating positions, appear now to take a secondary place. This does have an effect on negotiations, however, since in order to get the reputation for negotiating flexibility the Soviets seem to be seeking for propaganda purposes, they need to show some flexibility now and then.[30] This, of course, raises the duck question. If it swims like a duck, waddles like a duck, and quacks like a duck, but thinks it is a shark, should we consider it a duck or a shark? Kampelman and Nitze would argue, not without considerable justification, that past experience with this particular creature should warn us to wonder whether duck-like apparition paddling around the pond and uttering quacks is merely the surface ten percent of an entity with considerably more carnivorous appetites than a duck. They would like to have a look beneath the surface of the water before going swimming. In other words, they want to see the bottom line in the arms control negotiations before drawing any conclusions about changes in Soviet negotiating behavior.

While this is legitimate, it is also worthwhile to draw a distinction between Soviet intentions and Soviet behavior. Arms control negotiations are a case in point. The Soviets have not been reactive; if anything, they have been pushing the pace. They made a comprehensive proposal on offensive weapons in late September 1986. The United States offered a response in early November. Two months later, the Soviets offered a sweeping new proposal. In his moves at Reykjavik on strategic weapons systems, and later in accepting the zero option on intermediate range missiles, Gorbachev has shown a readiness to move rapidly off long-established Soviet positions. As we have seen, sudden, substantial shifts in Soviet negotiating positions are more the norm than the exception. What is unusual here is the shortness of the time frame within which these shifts are occurring. It suggests someone at the top impatient for results. Whether of the substantive or of the public relations variety is another question, although one which would seem to be answered at least in part, by the signature in December 1987 of the INF Treaty.

Soviet readiness at times even to preempt the U.S. agenda has also been evident at the Conference on Security and Cooperation in Europe (CSCE) in Vienna. During the Madrid CSCE session several years ago, the Soviet delegation sought to have nothing to do with the human rights issue, and resisted bitterly U.S. efforts to set up a follow-up human rights meeting. By contrast, they arrived in Vienna with a proposal for a follow-up human rights meeting in Moscow and tabled it on opening day.

Foreign Ministry officials at regional talks on southen Africa in which I participated in early 1986 conveyed this sense of higher-level impatience, searching for new ideas, readiness to take initiatives. Their mandate, they said, was to find ways to make progress on issues of conflict in U.S.-Soviet relations. What they actually had to offer in the way of new ideas at that point was meager, but more fruitful discussions took place subsequently. In late 1988, the United States publicly acknowledged the constructive role played by the Soviet Union and its Foreign Ministry representative, Vladilen Vasev, in moving the Angolan/South African talks on Cuban troop withdrawal and Namibian independence toward a successful conclusion. The major breakthrough in regional disputes has, of course, been Afghanistan, although periodic indications of Soviet willingness to rethink old positions on other regional issues emerge. One such was Gorbachev's indication, during a 1987 visit by President Assad of Syria, that the Soviet Union's lack of diplomatic relationships with Israel was abnormal, a statement given added significance by its timing.

A pattern has begun to emerge of a round of talks at the regional expert level (assistant secretaries on the U.S. side; either deputy ministers or division chiefs on the Soviet side, depending on the issue and the personalities), followed by an overall discussion headed on the U.S. side by the under secretary for political affairs. As in the case of human rights, the Soviets have moved from a primarily reactive posture to one of taking the initiative. In the early 1980s, their interest in regional discussions was limited, at least in part by a reluctance to have Afghanistan on the agenda. By contrast, during the first half of 1987, they approached the United States with a proposed schedule for the next round of talks, with specific dates on each issue, including Afghanistan.

The clear distinction that American Sovietologists sought to draw between increased diplomatic activity in regional conflicts, perhaps even an increased willingness to rethink old positions, and willingness to participate or acquiesce in resolutions of those conflicts along lines that the United States seems to consider acceptable had eroded considerably with the start of Soviet withdrawal from Afghanistan. We should remember, however, that Soviet reluctance to accept costly new commitments, à la Cuba and Vietnam, predated Gorbachev's accession to power. They are not, a senior American diplomat told me, looking for more military exposure in the Third World and may be less willing now than in the past to support communist guerilla movements in developing countries such as the Philippines. Afghanistan has shown them that putting in troops does not automatically lead to gains for the Soviet Union. They may now believe, the same diplomat added, that they moved prematurely in the 1970s, based on an incorrect assessment of the correlation of forces. This perception of limits coexists with a reluctance to be seen as willing to abandon current friends and clients. As Simes correctly points out, in Nicaragua, Angola, and Afghanistan the Soviet Union has, under Gorbachev, made considerable new investments to support its allies.[31] But these investments have their limits. The Soviets are getting out of Afghanistan. And their support for Angola, and for an increase in the size and combat activity of Cuban troops in Angola, was accompanied by support for an intensification of diplomatic contacts to explore settlement possibilities.

NEGOTIATING BEHAVIOR: CHANGE AND CONTINUITY

Present-day Soviet negotiating behavior arises out of the uncertain and changing domestic context we discussed above. Soviet diplomats and Soviet emigrés alike confess themselves amazed at what they are seeing and hearing. Yet, despite the winds of change currently blowing, many key elements remain intact. The Soviet system remains authoritarian. Mikhail Gorbachev is in the tradition of the reforming tsars; he is not a closet Jeffersonian. The intense awareness the Russian people have of issues of hierarchy, and their accompanying expectations of dominance or submission, continue to exist. It should not be surprising, then, to find much that is in flux, much that is contradictory—and not only in a dialectical sense—in current Soviet negotiating behavior. A British diplomat who has written on the subject told me that if asked about the current relevance of his earlier work he would say: "Under study. Come back in three years." What follows is a very speculative attempt to shorten that time frame.

It is probably reasonable to assume that the negotiating style that Mikhail Gorbachev would prefer his countrymen adopt is his own. It is evident that he has no small opinion of his own abilities and vision, and presumably he thinks well of his capability as an international statesman, as well as a domestic leader. Let us look first, then, at what we can conclude about Gorbachev's personal negotiating style. There are, to begin with, indications that he is uncomfortable with some of the crasser forms of public adulation his predecessors enjoyed. In his interpersonal relations and in his politicking among the people in the Soviet Union, Gorbachev conveys a sense of informality and a willingness to listen as well as to talk. Exaggerated references by other Soviet leaders to his person and accomplishments have diminished greatly, at his request it is generally assumed. He is evidently uncomfortable with the ritualistic applause that formerly greeted speeches by the Soviet Union's general secretary, a discomfort that manifested itself particularly during a May 1987 visit to Rumania, which had adopted and still adheres to the older Soviet protocols.[32] Accounts of his 1984 visit to Britain tell of an air of informality in how his staff dealt with him, which has been absent in the retinue of other Soviet leaders.[33]

If we take these rituals to manifest a Russian sense that power must not only exist, but be displayed prominently to stamp out any thoughts of rebellion, are we justified in concluding from their absence that Gorbachev has a different view of the fragility of authority from the traditional Russian one? If so, what is his view—that dominance can be retained without ritualistic displays of submission by the weaker party? Or that an alternative to total dominance/submission is possible in relationships involving authority? The latter would suggest a different, and less insecure, view of hierarchical relationships which could manifest itself in a different approach to international negotiations.[34] Stalin's insecurity manifested itself on the international scene in paranoid suspicion of the outside world, Khrushchev's in bombast, and Brezhnev's in a less conspicuous but nevertheless exaggerated concern for the honors and ceremonies associated with power. From the limited evidence available, it appears to me that in situations in which Gorbachev sees no challenge to his authority he is secure enough not to require the ritualistic displays of submission that had become an accepted part of Soviet political life. But he reacts strongly when challenged, perhaps more strongly than circumstances warrant, so as to assert or regain his position of authority or dominance.

American diplomats have found him, not surprisingly, nationalistic and concerned with his country's place in the world—a trait he probably shares with most other chiefs of state. Moreover, ensuring that place is one of the principal objectives of his reform program. Some of his negotiating behavior, however, seems to reflect more of the style of his predecessors than the common attributes of chiefs of state. He has, for example, been known in a high-level meeting to ask his interlocutors whether they thought the Soviet Union was some two-bit country like Tanganyika, a query that might as well have come from Stalin, Khrushchev, Brezhnev, Gromyko, or any other Soviet leader of earlier generations.[35] While Gorbachev appears not to like boot-licking, he also seems to have little patience for those with different views. British Labour Party leader Neil Kinnock was treated, a British diplomat told me, to the Gorbachev fist in the face when he raised human rights issues.

Gorbachev's handling of such bilateral mini-crises as arrests and expulsions also, in my view, reveals something about his view of authority relationships, as well as about other elements of his negotiating style. It should go without saying that it would be foolish simply to project that same behavior unchanged into a totally different context, one involving issues of war and peace for example. But it does seem worthwhile to glean what we can from how he handled these conflictual, adversarial negotiations. A high-ranking American diplomat, who has many years of experience in Soviet affairs, characterized Gorbachev's tough reaction on diplomatic expulsions as a fervor indicative of insecurity. Possibly, but the fact remains that Gorbachev, in contrast to his predecessors, did not submit to Western steps that assumed the Soviet Union would accept large-scale expulsions with only minimal retaliation. The Western assumption was not completely arbitrary. It was based on the argument that a far larger proportion of Soviet than of

Western diplomatic staffs was made up of undercover intelligence operatives. Whatever the merits of that argument, the factual disparity in the expulsions created the impression of Soviet second-class diplomatic status and lack of will in a crisis. Gorbachev may have shared the same concerns about Soviet insecurity, or inferiority, but he insisted on the principle of Soviet equality. And by tough negotiating tactics he made it stick. The international principle may have been one of equality, but to the extent there was a test of wills involved, his was dominant. In the British, French, and New Zealand cases, the application of that principle involved one-for-one retaliations. In dealing with the United States, where he wanted to avoid several rounds of mutual expulsions which could have crippled diplomatic contacts, he took a different tack, while asserting the same principle: equal ceilings on each side's employees, of whatever nationality, the numerical imbalance in favor of the United States to be redressed initially by withdrawal of the many Soviet citizen workers at the U.S. missions.

Gorbachev's personal style, in contrast to that of Stalin, is not that of a counterpuncher. He seeks to take and hold the initiative, to keep others reacting to him. He counterpunches effectively in response to initiatives from others—as we, the British, and the French have discovered on expulsions—but he does it as a means of retaking the initiative, rather than as a preferred style. Soviet arms control moves appear more characteristic of his style—bold, attention-getting steps that keep the other side in a reactive posture, a dramatic change from what Jonathan Dean has correctly identified as the traditional, incremental Soviet style.[36] This aspect of Soviet negotiating style is in flux, with some elements of the foreign policy establishment adapting to it with an appearance of ease and assurance, while others are obviously uncomfortable—understandable mixed reactions in a period of change.

The term *glasnost*, used to describe the direction of Soviet society under Gorbachev, implies a different view of facts and emotions from that which has characterized his countrymen's style of negotiating with foreigners. Whether the subject is alcohol abuse, Chernobyl, or the dismissal of the Minister of Defense,[37] Gorbachev's regime has been, if far from transparent, at least unprecedentedly candid in describing domestic developments and problems, both to its own people and to the world. The extent to which a decreased Soviet obsession with secrecy may affect its international negotiating style remains to be seen. There are often functional advantages, which have nothing to do with national style, to playing your cards close to the chest in international negotiations. At a minimum, we should expect to see less of the tendency noted in the past to refuse to share information, even when the sharing would appear to serve Soviet interests.

Gorbachev also appears to lack his countrymen's reluctance to compromise. In the arms negotiations area, he has certainly succeeded in creating a general impression of willingness to go more than half way, particularly in the eyes of the West European public.[38] He is, as one American diplomat put it, willing to rethink issues from the ground up. Aware that an expensive arms race with the

United States is not in the Soviet interest, he has come a long way toward the U.S. arms control position. Paul Nitze, who finds his performance to have less substance and to be even more for public consumption than that of his predecessors, acknowledges that the desire to create an impression of flexibility requires actual demonstrations of it from time to time.[39] However, while his willingness to rethink long-standing Soviet positions and his understanding of the necessity for compromise appear greater than what we have become accustomed to as the Soviet norm, Gorbachev's actual concession-making behavior during the Reykjavik negotiations with President Reagan was closer to the Soviet norm. He offered a compromise on INF only after making all of his arguments and trying very hard to get agreement on his terms. As soon as he proposed his compromise, he went on the offensive, asking what compromises the United States was prepared to make.[40] Gorbachev's penchant for the initiative and his willingness to compromise appear related. They suggest that he approaches the negotiating process with greater confidence and with less of his predecessors' belief that in dealing with the West he negotiates from a position of ineluctable technological and cultural backwardness. The most revealing thing about his April 1986 speech to workers at the Soviet space center extolling the world-class quality of the Soviet space effort and exhorting them not to accept the idea that they cannot produce advanced technology equal to that of the West is the demonstration of his awareness that the Soviet people do not share his confidence.

Scott Davis, who has studied Soviet negotiating behavior extensively, suggests that the rise to power of Gorbachev and the generational change in the Soviet Union is producing a trend away from the abusive, confrontational style that the Soviets often used in the past.[41] This would be consistent with the suggestion above that in situations where hierarchy is not at issue Gorbachev is comfortable with a relaxed, informal atmosphere. At the same time, when he believes hierarchy is at issue, he is tough and determined not to be dominated. It needs to be pointed out, however, that the evolution away from the more violently abusive aspects of Soviet negotiating style has been underway for some years. In his encyclopedic study of Soviet negotiating behavior, Joseph Whelan gives the mercurial Nikita Khrushchev credit for initiating a broadening of the intellectual standards of the foreign policy establishment which Brezhnev simply built upon and expanded.[42] Tony Bishop sees the more "unappealing" of Soviet negotiating traits most prominently associated with earlier periods of Soviet diplomacy. He believes that the promotion of younger people in the foreign policy establishment may call for a new look at his guide to negotiating with the Soviet Union.[43] If this assessment is correct, some elements of what may appear to be new in Soviet international behavior may be less a response to Gorbachev's preferences than to the fact that a generation of diplomats more acculturated to Western diplomatic practice has finally moved into policy-making positions.

The appointment of Eduard Shevardnadze to replace Andrei Gromyko as foreign minister in June 1985, originally a surprise since his foreign policy qualifications appeared to be nil, has also sent fresh, and not always welcome, breezes blowing through the Soviet foreign policy establishment. We have already mentioned the high-ranking Foreign Ministry official who, while visiting a Western country months after Gromyko's departure, proposed a toast to "my Foreign Minister, and I mean Foreign Minister Gromyko" and was shortly thereafter posted abroad, to the Soviet diplomatic equivalent of Siberia. A number of other hold-overs from the Brezhnev generation have been retired and replaced by younger people who appear less constrained to engage in set-piece expositions of Soviet positions. Even most skeptics about Soviet foreign policy under Gorbachev now concede that along with this difference in style is at least some greater flexibility on substance.

Changes in the Soviet diplomatic establishment during the Gorbachev era have without doubt reinforced his own negotiating propensities. One wonders what these aspects of Soviet foreign policy behavior would look like today if the more rough-hewn Grigoriy Romanov had achieved his ambition of becoming general secretary. Would different personality types have been promoted? Would the same people have been promoted and acted differently? Most of the institutional pressures on Soviet diplomats to conform with prevailing opinion at the top, or with what they believe it to be, remain. Loss of the perquisites of diplomatic life is about as serious a nonlegal sanction as a Soviet professional can face. They are highly responsive to changed signals from above—windmills, not compasses. They now face a dilemma. Avoiding initiatives was always the safest course. You might not become a star, but you minimized the downside risks, which were enormous. Soviet officials today, as one British diplomat put it, do not want to be viewed as old-thinking types.[44] They are being told that if they do not show more initiative, they may be replaced. Reports of Gorbachev's May 1986 meeting with the foreign policy establishment indicate that he was highly critical. He condemned the "Mister Nyet" approach of those Soviet diplomats incapable of distinguishing between persistence in defending a position and senseless stubbornness. He told them that they were expected to show more initiative and those who did would be rewarded for it. But it is not clear that they are also being assured that the greater risk-taking will be supported by a greater tolerance for error. If not, Gorbachev's exhortations are running against the very deep-seated Russian impulse to minimize risk, an impulse intensified by the repeated demographic catastrophes the country has suffered during this century. The result in everyday diplomatic contacts may turn out to be more motion without any real movement—a kind of diplomatic Brownian effect in which the heat Soviet officials are feeling produces considerable surface agitation, but never reaches the boiling point.

One thing does seem clear: Gorbachev's efforts to cajole, pressure, and persuade his countrymen to show more personal initiative in domestic affairs does have its foreign policy counterpart. Gorbachev apparently likes decisive people, and is one himself. As a State Department official who has seen him in action put it to me: "He does not dither; he cuts the knot." An American diplomat who has recently followed Soviet foreign policy both in Moscow and Washington suggested to me that Gorbachev may be more willing to follow the advice of his foreign policy advisers than Brezhnev was. He also allows his diplomats abroad more leeway in acting to advance Soviet interests, particularly in the public arena. The Soviet embassy's decision, shortly after the Chernobyl nuclear accident, to allow one of its officers—not coincidentally probably its most fluent and articulate English speaker—to testify before a congressional committee holding hearings on the subject, is illustrative of this new openness. Most objective observers would say that he handled himself with distinction. The Soviet ambassador in Lebanon is another example of this new breed of activist Soviet diplomat. A fluent Arabic speaker, he has become a significant player on the local scene, exploiting his country's lack of predominant ties to any particular Lebanese faction. This is not to say that Soviet diplomats and negotiators have any greater policy leeway. They are expected to carry out policy guidance with imagination, not to make policy. But in this age of rapid communications, this injunction is not so different from that laid on Western diplomats.

If the examples above illustrate the direction Gorbachev is pushing the Soviet foreign policy establishment, the everyday reality remains considerably different. The handling of foreign policy areas that do not have Gorbachev's regular personal attention often contrasts sharply from those that do. In the arms control area, Gorbachev has taken and maintained the initiative. He has been the primary source of movement and new ideas. The American bureaucracy has had its hands full simply in trying to get agreement on how to respond to his initiatives. This may, as Paul Nitze suggests, be primarily more effective use of public diplomacy rather than any greater commitment to arms control. But that it is effective seems not in much doubt. Moreover, given Gorbachev's evident interest in devoting additional resources and attention to the faltering Soviet economy, he would appear to have sufficient interest in heading off the necessity for a massively expensive Soviet Star Wars program to explain his intense activity in the arms control area. But the everyday reality of arms control negotiations presents a much more mixed picture. The Soviets tend to be less stilted and more willing to take part in informal exchange. But during three rounds of implementing discussions on the INF Treaty in which I participated during the first half of 1988, their style was predominantly reactive and counterpunching. Their efforts during implementation to redefine what U.S. negotiators considered firm and important treaty commitments eventually stalled the Senate ratification process and required a Shultz/Shevardnadze meeting to resolve.

American diplomats involved in negotiations on bilateral issues also find Soviet behavior generally proceeding along much more traditional lines—reactive, risk-avoiding, and nervous. A detailed U.S. proposal on opening new consulates in Kiev and New York went without a Soviet reply for a year, while Soviet diplomats responded to U.S. prodding with unimaginative *vranyo* about the numerous entities in their government involved in approving a response, including the local authorities in Kiev. Interestingly, what finally appeared to produce a response was the prospect of a high-level meeting, which brought with it high-level attention. Soviet diplomats then became sufficiently anxious that they began to pressure their U.S. counterparts to respond quickly to the Soviet position even before that position had been presented. The heat they were feeling was evidently producing motion. Effective American diplomacy in such circumstances could turn it into movement. Soviet diplomats are experienced and will negotiate with tactical effectiveness even with the uncertainties and changes around them. But when top-level attention is turned toward them and they feel the pressure to get results, to reach an agreement, they may have a tendency to give a bit more than they would have previously.

There is no easy way to summarize this picture. The signs of an opening of the Soviet Union to the outside world are exciting and offer badly needed hope for the future as we face the seemingly intractable problems of today. My own sense is that when we live through a period of change we tend to exaggerate its importance and permanence. With time and distance we begin to see more clearly the elements of continuity. The elements of traditional Soviet negotiating style we discussed in earlier chapters arise from deep roots and are likely to reassert themselves. Those aspects of Gorbachev's personal negotiating style that are most at variance with Russo-Soviet traditions—his preference for the initiative, readiness to compromise, relative openness—are least likely to survive his tenure. His own mixed reaction to issues of hierarchy, dominance/submission, and equality illustrates the hold traditional Russian views, reinforced by Leninist precepts, continue to have. And yet in another sense perhaps Gorbachev does represent the Soviet future. The information revolution is no respecter of national boundaries, a fact he recognizes. There exists no other educated, urbanized population so cut off from the stimulus for change that outside ideas represent. No one can predict what synthesis will emerge from the conflict of Russo-Soviet traditions and world intellectual currents. Gorbachev's policies are carrying that conflict into a new phase, changing it from implicit to actual. He may not know what the outcome will be, but he appears to know that the process is essential. Let us, then, choose to be optimistic about the outcome, if only because the alternative is too grim. But what about the process? What do we do in the meantime? Those are the questions to which we turn our attention in the concluding chapter.

CHAPTER 6

TACTICS, STRATEGY, AND OBJECTIVES

Don't try to skin a bear that's not dead.

—Russian proverb

THE TACTICAL LESSONS OF THIS ANALYSIS OF SOVIET NEGOTIATing behavior are generally too obvious to require extensive elaboration. Many of them apply to any negotiation, particularly to any cross-cultural negotiation. In a sense, they boil down to making sure that you are communicating what you intend to, that the signals you are sending out are adapted to the particular filters of your negotiating partner or adversary, and that you understand the signals coming your way.

One lesson that needs to be driven home is that a new negotiating relationship with the Soviets almost inevitably goes through a period of testing, much of which has to do with maneuvering to establish whether the relationship is to be one of dominance/submission or of equality. Soviet tactics during this period are likely to be tough: verbal aggressiveness, stonewalling, attempts at intimidation. Their objective is to establish the adversary's moral strength and determination. Sweet reasonableness in the face of such tactics risks being mistaken for weakness, with potentially very serious consequences. We have on several occasions gone astray as a new administration takes office in Washington because we have failed to understand the existence and nature of this period of testing. I have tried to show that the Kennedy administration's failure to understand this phenomenon led from the Bay of Pigs through the Vienna Summit and the Berlin Wall to the Cuban missile crisis. The administration was being tested and, in Soviet eyes, its failure prior to the missile crisis justified that uniquely high risk endeavor.

But we should not forget that the Soviets consider that they also are being tested in the early stages of a relationship. My first year at the U.S. embassy in Moscow coincided with the changeover between the Ford and Carter administrations. In April 1977, Secretary of State Vance arrived in Moscow for the new team's first serious arms control negotiations with the Soviets. Rather than attempting simply to push the previous regime's Vladivostok SALT II framework agreement to conclusion before tackling more ambitious goals, Vance brought with him a new proposal for deep cuts in both sides' strategic forces. The meeting was a failure; the Soviets stonewalled, and Vance left empty-handed. During a meeting at the Foreign Service Institute in late 1987, Paul Warnke, who, as the head of the Arms Control and Disarmament Agency, accompanied Vance to Moscow, reflected on this meeting and candidly admitted that it had been a mistake to begin with such an ambitious proposal. As he was riding out to the Moscow airport at the end of the visit, the high-ranking Foreign Ministry official accompanying him told him, in effect, that Brezhnev had had to spill a great deal of blood to get agreement to the Vladivostok framework, that he needed that finalized before he could move on. In Warnke's view, the failure of this initial effort set back the negotiating process for months, a delay that contributed substantially to the failure to obtain ratification of the SALT agreement eventually reached.

It is always easier to quarterback on Monday morning. And yet an analysis of the Soviet negotiating style should have led to the conclusion in advance that the Soviets would need some time to establish a relationship with the new team and that, if faced immediately with major new proposals, they would feel threatened and react, predictably, by stonewalling. There was nothing wrong with the substance of the Carter team proposals. There was something deeply wrong with the failure to analyze how the timing and content of those proposals would look to a Soviet mind.

While firmness in the face of aggressive Soviet negotiating tactics is essential, particularly at the earlier stages of a relationship, this does not necessarily mean that the American negotiator's response to stonewalling should be to adopt the same tactics. You may want to allow your Soviet counterpart to draw you out somewhat at the earlier stages of a negotiation, since an assessment that you are serious about the negotiation, that you are prepared to offer something of interest to his side, may be an essential precondition for the Soviet to begin to open up. Until he can assure his superiors that the Americans are serious, he may be required to stonewall, to refuse to engage the substance of the issues on the table. He may have arrived with a portfolio of trading items, but may not be authorized to open the portfolio until Moscow is satisfied that there is something to be gained.

If there is one thing that cries out from this analysis of Soviet negotiating behavior it is that negotiators who are perceived as confused, weak, vacillating, or uncertain will be both exploited and scorned. The opposite of these qualities is not hostile, aggressive, and threatening. Rather, it is determined, competent, and strong. Clear signals, consistent signals—how do we send them? Ultimately, on an individual basis, this is something that the negotiator will have to decide. But what about the larger context? How do we project a sense of national will, purpose, and determination?

We are hampered greatly in this area by the lack of a bipartisan foreign policy consensus. Lest we forget, there was a time when we had one. It is not that foreign policy was immune from partisan conflict, particularly during election campaigns, but rather that there was a widespread consensus about basic objectives and the means used to achieve them, and about how the legislative and executive branches could properly and effectively play their constitutional foreign policy roles. The erosion and ultimate dissolution of that consensus as we traveled the road between the New Frontier and the Tehran hostages is not the subject of this study. What is of concern is the implication of the lack of such a consensus for our negotiating effectiveness. Determination, competence, and strength cannot be projected by a country such as ours when the executive and legislative branches are at loggerheads both over the objectives of policy and the means to be used to achieve them; when within Congress the center will not hold and executive branch goals are whipsawed between small but passionate minorities on the left and right extremes; when the executive branch exhausts itself with its own infighting between those desperate to have an agreement, any agreement, and those determined to have no agreement, on any terms.

The more important implications of this analysis are for the development of a long-term strategy for negotiating more effectively with the Soviet Union. The shorthand for such a strategy is tactical toughness/strategic flexibility. Without tough negotiating tactics, we will not be taken seriously by the Soviet Union. Flabby negotiating tactics, indecisiveness, waffling are signs of weakness, and those who exhibit them will be treated with contempt, a dangerous attitude toward a nuclear superpower. Tough negotiating does not make it more difficult to get agreements with the Soviets; it makes it easier, provided the negotiator does not confuse tactics with strategy. Strategic flexibility implies a willingness, first, to reach agreements with the Soviets and, second, an ability to communicate that willingness.

What are our objectives in negotiating with the Soviet Union? First, to advance our interests. Second, to lessen the likelihood that conflicts will spiral into violence. Third, to advance our values. Fourth, to promote an evolution in Soviet society that will ease achievement of the first three. Many persons, both within government and outside, would argue that the last objective is unachievable and even undesirable. Their argument would be that we know so little about the internal workings of Soviet society and of the Soviet decision-making process that any efforts we might make to influence it would be ham-handed and as likely as not to produce negative rather than positive effects. The essential thing for us, they would argue, is to keep our own objectives in focus and to pursue them in a sensible way.

There is a lot of merit to this argument. Soviet society will evolve largely at its own pace and in its own way. Our ability to affect the pace and direction of that evolution is very limited. But it is not nonexistent. Educated Soviets still look to the West for models either to be emulated or to be scorned. By better understanding the forces at work in Soviet society and exercising our admittedly limited leverage at the right fulcrum points, we may be able to exercise an influence greater than the sheer weight of our efforts.

Any negotiation with the Soviet Union, on any subject, should include an underlying agenda. That agenda can be summed up in two words: transparency and predictability. We need to know a lot more about what is really happening in Soviet society, about the desires of its people and the goals of its leaders. We need to understand Soviet intentions and to have confidence that if those intentions should change we will know about it in time to do what is necessary to ensure our security and that of our allies. There are those who would argue that we already do know Soviet intentions. They can be summed up very simply: to take over the world. While many others might scoff at attempting to develop a foreign policy around such a simplistic analysis, in fact the essence of our national security policy, whether under a Democratic or a Republican administration, is based on such a view. We make a worst-case assumption about Soviet intentions. We assume that whatever the Soviets are capable of doing to us militarily, they will do unless deterred by the prospect of suffering equal or greater harm.

It is not difficult to understand why, in the face of Soviet tendencies toward secretiveness, control, and security overkill, American military planners are virtually driven to worst-case assumptions about Soviet intentions. We are living in an age in which the speed and destructiveness of military weapons means that underestimation of Soviet capabilities, misestimation of Soviet intentions, and insufficient American readiness could result in the elimination of the United States as a functioning society. We would not survive another Pearl Harbor. In a sense, it is not what we know about the Soviet Union that makes us consider it dangerous. It is what we do not know. And what we do not know is a great deal.

Thus, one of the principal long-term objectives of U.S. policy should be to facilitate a gradual opening of Soviet society to the outside world. Our policies should encourage those elements of Soviet society that are arguing for greater access to the Western world and less control by the political authorities over information flow and organized social activities. Such an opening offers the best prospects of eroding the deeply engrained traits of authoritarianism, risk-avoidance, and control which greatly complicate our ability to develop a more normal relationship with this military giant. The Soviet penchant, embedded in the Russian political culture and reinforced by Marxism-Leninism, for interpreting relationships as struggles for dominance, and for seeing them as polarized between complete dominance and complete submission, contributes to a world view that lacks limits. The notion of finding its appropriate place in the community of nations is not one that comes naturally to the Soviet mind.

The Russian tendency toward risk-avoidance is not without its positive features in an era of massive nuclear overkill. But again, it contributes toward an open-ended outlook on what constitutes sufficient security. Gorbachev's effort to inculcate the concept of "reasonable sufficiency" into Soviet strategic thought runs against the grain of Russian risk-avoidance. Sufficiency is not measured in reasonable terms. It equates to what others would probably consider massive superiority. When this trait encounters the American military planner's worst-case scenarios, the implications for circular arms spirals are obvious.

Control has to do in large part with the Party's control of all aspects of Soviet political and social life. Particularly relevant is the realization that information is an aspect of both power and control. The Soviet penchant for secrecy and control of information both extends and qualitatively transforms the Russian tradition of "*neglasnost.*" Outsiders must not learn how the society really works. Those in the society must not learn the reality of the outside world. Secrecy encompasses not only military planning, supply, and technology. It extends even to the basic elements of the political decision-making process.

Worst-case assumptions are not required by the fact that another nation has a large stockpile of nuclear weapons and the ability to deliver them on the United States. Britain and France fit in that category, but historical, cultural, and economic ties give us confidence that they will not attack us. But though these factors may be sufficient to obviate worst-case assumptions, they are not necessary. China is a case in point. Few countries could be more distant from us historically and culturally. China, lest we forget, is still ruled by a communist party. It is the most populous country in the world. Its interests do not always coincide with ours. Less than two decades ago, China—not the Soviet Union—was considered our most virulent, if not most dangerous, adversary. In the films and spy novels of the period, the Chinese were the crazed threats to world peace, while the U.S. and Soviet intelligence services often worked quietly together to avoid a Chinese-inspired catastrophe. Our ABM system was justified not as a protection against a Soviet attack, but as insurance against a Chinese strike.

The normalization of U.S.-Chinese relationships reduced the necessity for worst-case assumptions by producing predictability, or at least the belief in it. We and the Chinese developed a concept of certain basic shared interests, a view of the world that saw the Soviets as the basic danger. We developed a set of trading relationships that intensified our interactions. Our people began to travel in fairly large numbers to one another's countries. There are now over twenty thousand Chinese students in the United States. Our two countries are now far more open to one another than they were twenty years ago. We believe we understand one another's goals and intentions and that we have sufficient knowledge of one another's decision-making processes that if those intentions began to change we would know about it in adequate time to adjust our expectations and behavior appropriately.

Is such a transformation possible in our relations with the Soviet Union? If our definition of a changed relationship is the millennium—the lamb lying down with the lion, or the bear with the eagle—the answer is no. Neither the United States nor the Soviet Union intends anytime in the foreseeable future to cease being a major power. On this small planet, that implies interests that are sometimes opposed, and conflict over them. But we should not confuse conflict with hostility. Conflict arises from opposed interests, but there are few relationships, whether personal or international, in which interests are always and everywhere harmonious. The nature of the relationship is determined more by how conflicts are resolved than by their frequency. The absence of conflict is as likely to signify indifference as harmony.

The development of a more normal relationship requires a change both in the reality of our ability to destroy one another and in the perception of our willingness to do so. Sharp reductions in offensive strategic nuclear arms, accompanied at some point by a carefully orchestrated and nondestabilizing shift to effective defensive systems, would substantially change the reality. But such a change is unlikely to occur, or to be believed if it should occur, unless it is accompanied by changed perceptions. Even deep reductions in strategic weapons will not by themselves change worst-case assumptions. Rather, they will change the arena of competition. Instead of nuclear delivery systems, we will require smarter, more accurate conventional delivery systems. If conventional forces are drastically reduced, those remaining will have to be vastly improved in quality.

Military interventions in the Third World are one obstacle to changed perceptions. Secrecy, closed borders, travel restrictions, these and all of the other paraphernalia of the society that seeks to avoid risk by imposing control, also stand in the way of changed perceptions. We, ourselves, are not immune from such impulses in our more insecure moments. At such times, our own streak of isolationism predominates, and we are more concerned to protect ourselves against hostile outside penetrations than to project our influence and values outward. Yet the reality is that our open society has little to fear from either outside ideas or values. We should not, in the name of ensuring our security, deprive ourselves of the best tools we have to shape a safer and more just world—our openness, our democratic values, our respect for individual rights.

In the long run, in dealing with the Soviet Union, the advancement of our interests and the advancement of our values are inseparable. Predictability in the relationship can only be assured by increasing the permeability of the two societies. We must have a level of trade, travel, and exchanges that vastly increases what we know about one another. We must have sufficient access to one another's decision-making processes that we have confidence in one another's intentions, and in our ability to predict at least the outside limits of one another's behavior. This will require some risks on our part. Increased openness brings with it the possibility of increased hostile intelligence activity. We are facing these risks as we conduct the on-site inspections required in the Treaty on the Elimination of Intermediate and Shorter-Range Weapons. Far greater risks will have to be run to ensure verification of a START Treaty. But the tradeoffs in terms of increased access to the much more closed Soviet society can be enormous.

These are steps that will require a far greater and more painful break with tradition for the Soviets than for us. Are they ready for such steps? Part of the answer, of course, is that they have already come a long way. Their agreement to the verification provisions of the INF Treaty testifies eloquently to that. Even some Americans involved in the arms negotiation process still shake their heads in wry amusement about leaving out on their desks a thick document, the Memorandum of Understanding section of the INF Treaty, which contains many pages of Soviet-supplied photographs of their missiles and launchers, maps pinpointing the location of their installations, and diagrams of the installations—information which, to understate the point considerably, in the past U.S. intelligence agencies would have given a great deal to obtain. As one Soviet negotiator put it as the documents were exchanged, "If I had given you even one of these pictures a week ago, I would have been shot."

Gorbachev's internal reform program has focused exactly on the Soviet traits of authority, risk-avoidance, and control that we have discussed. Because those traits are so central to Soviet society, attempts to change them have potentially profound significance. But because the traits are so deep-rooted, they will be among the most difficult to change. Thus, Gorbachev's reforms involve their own dialectic in which certainty of rule implies ineffectuality, while pressing for change carries greater risk of overthrow. Brezhnev's stability eventually came to be seen as stagnation; Khrushchev's innovations as hare-brained schemes. Stalin found a way to force the Soviet Union to change while ensuring his own hold on power, but at enormous costs. Some of those costs, in the Soviet system's inability to compete effectively in an era of information and technological explosion, are still being borne. Gorbachev is trying to find a way to stimulate innovation and change, without changing the basic socioeconomic system or its style of rule. He has a tough row to hoe.

What should be the U.S. strategy in light of this? Always, our strategy should be to contribute to an opening of Soviet society. This strategy happens to coincide, at least in part, with Gorbachev's, even though our objectives are greatly dissimilar. Gorbachev, analyzing Soviet society in the late 1970s and early 1980s as in a precrisis situation, seeks to strengthen its economic and technological infrastructure and create institutions that can stimulate innovation, so as to strengthen the socialist system and Communist Party rule and ensure his country's ability to function as a major world power in the next century. Ours is to create a more stable international system and reduce the threat of war by increasing Soviet transparency and predictability. A more efficient and competitive Soviet system might indeed be a greater threat. But this is not the issue. In order to become more efficient and competitive, the Soviet system is going to have to change in some fundamental ways. As the next century opens, either we will be dealing with a Soviet Union that is more efficient and competitive, but qualitatively different—substantially open to the outside world and engaged positively in the world political and economic system—or a Soviet Union that remains a potentially mortal military threat, but one that is increasingly irrelevant to developments at the cutting edge of human progress.

Writing in *Foreign Affairs* more than forty years ago, George F. Kennan advised a U.S. policy of patient, persistent, long-term counterpressure to Soviet expansionist probes. Over the long term, he felt, such a policy, without directly forcing change on the Soviet Union, would nevertheless force it to confront its own internal contradictions and in that way contribute to an evolution in Soviet society toward a system with which we might more productively and peacefully share this planet. The American government adopted this advice, in the form of a policy of containment with which the original author may not always have agreed, and it has since been the leitmotif of U.S. strategy for dealing with the Soviet Union.

As Soviet ability to project military power worldwide has increased, and as the Soviet Union has become increasingly active in the Third World, some have questioned whether containment has failed. Perhaps, though, in light of Gorbachev's efforts to restructure basic elements of the Soviet system, we should instead be asking whether containment has succeeded and, if so, what the implications of that success are for future American policy. To the extent that we have treated containment as simply a reactive, defensive strategy of responding to Soviet efforts to subvert or disrupt the international system, we have underestimated its potential for forcing to the surface currents for change in Soviet society. Gorbachev's policy of *perestroika* acknowledges that the Stalinist system, whatever its achievements may have been in force-marching the Soviet Union into industrialization, was ultimately a dead end. Despite the Soviet Union's current receptivity to change, the inheritance of Soviet political culture weighs heavily against creation of a significantly more open and tolerant society, particularly when the resistance of vested interests is added to the scale.

Our task is not to help Gorbachev, or to hinder him. Rather, it is to persistently and patiently provide opportunities for greater information about alternatives to permeate Soviet society. When the Soviet Union is in a reformist mode, such a strategy will reinforce and perhaps deepen it; when it is in an autarchic or Stalinist phase, such a strategy may limit it and keep alive the knowledge that alternatives exist. Perhaps the most important part of what Kennan had to say is also the hardest for Americans to internalize. Our policy must be patient, persistent, and long-term. There are no quick fixes. This is the work of generations. We say "Rome was not built in a day." The Soviets say the same thing, except, revealingly, that they substitute Moscow for Rome. The roots of present-day Moscow are fixed in soil that is both ancient and very different from our own. In negotiating with the Soviet Union, we must both understand this and seek to transcend it.

NOTES

1. NEGOTIATING WITH THE SOVIETS

1. Anton Antonov-Ovseyenko, *The Time of Stalin* (New York: Harper and Row, 1981); Isaac Deutscher, *Stalin: A Political Biography* (New York: Oxford University Press, 1967); W. A. Harriman and Elie Abel, *Special Envoy to Churchill and Stalin, 1941–1946* (New York: Random House, 1975); Seweryn Bialer, *Stalin and His Generals* (Boulder, Colo.: Westview Press, 1984).

2. Joseph Whelan, *Soviet Diplomacy and Negotiating Behavior: Emerging New Context for U.S. Diplomacy*, Special Studies Series on Foreign Affairs Issues, Vol. 1, Committee on Foreign Affairs, House of Representatives, 1979, p. 101. Study prepared by Joseph Whelan, Senior Specialists Division, Congressional Research Service, Library of Congress.

3. This description of the meeting draws heavily on Whelan and on Harriman and Abel.

4. Harriman and Abel, p. 92.

5. Whelan, pp. 109–10.

6. When I do not give the identity of my source, the reader should understand that it is because the conversation was conducted on a background basis (i.e., the source was not to be identified).

7. Edward T. Hall has developed the concepts of high-, middle-, and low-context cultures and transactions in *Beyond Culture* (Garden City, N.Y.: Anchor Press/Doubleday, 1976).

2. CHAMELEONS, SAUSAGES, AND SOVIET NEGOTIATING STYLE

1. Ronald Hingley, *The Russian Mind* (New York: Charles Scribner and Sons, 1977), p. 172.

2. Ibid., p. 34.

3. Geoffrey Gorer and John Rickman, *The People of Great Russia* (New York: Chanticleer Press, 1950), p. 177.

4. Hingley, *The Russian Mind*, p. 260.

5. Edward T. Hall, *Beyond Culture* (Garden City, N.Y.: Anchor Press/Doubleday, 1976), pp. 115, 117.

6. Hingley, *The Russian Mind*, p. 196.

7. Robert C. Tucker, *The Soviet Political Mind: Studies in Stalinism and Post-Stalinist Change* (New York: W. W. Norton and Co., 1971), p. ix.

8. Stephen F. Cohen, *Rethinking the Soviet Experience: Politics and History Since 1917* (New York: Oxford University Press, 1985), pp. 146–48.

9. Nicholas Vakar, *The Taproot of Soviet Society* (New York: Harper & Brothers, 1961), pp. 17–18. Edward Keenan shares this general view of the split in Russian society and of the importance of hierarchical patterns. He argues, however, that within the innermost circles at the top the tsar was not all-powerful, though this might be the impression conveyed to the outside world. Edward Keenan, "Muscovite Political Folkways," *Russian Review* 45 (April 1986): pp. 115–81.

10. Dinko Tomasic, *The Impact of Russian Culture on Soviet Communism* (Glencoe: The Free Press, 1953), p. 16. Tomasic's general idea was to contrast the idyllic, peaceful Old Slavonic culture of the settled agricultural communities with the gloom, plundering,

pillage, rape, and autocracy of the steppe horsemen. This scheme is a bit too pat, but the fact that the church, the state, and the landlords might have had a common interest in promoting authoritarianism is believable.

11. Vakar, p. 8.

12. Nicholas Berdyaev, *The Russian Idea* (New York: Macmillan, 1948), p. 16.

13. Hingley, *The Russian Mind*, p. 197. See also Tucker's discussion of the influence of the Mongol domination and the reaction of the Russian princes to it. Robert C. Tucker, *Political Culture and Leadership in Soviet Russia* (New York: W. W. Norton, 1987), pp. 88–89.

14. Gorer and Rickman, p. 174. Gorer's study of Russian national character was roundly criticized, perhaps most devastatingly by Irving Goldman, who accused him of piling a "towering structure of unproved assumptions and vast hypotheses . . . upon a very frail and unreliable base of descriptive data." "Psychiatric Interpretation of Russian History: A Reply to Geoffrey Gorer," *American Slavic and East European Review* 9 (1950): pp. 151–61. But one does not have to accept the swaddling hypothesis to recognize that Gorer had some valid insights.

15. Tomasic, p. 152.

16. Hedrick Smith, *The Russians* (New York: Quadrangle, 1976), pp. 259, 264, 265.

17. Leon Sloss and M. Scott Davis, eds., *A Game for High Stakes: Lessons Learned in Negotiating with the Soviet Union* (Cambridge, Mass.: Ballinger, 1986), findings summarized pp. 6–11.

18. Robert Jervis, *Perception and Misperception in International Politics* (Princeton: Princeton University Press, 1976), p. 87.

19. Discussions, respectively, with Robert Bathurst, professor at the Naval Postgraduate Institute, Monterey, California, and with Jim Garrison, director of the Esalen Institute, San Francisco, California, in January 1987.

20. "Traditional Soviet ideas about the hierarchical structure of the international order were strongly conditioned by Bolshevik conceptions of power." William Zimmerman, "Elite Perspectives and the Explanation of Soviet Foreign Policy," in *The Conduct of Soviet Foreign Policy*, ed. Erik Hoffman and Frederick J. Fleron, Jr. (New York: Aldine, 1980), p. 22.

21. Gorer and Rickman, p. 174.

22. Conversation with Vladimir Bukovsky, Cambridge, England, January 1987.

23. Margaret Mead and Rhoda Metraux, eds., *The Study of Culture at a Distance* (Chicago: University of Chicago Press, 1953), p. 213.

24. Lenin, *What Is to Be Done?*, in *Collected Works of V. I. Lenin* (New York: International Publishers, 1929), vol. 4, book 2, p. 126.

25. Lenin, in a letter to S. I. Gusev of 11 March 1905. *Collected Works*, from the Russian 4th Edition (London: Lawrence and Wishart, 1966), vol. 34, p. 302.

26. John R. Deane, *The Strange Alliance* (New York: Viking Press, 1947), p. 33.

27. Conversation, February 1987.

28. Jonathan Dean, "East-West Arms Controls Negotiations: The Multilateral Dimension," in Sloss and Davis, p. 88.

29. Arthur M. Schlesinger, Jr., *A Thousand Days* (Boston: Houghton Mifflin, 1965); Maxwell Taylor, *Swords and Plowshares* (New York: W. W. Norton Company, 1972); Roger Hilsman, *To Move a Nation* (Garden City, N.J.: Doubleday and Company, 1967).

30. Christer Jönsson, *Soviet Bargaining Behavior: The Nuclear Test Ban Case* (New York: Columbia University Press, 1979); and Graham T. Allison, *Essence of Decision: Explaining the Cuban Missile Crisis* (Boston: Little, Brown, 1971).

31. Nikita Khrushchev, *Khrushchev Remembers* (Boston: Little, Brown and Company, 1970), p. 493.

32. Conversation with William Stearman, November 1986.

33. Schlesinger, p. 359.

34. Gordon R. Weihmiller and Dusko Doder, *U.S.-Soviet Summits: An Account of East-West Diplomacy at the Top, 1955–1985* (Lanham, Md.: University Press of America/ Institute for the Study of Diplomacy, 1986), p. 43.

35. Conversation with Paul Nitze at the State Department, February 1987.

36. See the discussion in chapter 1 of high-context and low-context cultures drawn from Edward Hall's *Beyond Culture.*

37. Jönsson, p. 192, and *Soviet Diplomacy and Negotiating Behavior: Emerging New Context for U.S. Diplomacy,* Special Studies Series on Foreign Affairs Issues, Vol. 1, prepared by Joseph Whelan, Senior Specialists Division, Congressional Research Service, Library of Congress, for the Committee on Foreign Affairs, House of Representatives, 1979, p. 357.

38. Taylor, p. 278; Hilsman, p. 182.

39. Arkady N. Shevchenko, *Breaking with Moscow* (New York: Alfred A. Knopf, 1985), p. 117.

40. Ibid.

41. James G. Blight, Joseph S. Nye, Jr., and David A. Welch, "The Cuban Missile Crisis Revisited," *Foreign Affairs* 66, no. 1 (Fall 1987): p. 173.

42. Theodore Sorensen says that majority opinion initially favored an air strike, but some views changed because of the difficulty of a "surgical" strike. Moreover, Acheson, a consistent proponent of an air strike, no doubt chilled his Excom colleagues with his scenario of a Soviet counterstrike against U.S. missiles in Turkey, a U.S. retaliatory strike against Soviet territory, followed, hopefully, by cooler heads prevailing. Theodore Sorensen, recorded interview by Carl Kaysen, March 26, 1964, John F. Kennedy Library Oral History Program, pp. 50–51. Whelan, p. 350.

43. Schlesinger, p. 823. Adam Ulam considers, in fact, that the intention of the Soviet Union was to force the United States to agree to a German peace treaty on Soviet terms in return for removal of the missiles. "Forty Years of Troubled Coexistence," *Foreign Affairs* 64, no. 1 (Fall 1985): p. 24. I am not aware of the circumstantial evidence to which Ulam refers, and my analysis of Soviet motives leads me to different conclusions.

44. Blight, Nye, and Welch, p. 182.

45. Alexander L. George, " 'The Operational Code': A Neglected Approach to the Study of Political Leaders and Decision-Making," in Hoffman and Fleron.

46. Strobe Talbott, *Deadly Gambits* (New York: Alfred A. Knopf, 1984), p. 206.

47. Schlesinger. The reaction of the Soviet diplomat to the mention of Berlin brings to mind Leites's discussion of the obligation of Bolsheviks not to allow themselves to be manipulated by the adversary's "provocations." Nathan Leites, *A Study of Bolshevism* (Glencoe: The Free Press, 1953), p. 46.

48. Jönsson.

49. Several of those who took part in the crisis acknowledged this in their memoirs, and U. Alexis Johnson, former Under Secretary of State for Political Affairs, reiterated it in November 1986 at a discussion on the Cuban missile crisis sponsored by Georgetown University's Institute for the Study of Diplomacy.

50. Blight, Nye, and Welch, pp. 178–80.

51. Ibid., p. 181.

52. Lenin, *Against Boycott: Notes of a Social-Democratic Publicist,* in *Collected Works,* translated from the Russian 4th Edition (London: Lawrence and Wishart, 1962), vol. 13, p. 23.

53. Lenin, *We Have Paid Too Much,* in *Selected Works* (New York: International Publishers, 1943), vol. 10, p. 303.

54. Bryant Wedge and Cyril Muromcew, "Psychological Factors in Soviet Disarmament Negotiations," *Journal of Conflict Resolution* 9, no. 1, (March 1965): p. 33.

55. Howard J. Stoertz, "Observations on Soviet Negotiating Practice," in Sloss and Davis, p. 44. Walter Slocombe, "Negotiating with the Soviets: Getting Past No," in Sloss

and Davis, p. 69. Jonathan Dean, "East-West Arms Control Negotiations: The Multilateral Dimension," in Sloss and Davis, p. 88.

56. See Jonathan Dean's discussion of this in "Negotiation by Increment," *Foreign Service Journal* 60, no. 7 (July/August, 1983): p. 29.

57. Jervis, pp. 84–85.

58. Interview with Vladimir Bukovsky, Cambridge, England, January 1987.

59. Background interview with a U.S. official, January 1987.

60. "The Soviet tendency to equate compromise in negotiations with weakness has been evidenced by their reluctance to make concessions and their frequent denial that they have conceded when they in fact have done so." Leon Sloss and M. Scott Davis, "The Soviet Union: The Pursuit of Power and Influence through Negotiation," in *National Negotiating Styles,* ed. Hans Binnendijk (Washington, D.C.: Center for the Study of Foreign Affairs, Foreign Service Institute, U.S. Department of State, 1987), p. 25.

61. Interview in Geneva, January 1987.

62. Whelan, pp. 344–45.

63. Leites, p. 62.

64. Hannes Adomeit, *Soviet Risk-Taking and Crisis Behavior* (London: George Allen & Unwin, 1982), p. 320.

65. Herbert York, "Negotiating and the U.S. Bureaucracy," in Sloss and Davis, p. 132.

66. Lenin, "From a Publicist's Diary," *Rabochii* 10 (September 14, 1917); reproduced in *Collected Works of V. I. Lenin* (New York: International Publishers, 1932), vol. 21, book 1, p. 143.

67. Hingley, *The Russian Mind*, p. 9.

68. Whelan, p. 109.

69. Gorer and Rickman, pp. 189–90.

70. Hingley, *The Russian Mind*, p. 46.

71. Tucker, *The Soviet Political Mind*, pp. 122–24, 140–41.

72. Wright Miller, *Russians as People* (New York: Dutton, 1961), p. 35. Vakar.

73. Leites, pp. 40–41, 46, 237.

74. Tony Bishop, "A Guide to Negotiating with the Soviets," unpublished paper. Conversation with author in September 1986.

75. Smith, p. 105.

76. I am certain that a number of my Russian friends would assert that in the Russian tradition both chameleons and sausages were considered contemptible, citing Chekhov's satiric story "The Chameleon" as evidence. I can only say that Soviet life may have exaggerated these traits, perhaps considerably, but it did not create them. Perhaps the process was circular. The new Soviet state drew on, and rewarded, those traits that strengthened its hold on power, thereby strengthening the traits, etc.

77. Lenin, "The Chief Task of Our Day," *Izvestia* (12 March 1918); reproduced in *Collected Works,* 4th Edition (London: Lawrence and Wishart, 1965), vol. 27, p. 160.

78. Adomeit, p. 320.

79. Interview with Robert Bathurst, Naval Postgraduate Institute, Monterey, California, January 1987.

80. John R. Deane, pp. 278–79.

81. Ibid.

82. Bishop.

83. John R. Deane, p. 258.

84. Interview with Vladimir Bukovsky, Cambridge, England, January 1987.

85. Seweryn Bialer, *The Soviet Paradox: External Expansion, Internal Decline* (New York: Alfred A. Knopf, 1986), pp. 161–62. While not explicitly mentioning "*chinovnichestvo*," Bialer describes the importance of service to the state for social status and its negative implications for initiative. Tomasic (p. 70) discusses the introduction of

"chinovnichestvo" by Peter the Great and the extent to which it built upon even earlier systems of rank and service.

86. Sloss and Davis, from summary of Soviet negotiating characteristics, pp. 6–11. Dean, "East-West Arms Control Negotiations," p. 84.

87. Interview with Paul Nitze at State Department, January 1987.

88. A point Bishop also makes.

89. Leites, pp. 52–53.

90. Wedge and Muromcew, p. 34.

91. Christer Jönsson's review of the literature on negotiating with the Soviets led him to a lengthy description of typical Soviet negotiating behavior, which included the following: "reliance on a cycle of commitment to positions which are repeated numerous times and for an extended period of time, eventually to be abandoned and taken up by a new commitment which is just as stubbornly pursued." Jönsson, pp. 41–54. He concluded that his case study did not provide evidence that this trait existed. I admire his efforts to test stereotypes about Soviet negotiating behavior but in this case find the repeated assertions of those who have sat across the table from Soviet negotiators more persuasive.

92. Max Kampelman, "Madrid Conference: How to Negotiate with the Soviets," *Law and National Security Intelligence Report,* American Bar Association, vol. 7. no. 2.

93. Jönsson, pp. 72, 73.

94. Keenan, pp. 119–20.

95. Hingley, *The Russian Mind,* pp. 70–71.

96. Interview at Naval Postgraduate Institute, Monterey, California, January 1987.

97. See Tucker's contrast between the Western problem-solving, instrumentalist approach and the Soviet view that theory must precede action. (Robert C. Tucker *The Soviet Political Mind,* pp. 262–65). Some American negotiators also consider this crucial. In discussing Henry Kissinger's Mideast shuttle diplomacy at Georgetown University in April 1987, Harold Saunders stressed that numerous initial shuttles were concerned with establishing the principles upon which a peace negotiation might be conducted, not the terms of an agreement. American journalists accompanying the mission had great difficulty in dealing with this concept. Kissinger's stress on the importance of reaching agreement on principles meshed well with Soviet needs and probably accounted for the relative ease with which he and Soviet leaders dealt with one another.

98. Wedge and Muromcew, p. 31.

99. John R. Deane, pp. 100, 296.

100. A Soviet negotiator, I was told, remarked to his American counterpart that he (the Soviet) would have been shot if he had handed over so much as a single page of the Memorandum even a week prior to signature of the Treaty.

101. Wedge and Muromcew, p. 25.

102. Interview at Naval Postgraduate Institute, January 1987.

103. John R. Deane, pp. 58–59.

104. Hingley, *The Russian Mind,* p. 91.

105. John R. Deane, p. 203.

106. Hingley, *The Russian Mind,* pp. 94–95.

107. Ronald Hingley, "That's No Lie, Comrade," *Problems of Communism,* vol. 11, no. 2 (1962): p. 50.

108. Charles J. Halperin, *Russia and the Golden Horde* (Bloomington: Indiana University Press, 1986), p. 74.

109. Ibid., p. 104.

110. Leonid Andreyev, *Polnoe sobranie sochinenii* (St. Petersburg, 1913), vol. V, pp. 226, 227.

111. Feodor Dostoevsky, "Something About Lying," in *Diary of a Writer* (New York: Octagon Books, 1973), p. 135.

112. Bishop.
113. Smith, p. 17.
114. John R. Deane, p. 303.
115. Interview at Naval Postgraduate Institute, January 1987.
116. Hingley, "That's No Lie, Comrade," p. 102.
117. Whelan, p. 334.
118. Dostoevsky, pp. 131–35.

3. THE BIRD IN THE HAND AND OTHER SOVIET NEGOTIATING TACTICS

1. Joseph Whelan, *Soviet Diplomacy and Negotiating Behavior: Emerging New Context for U.S. Diplomacy,* Committee on Foreign Affairs, U.S. House of Representatives, Special Studies Series on Foreign Affairs Issues, vol. 1, pp. 109–10.
2. Ibid., p. 413.
3. Herb Cohen, *You Can Negotiate Anything* (New York: Bantam Books, 1982), p. 121.
4. Christer Jönsson, *Soviet Bargaining Behavior: The Nuclear Test Ban Case* (New York: Columbia University Press, 1979), pp. 41–54.
5. Tony Bishop, "A Guide to Negotiating with the Soviet Union," unpublished manuscript, London, British Foreign Office, n.d.
6. START negotiator Ambassador James Goodby told me he believes the criticism that U.S. negotiators allow time to be used against them is badly outdated, the MBFR and START talks being clear evidence against the criticism. Walter Slocombe has made the point that in some cases deadlines have clearly worked against the Soviets ("Negotiating with the Soviets: Getting Past No," in Leon Sloss and M. Scott Davis, *A Game for High Stakes: Lessons Learned in Negotiating with the Soviet Union* [Cambridge, Mass.: Ballinger, 1986], pp. 70–71).
7. Interview with Robert Bathurst, Naval Postgraduate Institute, Monterey, California, January 1987.
8. Raymond L. Garthoff, "Negotiating with the Russians: Some Lessons from SALT," *International Security* 1, no. 4 (Spring 1977): p. 5.
9. Howard J. Stoertz, "Observations on Soviet Negotiating Practice," in Sloss and Davis, p. 44. See also Bishop.
10. Bishop.
11. Lenin, "The War and the Provisional Government," *Pravda,* no. 31, April 26, 1917; reproduced in *Collected Works of V. I. Lenin* (New York: International Publishers, 1929), vol. 20, book 1, p. 173.
12. Bishop.
13. Sloss and Davis, *A Game for High Stakes,* pp. 6–11.
14. Bishop.
15. Interview with Robert Bathurst, Naval Postgraduate Institute, January 1987.
16. Bryant Wedge and Cyril Muromcew, "Psychological Factors in Soviet Disarmament Negotiations," *Journal of Conflict Resolution* 9, no. 1 (March 1965): p. 35.
17. Bishop.
18. John R. Deane, *Strange Alliance* (New York: Viking Press, 1947), p. 297.
19. Bishop.
20. Jönsson, pp. 72–73.
21. Max Kampelman, "Madrid Conference: How to Negotiate with the Soviets," *Law and National Security Intelligence Report,* vol. 7, no. 2, American Bar Association.
22. John R. Deane, p. 139.
23. Bishop.

24. Herb Cohen, p. 121.
25. Jönsson, p. 211.
26. Bishop.

4. TRUTH, REALITY, AND POWER

1. This view has much in common with that of Wedge and Muromcew, who based their research on Soviet negotiating behavior during the SALT talks on the "thesis that the Soviet government views the world in terms of assumptions which are generally shared within its own social framework. Soviet representatives must interpret the negotiations in terms of the reality world of the Soviet government; this is the only world they know." Bryant Wedge and Cyril Muromcew, "Psychological Factors in Soviet Disarmament Negotiations," *Journal of Conflict Resolution* 9, no. 1 (March 1965), pp. 18–19.

2. One distinction which has been proposed is between cognitive standards, appreciative standards, knowledge, and power. The first, which has to do with criteria for establishing the validity of information and is not itself subject to ultimate verification, should be far less susceptible to change than the last, which has to do with an individual's perception of his capacity to affect his environment. Rita M. Kelley and Frederick J. Fleron, Jr., "Personality, Behavior, and Communist Ideology," in *The Conduct of Soviet Foreign Policy*, ed. Erik Hoffman and Frederick J. Fleron, Jr. (New York: Aldine, 1980), pp. 195–96.

3. *The Conduct of Soviet Foreign Policy* reprints a classic debate between scholars holding the ideological and the national interest views of Soviet foreign policy. On the functions of ideology, see in that text John A. Armstrong, "The Domestic Roots of Soviet Foreign Policy," esp. pp. 93–95, and Richard Lowenthal, "The Logic of One-Party Rule," p. 119. See also, Alexander Dallin, "The Domestic Sources of Soviet Foreign Policy," in *The Domestic Context of Soviet Foreign Policy*, ed. Seweryn Bialer (Boulder, Colo.: Westview Press, 1981), p. 335; and Hannes Adomeit, *Soviet Risk-Taking and Crisis Behavior: A Theoretical and Empirical Analysis* (London: George Allen & Unwin, 1982), p. 330.

4. R. N. Carew Hunt, "Ideology and Power Politics: A Symposium," in Hoffman and Fleron, p. 103.

5. Adam B. Ulam, "Soviet Ideology and Soviet Foreign Policy," in Hoffman and Fleron, p. 141.

6. John A. Armstrong's essay, "The Domestic Roots of Soviet Foreign Policy," points out the various distinctions scholars have made between ideology, doctrine, dogma, and various other permutations of what the Soviet leaders think versus what they say. I like the distinction between unverifiable beliefs (grand ideology) and verifiable but unverified beliefs (petty ideology or dogma). Grand ideology includes the concepts we will be discussing below about the nature of reality. Doctrine, or petty ideology, comprises propositions such as the inevitability of war, or peaceful coexistence.

7. Ronald Hingley, "That's No Lie, Comrade," *Problems of Communism* 11, no. 2 (March/April 1962): p. 54.

8. Raymond L. Garthoff, "American-Soviet Relations in Perspective," *Political Science Quarterly* 100, no. 4 (Winter 1985–1986): p. 546.

9. Ibid., pp. 550–51.

10. Alfred G. Meyer, "The Functions of Ideology in the Soviet Political System," *Soviet Studies* 17, no. 3 (January 1966): p. 276.

11. James H. Billington, *The Icon and the Axe: An Interpretive History of Russian Culture* (New York: Alfred A. Knopf, 1966), p. 324.

12. Ibid., p. 266. Mead and Metraux make essentially the same point: "Empirical ways of thinking, which stress the detailed steps through which something happens and the

detailed clues by which it is found out, have had less time to take hold in Russia than in the West. The ideal of knowledge remains much more an immediate and complete revelation of the core of events, of the soul of another person." Margaret Mead and Rhoda Metraux, eds., *The Study of Culture at a Distance* (Chicago: University of Chicago Press, 1953), pp. 439–40.

13. Geoffrey Gorer and John Rickman, *The People of Great Russia* (New York: Chanticleer Press, 1950), pp. 186–88.

14. Robert Kennedy, *Thirteen Days* (New York: W. W. Norton & Co., 1969), p. 64.

15. Ibid., p. 65, emphasis added.

16. Tibor Szamuely, *The Russian Tradition* (New York: McGraw-Hill, 1974), p. 157.

17. Nicholas Berdyaev, *The Russian Idea* (New York: Macmillan, 1948), p. 31.

18. The following discussion draws substantially on Thomas J. Blakeley's excellent *The Soviet Theory of Knowledge* (Dordrecht, Holland: Reidel, 1964).

19. Edward T. Hall, *Beyond Culture* (Garden City, N.J.: Anchor Press/Doubleday, 1976), pp. 114–15.

20. Lenin, "Materialism and Imperio-Criticism," in *Selected Works* (New York: International Publishers, 1943), pp. 317–19.

21. Blakeley, *The Soviet Theory of Knowledge*, pp. 95–99, 114–21.

22. A. J. Ayer, *The Central Questions of Philosophy* (London: Weidenfeld and Nicolson, 1973), p. 8.

23. Ibid., p. 60.

24. Lenin's widow, Krupskaya, speaking at the 14th Party Congress in 1925, quoted in Margaret Mead, *Soviet Attitudes toward Authority* (New York: McGraw-Hill, 1951), p. 15.

25. Lenin, *Conspectus of Hegel's Book "The Science of Logic,"* in *Collected Works*, from the Russian 4th Edition (London: Lawrence and Wishart, 1961), vol. 38, p. 171.

26. Ulam, p. 140.

27. Peter B. Reddaway, "Aspects of Ideological Belief in the Soviet Union; Comments on Professor Meyer's Essay," *Soviet Studies* 17, no. 4 (April 1966): pp. 482–83. Uri Ra'anan, "Soviet Decision-making and International Relations," *Problems of Communism* 29 (November/December 1980): p. 41.

28. Steven White, "The USSR: Patterns of Autocracy and Industrialism," in *Political Culture and Political Change in Communist States,* ed. Archie Brown and Jack Gray (London: Macmillan, 1977), p. 47.

29. Daniel Bell, "Ideology and Soviet Politics," *Slavic Review* 24, no. 4, (December 1965): pp. 591–603.

30. Adomeit, p. 333.

31. Bialer, pp. 263–65.

32. On this, the author speaks from experience.

33. The Soviet official told this anecdote to his State Department counterpart, who related it to me during a background interview in December 1986.

34. Conversation with Vladimir Bukovsky, Cambridge, England, January 1987.

35. Tucker notes that Soviet theorists point out this difference between their "dialectical" approach to coexistence and the "metaphysical" approach of "bourgeois ideologues." Robert Tucker, *The Soviet Political Mind: Studies in Stalinism and Post-Stalinist Change* (New York: W. W. Norton and Co., 1971), pp. 246–47.

36. Conversation with Vladimir Bukovsky, Cambridge, England, January 1987.

37. Jonathan Dean, "East-West Arms Control Negotiations: The Multilateral Dimension," in *A Game for High Stakes,* ed. Leon Sloss and M. Scott Davis (Cambridge, Mass.: Ballinger, 1986), p. 86.

38. Wedge and Muromcew, p. 33.

39. Lenin, in *Proletarskaya Pravda,* 7 December 1913; reproduced in *Collected Works* (London: Lawrence and Wishart, 1963), vol. 19, p. 523.

40. Adomeit, p. 324.

41. John R. Deane, *The Strange Alliance* (New York: Viking Press, 1947), p. 297.

42. Tony Bishop, *A Guide to Negotiating with the Soviets,* unpublished paper. Conversation with author in September 1986.

43. Conversation at British Cabinet Office, January 1987.

44. Max Kampelman, "Madrid Conference: How to Negotiate with the Soviets," American Bar Association, *Law and National Security Intelligence Report,* vol. 7, no. 2. Ambassador Kampelman made the comment on dialectics during a meeting with the author in December 1986.

45. Conversation in January 1987.

46. Leon Sloss and M. Scott Davis, "The Soviet Union: The Pursuit of Power and Influence through Negotiation," in *National Negotiating Styles,* ed. Hans Binnendijk (Washington, D.C.: Center for the Study of Foreign Affairs, Foreign Service Institute, U.S. Department of State, 1987), p. 29.

47. Wedge and Muromcew, p. 33.

48. On negotiation as process, see the popular work by Herb Cohen, *You Can Negotiate Anything* (New York: Bantam Books, 1982), p. 102.

49. Julian Lider, *Correlation of Forces: An Analysis of Marxist-Leninist Concepts* (New York: St. Martin's Press, 1986).

50. Ibid., p. 10.

51. Robert V. Daniels, "Doctrine and Foreign Policy," in *The Conduct of Soviet Foreign Policy,* ed. Hoffman and Fleron (New York: Aldine, 1980), p. 164.

52. Lider, pp. 67–68.

53. Lenin, "A Poor Defense of a Liberal Labour Policy," *Zvezda,* April 1, 1912; as reproduced in *Collected Works* (Moscow: Foreign Languages Publishing House, 1963), vol. 17, p. 560.

54. Lider, p. 124.

55. Ibid., pp. 145–46.

56. Ibid., p. 217. Lider's reference to "both approaches" is a comparison of Western balance of power theory with the Soviet correlation of forces.

57. Ibid., p. 233.

58. Ibid., p. 261.

59. Thomas W. Wolfe, "Concluding Reflections on the SALT Experience," in Hoffman and Fleron, p. 413.

60. Conversation with Paul Nitze in Washington, D.C., February 1987.

61. Comments at American Political Science Association annual meeting, September 1986, Washington, D.C.

62. Edward Hallet Carr, *Socialism in One Country, 1924–1926* (London: Macmillan & Co., 1958), p. 4. Brzezinski shares Carr's view that over time, the more enduring patterns of Russian political culture have begun to exert greater influence. Zbigniew Brzezinski, "Soviet Politics: From the Future to the Past?" in *The Dynamics of Soviet Politics,* ed. Paul Cocks, Robert V. Daniels, and Nancy Whittier Heer (Cambridge, Mass.: Harvard University Press, 1976), p. 337.

63. Billington, p. ix. Steven White, "The USSR: Patterns of Autocracy and Industrialism," in Brown and Gray, p. 34.

64. Carr, pp. 9–10.

65. Robert C. Tucker, *Political Culture and Leadership in Soviet Russia: From Lenin to Gorbachev* (New York: W. W. Norton, 1987), pp. 88–89. Szamuely, *The Russian Tradition,* pp. 15, 19–20, 24–25. George Vernadsky, *The Mongols and Russia* (New Haven: Yale University Press, 1953), esp. pp. 335–349. Another who has stressed the impact of Mongol/Tatar rule on Russia's authoritarian political traditions is Ronald Hingley, *The Russian Mind* (New York: Charles Scribner's Sons, 1977), p. 197. For a dissenting view,

see Charles J. Halperin, *Russia and the Golden Horde: The Mongol Impact on Medieval Russian History* (Bloomington: Indiana University Press, 1986). Brzezinski also considers that the central reality of Russian politics has been its predominantly autocratic character (p. 337).

66. Halperin, pp. 102–03. Edward L. Keenan, "Muscovite Political Folkways," *The Russian Review* 45 (April 1986): pp. 115–81, especially p. 118.

67. Keenan, pp. 155–57.

68. Ibid. For more on the subordination of the interests of the individual to those of society in the Russian dissident tradition, see Szamuely, pp. 170–71.

69. Halperin, p. 126.

70. Seweryn Bialer, *The Soviet Paradox: External Expansion, Internal Decline* (New York: Alfred A. Knopf, 1986), p. 200.

71. Ibid., p. 240.

72. See, for example, Nicholas Vakar's, *The Taproot of Soviet Society* (New York: Harper & Brothers, 1961), p. 17. Keenan's view is essentially the same, although he distinguishes two elements of the early upper classes—court and bureaucratic—which over time melded (Keenan).

73. Berdyaev, p. 16.

74. Billington, p. 123.

75. Ibid., p. 198. See also Szamuely, p. 72.

76. George Kennan, "The Sources of Soviet Conduct," *Foreign Affairs* 65, no. 4 (Spring 1987): p. 852; (a reprint of the 1947 "X" article).

77. Lenin, of course, stood on the shoulders of others. He acknowledged his debt to Plekhanov, the father of Russian Marxism. And many of his organizational principles had antecedents in the principles of *"Narodnaya volya,"* a debt that he also acknowledged. See the discussion in Szamuely, pp. 354–69.

78. Nikolai Aleksandrovich Berdyaev, "The Origin of Russian Communism," in *The Mind of Modern Russia,* ed. Hans Kohn (Rutgers, N.J.: Rutgers University Press, 1955), p. 254. Billington, p. 524. J. N. Bochenski, *Soviet Russian Dialectical Materialism* (Dordrecht, Holland: Reidel, 1963), p. 28.

79. Quoted in Kohn, p. 244.

80. Thomas T. Hammond, "Leninist Authoritarianism before the Revolution," in *Continuity and Change in Russian and Soviet Thought,* ed. Ernest J. Simmons (Cambridge, Mass.: Harvard University Press, 1955), p. 154.

81. Carr, p. 16. For further on Lenin's view of party organization and its influence on communism, see Robert C. Tucker "Lenin's Bolshevism as a Culture in the Making," in *Bolshevik Culture: Experiment and Order in the Russian Revolution,* ed. Abbott Gleason, Peter Kenez, and Richard Stites (Bloomington: Indiana University Press, 1985).

82. Lenin, "On the Eve of October, 1917," in Kohn, p. 235.

83. Nathan Leites, *A Study of Bolshevism* (Glencoe: The Free Press, 1953).

84. Ibid., pp. 148, 152, 155, 162.

85. John A. Armstrong, who is sympathetic to Leites's work, at least insofar as he considers the study of psychological processes relevant to international affairs, concedes the approach fell into disrepute following the appearance of *A Study of Bolshevism* ("The Domestic Roots of Soviet Foreign Policy," in Hoffman and Fleron, p. 96). Samuel L. Sharp, "National Interest: Key to Soviet Politics," in Hoffman and Fleron, p. 110. Robert Jervis, *Perception and Misperception in International Politics* (Princeton: Princeton University Press, 1976), p. 103, note 88.

86. Alexander L. George, " 'The Operational Code': A Neglected Approach to the Study of Political Leaders and Decision-Making," in Hoffman and Fleron, p. 166.

87. Ibid., p. 178.

88. Adomeit, p. 328.

89. Keenan, p. 168.

90. Archie Brown, ed., *Political Culture and Communist Studies* (New York: M. E. Sharpe, 1985), p. 156.

91. Bialer, *The Soviet Paradox*, pp. 263–65.

92. On the Revolution as a movement of restoration, see Brzezinski, p. 340. *Bolshevik Culture*, by Abbott Gleason, Peter Kenez, and Richard Stites (Bloomington: Indiana University Press, 1985) discusses the interaction of the intellectual and peasant cultures.

93. Vakar, pp. 8, 17–18. Billington, pp. 534, 539.

94. Tucker, *The Soviet Political Mind*, p. ix. Bialer, *The Soviet Paradox*, pp. 24, 31.

95. Keenan, p. 168. Joyce also stresses the central role risk-avoidance plays in the Soviet political culture (John Michael Joyce, "The Old Russian Legacy," *Foreign Policy*, No. 55 [Summer 1984], pp. 132–153).

96. Stephen F. Cohen, *Rethinking the Soviet Experience: Politics and History Since 1917* (New York: Oxford University Press, 1985), p. 146.

97. Tucker, *The Soviet Political Mind*, pp. 175, 229.

98. Bialer, *The Soviet Paradox*, pp. 161–62.

5. BALALAIKA, BROWNIAN MOTION, AND MOVEMENT

1. Former Washington Post correspondent Dusko Doder, speaking to a group at Georgetown University, April 22, 1987.

2. Daniel Bell, "Ideology and Soviet Politics," *Slavic Review* 24, no. 4 (December 1965): pp. 591–603.

3. Morton Schwartz, *The Foreign Policy of the U.S.S.R.: Domestic Factors* (Encino, Calif.: Dickenson, 1975), pp. 90–92.

4. Some Soviet emigrés believe that the regime's awareness of Sakharov's opposition to the U.S. Strategic Defense Initiative was the key to the decision both to end his exile and to assist the interview. The regime was willing to take the heat for his comments on human rights and Afghanistan in order to reap the benefits of his opposition to SDI. I do not find this persuasive. The real change was the voluntary relinquishment of control over what would be said to the outside world. They could not be certain what he would say about SDI, or about any of the other issues likely to be raised.

5. Bialer calls these discussions the most free and far-reaching of the post-Stalin era. Seweryn Bialer, *The Soviet Paradox: External Expansion, Internal Decline* (New York: Alfred A. Knopf, 1986), p. 123.

6. Interview with Joel Schatz, President, Moscow/San Francisco Teleport, San Francisco, January 1987.

7. Interview at Oxford University, England, January 1987.

8. Archie Brown, ed., *Political Culture and Communist Studies* (New York: M. E. Sharpe, 1985), p. 185.

9. Robert Jervis, *Perception and Misperception in International Politics* (Princeton: Princeton University Press, 1976), pp. 239, 253. Alexander L. George, " 'The Operational Code': A Neglected Approach to the Study of Political Leaders and Decision-Making," in *The Conduct of Soviet Foreign Policy*, ed. Erik Hoffman and Frederic J. Fleron, Jr. (New York: Aldine, 1971), pp. 186–87. See also Zbigniew Brzezinski, "Soviet Politics: From the Future to the Past?" in *The Dynamics of Soviet Politics*, ed. Paul Cocks, Robert V. Daniels, and Nancy Whittier Heer (Cambridge, Mass.: Harvard University Press, 1976), p. 345.

10. Gorbachev speech to GOSR Meeting, Foreign Broadcast Information Service, Soviet Union, November 3, 1987, p. 38.

11. Conversation with Vladimir Bukovsky, Cambridge, England, January 1987.

12. Bialer, *The Soviet Paradox*, pp. 119–21.

13. Ibid., p. 141. Zhores A. Medvedev, *Gorbachev* (New York: W. W. Norton, 1986), pp. 186, 223.

14. *Komsomolskaya Pravda*, June 29, 1988, page A9.

15. See particularly the discussion in chapter 4 of political culture and in chapter 2 of authority relationships.

16. Stephen F. Cohen, *Rethinking the Soviet Experience: Politics and History Since 1917* (New York: Oxford University Press, 1985), p. 146.

17. Nicholas Vakar, *The Taproot of Soviet Society* (New York: Harper & Brothers, 1961), p. 153. Brzezinski, p. 349.

18. Edward Keenan, "Muscovite Political Folkways," *Russian Review* 45 (1986): p. 171.

19. Ibid., pp. 176–77.

20. *Washington Post*, May 21, 1987, page A49.

21. Former Washington Post correspondent Dusko Doder, speaking to a group at Georgetown University, April 22, 1987.

22. Ibid.

23. T. Trister Gati, "Gorbachev and Russia's Future," in *Surviving Together: A Journal on Soviet-American Relations* (Washington, D.C.: Institute for Soviet-American Relations, March 1987), pp. 10–11.

24. Mikhail Gorbachev. *Perestroika: New Thinking for Our Country and the World* (New York: Harper & Row, 1987), pp. 63, 79.

25. Dimitri K., Simes, "Gorbachev: A New Foreign Policy?" *Foreign Affairs* 65 (1986): pp. 478–79.

26. Interview with Tony Bishop, British Foreign Office, London, January 1987.

27. *Washington Post*, September 2, 1986, p. 1.

28. This thought was suggested to me by British Foreign Office Counsellor Tony Bishop during a discussion in his office in January 1987.

29. Simes, p. 492. Interview with Ambassador Kampelman at State Department, December 1986.

30. Interview at State Department, February 1987.

31. Simes, p. 489. Angola may be different from the others, however, since it has substantial foreign currency earnings. Rather than representing a drain on Soviet resources, it may represent a supplier of hard currency in return for second-hand military merchandise.

32. *Washington Post*, May 28, 1987, p. A21; *Wall Street Journal*, May 29, 1987, p. 22.

33. Interview with Archie Brown, Oxford, England, January 1987.

34. Of course, this too could be seen as a further modification of trends that have been occurring throughout the post-Stalin period. Alex George, reporting Leites's findings that during the Khrushchev era Bolshevik "fears of annihilation" declined, decreasing the urgency of total victory, sees those changes as significant, but more in the nature of modifications of the classical Bolshevik belief system than in its radical transformation (George, p. 188). Does Gorbachev's approach represent further modification—not the only possible, but certainly a very possible evolution of the system at this stage in its history—or radical transformation?

35. The account of Gorbachev's remark was from a State Department official who was in a position to know.

36. Jonathan Dean, "Negotiation by Increment," *Foreign Service Journal* 60, no. 7 (July/August 1983): p. 29.

37. *New York Times*, May 31 and June 1, 1987; *Washington Post*, June 1, 1987.

38. *New York Times*, June 7, 1987, p. 7; *Los Angeles Times*, June 14, 1987, V:4.

39. Interview, February 1987.

40. Background interview with State Department official.

41. Remarks at a conference on National Negotiating Style sponsored by the Department of State's Foreign Service Institute, Rosslyn, Virginia, October 29, 1985.

42. Joseph Whelan, *Soviet Diplomacy and Negotiating Behavior: Emerging New Context for U.S. Diplomacy,* Special Studies on Foreign Affairs Issues, Vol. 1 (Senior Specialists Division, Congressional Research Service, Library of Congress, for the Committee on Foreign Affairs, House of Representatives, 1979), p. 404.

43. The initial point is made in Bishop's negotiating guide; he suggested the second in a discussion with me in January 1987.

44. Interview with Bishop, January 1987.

BIBLIOGRAPHY

BOOKS

Adomeit, Hannes. *Soviet Risk-Taking and Crisis Behavior: A Theoretical and Empirical Analysis*. London: George Allen & Unwin, 1982.

Allison, Graham T. *Essence of Decision: Explaining the Cuban Missile Crisis*. Boston: Little, Brown, 1971.

American Bibliography of Slavic and East European Studies. Chicago: American Association for the Advancement of Slavic Studies, Library of Congress, 1981/1982.

Andreyev, Leonid. *Polnoe Sobranie Sochinenii*, vol. V. St. Petersburg, 1913.

Antonov-Ovseyenko, Anton. *The Time of Stalin*. New York: Harper and Row, 1981.

Ayer, A. J. *The Central Questions of Philosophy*. London: Weidenfeld and Nicolson, 1973.

Berdyaev, Nicholas. *The Russian Idea*. New York: Macmillan, 1948.

Berlin, Isaiah. *Russian Thinkers*. London: Hogarth Press, 1979.

Bialer, Seweryn, ed. *The Domestic Context of Soviet Foreign Policy*. Boulder, Colo.: Westview Press, 1981.

Bialer, Seweryn. *The Soviet Paradox: External Expansion, Internal Decline*. New York: Alfred A. Knopf, 1986.

————. *Stalin and His Generals*. Boulder, Colo.: Westview Press, 1984.

————. *Stalin's Successors: Leadership, Stability and Change in the Soviet Union*. Cambridge and New York: Cambridge University Press, 1980.

Billington, James H. *The Icon and the Axe: An Interpretive History of Russian Culture*. New York: Alfred A. Knopf, 1966.

Binnendijk, Hans, ed. *National Negotiating Styles*. Washington, D.C.: Center for the Study of Foreign Affairs, Foreign Service Institute, U.S. Department of State, 1987.

Blakely, Thomas J. *Soviet Philosophy: A General Introduction to Contemporary Soviet Thought*. Dordrecht, Holland: Reidel, 1964.

————. *The Soviet Theory of Knowledge*. Dordrecht, Holland: Reidel, 1964.

Bochenski, J. N. *Soviet Russian Dialectical Materialism*. Dordrecht, Holland: Reidel, 1963.

Bronfenbrenner, Urie. *Two Worlds of Childhood*. New York: Russell Sage Foundation, 1970.

Brown, Archie, ed. *Political Culture and Communist Studies*. New York: M. E. Sharpe, 1985.

Brown, Archie and Jack Gray, eds. *Political Culture and Political Change in Communist States*. London: Macmillan, 1977.

Carr, E. H. *Socialism in One Country*, vol. 1. London: Macmillan and Co., 1958.

Cocks, Paul, Robert V. Daniels, and Nancy Whittier Heer, eds. *The Dynamics of Soviet Politics*. Cambridge, Mass.: Harvard University Press, 1976.

Cohen, Herb. *You Can Negotiate Anything*. New York: Bantam Books, 1982.

Cohen, Stephen F. *Bukharin and the Bolshevik Revolution*. New York: Alfred A. Knopf, 1973.

————. *Rethinking the Soviet Experience: Politics and History Since 1917*. New York: Oxford University Press, 1985.

————. *Sovieticus: American Perceptions and Soviet Realities*. New York: W. W. Norton and Co., 1984.

Deane, John R. *The Strange Alliance*. New York: Viking Press, 1947.

Dennett, Raymond, and Joseph E. Johnson, eds. *Negotiating with the Russians.* Boston: World Peace Foundation, 1951.

Deutscher, Isaac. *Stalin: A Political Biography.* New York: Oxford University Press, 1967.

Fisher, Roger, and William Ury. *Getting to Yes.* New York: Penguin Books, 1983.

Gleason, Abbott, Peter Kenez, and Richard Stites. *Bolshevik Culture: Experiment and Order in the Russian Revolution.* Bloomington: Indiana University Press, 1985.

Gorbachev, Mikhail. *Perestroika: New Thinking for Our Country and the World.* New York: Harper and Row, 1987.

Gorer, Geoffrey, and John Rickman. *The People of Great Russia.* New York: Chanticleer Press, 1950.

Hall, Edward T. *Beyond Culture.* Garden City, N.Y.: Anchor Press/Doubleday, 1976.

Halperin, Charles J. *Russia and the Golden Horde: The Mongol Impact on Medieval Russian History.* Bloomington: Indiana University Press, 1986.

Harriman, W. A., and Elie Abel. *Special Envoy to Churchill and Stalin, 1941–1946.* New York: Random House, 1975.

Hilsman, Roger. *To Move a Nation.* Garden City, N.Y.: Doubleday and Company, 1967.

Hingley, Ronald. *The Russian Mind.* New York: Charles Scribner and Sons, 1977.

Hnik, T. ed. *European Bibliography of Soviet, East European and Slavonic Studies.* Birmingham, England: University of Birmingham, International Committee for Soviet East European Studies, 1981/82.

Hoffman, Erik, and Frederic J. Fleron, Jr., eds. *The Conduct of Soviet Foreign Policy.* New York: Aldine, 1980.

Hofstede, Geert. *Culture's Consequences: International Differences in Work-Related Values.* Beverly Hills: Sage Publications, 1980.

Jervis, Robert. *Perception and Misperception in International Politics.* Princeton: Princeton University Press, 1976.

Jönsson, Christer. *Soviet Bargaining Behavior: The Nuclear Test Ban Case.* New York: Columbia University Press, 1979.

Joyce, John M. "The Old Russian Legacy," *Foreign Policy,* No. 55 (Summer 1984): pp. 132–153.

Kennedy, Robert. *Thirteen Days.* New York: W. W. Norton and Co., 1969.

Khrushchev, Nikita. *Khrushchev Remembers.* Boston: Little, Brown and Company, 1970.

Kohn, Hans, ed. *The Mind of Modern Russia.* Rutgers, N.J.: Rutgers University Press, 1955.

Leites, Nathan. *A Study of Bolshevism.* Glencoe: The Free Press, 1953.

Leonhard, Wolfgang. *The Kremlin and the West: A Realistic Approach.* New York: W. W. Norton and Co., 1986.

Lider, Julian. *Correlation of Forces: An Analysis of Marxist-Leninist Concepts.* New York: St. Martin's Press, 1986.

Mandelstam, Nadezhda. *Hope against Hope.* London: Collins, Harvill Press, 1971.

Mead, Margaret. *Soviet Attitudes toward Authority.* New York: McGraw-Hill, 1951.

Mead, Margaret, and Rhoda Metraux, eds. *The Study of Culture at a Distance.* Chicago: University of Chicago Press, 1953.

Medvedev, Roy A. *On Stalin and Stalinism.* Oxford: Oxford University Press, 1979.

Medvedev, Zhores A. *Gorbachev.* New York: W. W. Norton, 1986.

Mehnert, Klaus. *The Russians and Their Favorite Books.* Stanford: Hoover Institution Press, Stanford University, 1983.

Miller, Wright. *Russians as People.* New York: Dutton, 1961.

Newhouse, John. *Cold Dawn: The Story of SALT.* New York: Holt, Rinehart and Winston, 1973.

Pipes, Richard. *Russia under the Old Regime.* London: Weidenfeld and Nicolson, 1974.

Raiffa, Howard, *The Art and Science of Negotiation.* Cambridge, Mass.: Belknap/Harvard University Press, 1982.

Schlesinger, Arthur M., Jr. *A Thousand Days.* Boston: Houghton Mifflin, 1965.
Schwartz, Morton. *The Foreign Policy of the U.S.S.R.: Domestic Factors.* Encino, Calif.: Dickenson, 1975.
Shevchenko, Arkady N. *Breaking with Moscow.* New York: Alfred A. Knopf, 1985.
Simmons, Ernest J., ed. *Continuity and Change in Russian and Soviet Thought.* Cambridge, Mass.: Harvard University Press, 1955.
Sloss, Leon, and M. Scott Davis, eds. *A Game for High Stakes: Lessons Learned in Negotiating with the Soviet Union.* Cambridge, Mass: Ballinger, 1986.
Smith, Hedrick. *The Russians.* New York: Quadrangle, 1976.
Sonnenfeldt, Helmut. *Soviet Style in International Politics.* Washington, D.C.: The Washington Institute for Values in Public Policy, 1985.
Szamuely, Tibor. *The Russian Tradition.* New York: McGraw-Hill, 1974.
Talbott, Strobe. *Deadly Gambits: The Reagan Administration and the Stalemate in Nuclear Arms Control.* New York: Alfred A. Knopf, 1984.
Taylor, Maxwell. *Swords and Plowshares.* New York: W. W. Norton Company, 1972.
Tomasic, Dinko. *The Impact of Russian Culture on Soviet Communism.* Glencoe: The Free Press, 1953.
Tucker, Robert C. *The Soviet Political Mind: Studies in Stalinism and Post-Stalinist Change.* New York: W. W. Norton, 1971.
———. *Political Culture and Leadership in Soviet Russia.* New York: W. W. Norton, 1987.
Vakar, Nicholas. *The Taproot of Soviet Society.* New York: Harper & Brothers, 1961.
Verian, Graham D., ed. *Soviet Perception of War and Peace.* Washington, D.C.: National Defense University Press, 1981.
Vernadsky, George. *The Mongols and Russia.* New Haven: Yale University Press, 1953.
Voslensky, Michael. *Nomenklatura.* Garden City, N.Y.: Doubleday and Co., 1984.
Walicki, Andrzej. *A History of Russian Thought from the Enlightenment to Marxism.* Stanford: Stanford University Press, 1979.
Weihmiller, Gordon R., and Dusko Doder. *U.S.-Soviet Summits: An Account of East-West Diplomacy at the Top, 1955–1985.* Lanham, Md.: University Press of America/Institute for the Study of Diplomacy, 1986.
Weller, Gustav A. *Dialectical Materialism.* New York: Frederic A. Praeger, 1958.
Whelan, Joseph. *Soviet Diplomacy and Negotiating Behavior: Emerging New Context for U.S. Diplomacy.* vol. 1, Special Studies Series on Foreign Affairs Issues, Committee on Foreign Affairs, House of Representatives, Washington, D.C.: U.S. Government Printing Office, 1979.
White, Stephen. *Political Culture and Soviet Politics.* New York: St. Martin's Press, 1979.

ARTICLES

Almond, Gabriel. "Communism and Political Culture Theory." *Corporate Politics* 17 (January 1983): pp. 127–38.
Armstrong, John A. "The Domestic Roots of Soviet Foreign Policy." In *The Conduct of Soviet Foreign Policy,* edited by Erik Hoffman and Frederic J. Fleron, Jr. New York: Aldine, 1980.
Aspaturian, Vernon V. "Soviet Global Power and the Correlation of Forces." *Problems of Communism* 29 (May/June 1980): pp. 1–18.
Bell, Daniel. "Ideology and Soviet Politics." *Slavic Review* 24, no. 4 (December 1965): pp. 591–603.
Berdyaev, Nicholas. "The Origin of Russian Communism." In *The Mind of Modern Russia,* edited by Hans Kohn. Rutgers, N.J.: Rutgers University Press, 1955.
Bishop, Tony. "A Guide to Negotiating with the Soviet Union." Unpublished manuscript, London, British Foreign Office, n.d.

Blight, James G., Joseph S. Nye, Jr., and David A. Welch, "The Cuban Missile Crisis Revisited." *Foreign Affairs* 66, no. 1 (Fall 1987): pp. 170–88.

Brown, Archie. "Change in the Soviet Union." *Foreign Affairs* 64 (Summer 1986): pp. 1048–65.

———. "Gorbachev: New Man in the Kremlin." *Problems of Communism* 34 (May/June 1985): pp. 1–23.

Brzezinski, Zbigniew. "Soviet Politics: From the Future to the Past?" In *The Dynamics of Soviet Politics,* edited by Paul Cocks, Robert V. Daniels, and Nancy Whittier Heer. Cambridge, Mass.: Harvard University Press, 1976.

Carr, E. H. "The Legacy of History." In *Socialism in One Country.* Vol. 1, 1924–26. London: Macmillan and Co., 1964.

Comey, David Dinsmore. "Marxist-Leninist Ideology and Soviet Policy." *Studies in Soviet Thought* 2 (December 1962): pp. 301–20.

Craig, Gordon. "Techniques of Negotiating." In *Russian Foreign Policy: Essays in Historical Perspective,* edited by Ivo J. Lederer. New Haven: Yale University Press, 1972.

Dallin, Alexander. "The Domestic Sources of Soviet Foreign Policy." In *The Domestic Context of Soviet Foreign Policy,* edited by Seweryn Bialer. Boulder, Colo.: Westview Press, 1981.

Daniels, Robert V. "Doctrine and Foreign Policy." In *The Conduct of Soviet Foreign Policy,* edited by Erik Hoffman and Frederic J. Fleron, Jr. New York: Aldine, 1980.

Dean, Jonathan. "East-West Arms Controls Negotiations: The Multilateral Dimension." In *A Game for High Stakes: Lessons Learned in Negotiating with the Soviet Union,* edited by Leon Sloss and M. Scott Davis. Cambridge, Mass.: Ballinger, 1986.

———. "Negotiation by Increment." *Foreign Service Journal* 60, no. 7 (July/August 1983): pp. 26–34.

Deane, Michael J. "The Soviet Assessment of the 'Correlation of World Forces': Implications for American Foreign Policy." *Orbis* 20 (Fall 1976): pp. 625–36.

———. "Soviet Perceptions of the Military Factor in the 'Correlation of World Forces.' " In *International Perceptions of the Superpower Military Balance,* edited by Donald C. Daniel. New York: Praeger, 1978.

Dostoevsky, Feodor. "Something About Lying." In *Diary of a Writer.* New York: Octagon Books, 1973.

Fukuyama, Francis. "Gorbachev and the Third World." *Foreign Affairs* 64 (Spring 1986): pp. 715–31.

Garthoff, Raymond L. "American-Soviet Relations in Perspective." *Political Science Quarterly* 100, no. 4 (Winter 1985): pp. 541–59.

———. "Negotiating with the Russians: Some Lessons from SALT." *International Security* 1, no. 4 (Spring 1977): pp. 3–24.

Gati, Charles. "What Containment Meant." *Foreign Policy* 7 (Summer 1972): pp. 22–40.

Gati, T. Trister. "Gorbachev and Russia's Future." *Surviving Together: A Journal on Soviet-American Relations.* Washington, D.C.: Institute for Soviet-American Relations, March 1987.

George, Alexander L. " 'The Operational Code': A Neglected Approach to the Study of Political Leaders and Decision-Making." In *The Conduct of Soviet Foreign Policy,* edited by Erik Hoffman and Frederic J. Fleron, Jr. New York: Aldine, 1980.

Gitelman, Zvi. "Soviet Political Culture: Insights from Jewish Emigrés." *Soviet Studies* 29 (October 1977): 543–64.

Glagolev, Igor S. "The Soviet Decision-Making Process in Arms Control Negotiations." *Orbis* 21 (Winter 1978) pp. 767–76.

Goldman, Irving. "Psychiatric Interpretation of Russian History: A Reply to Geoffrey Gorer." *American Slavic and East European Review* 9 (1950).

Hammond, Thomas T. "Leninist Authoritarianism before the Revolution." In *Continuity and Change in Russian and Soviet Thought*, edited by Ernest J. Simmons. Cambridge, Mass.: Harvard University Press, 1955.

Hingley, Ronald. "That's No Lie, Comrade." *Problems of Communism* 11 (March/April 1962): pp. 47–55.

Hyland, William G. "The Gorbachev Succession." *Foreign Affairs* 63 (Spring 1985): pp. 800–9.

Joyce, John M. "The Old Russian Legacy." *Foreign Policy* 55 (Summer 1984): pp. 132–53.

Kampelman, Max. "Madrid Conference: How to Negotiate with the Soviets." *Law and National Security Intelligence Report*, vol. 7, no. 2 (February 1985). American Bar Association.

———. Remarks at Royal College of Defense Studies, London, England. October 30, 1986.

Keenan, Edward. "Muscovite Political Folkways." *Russian Review* 45 (April 1986): pp. 115–81.

Kelly, Rita M., and Frederic J. Fleron, Jr. "Personality, Behavior, and Communist Ideology." In *The Conduct of Soviet Foreign Policy*, edited by Erik Hoffman and Frederic J. Fleron, Jr. New York: Aldine, 1980.

Kennan, George F. "The Sources of Soviet Conduct." *Foreign Affairs* 65, no. 4 (Spring 1987): pp. 852–68. (A reprint of the 1947 "X" article.)

Kluckholn, Clyde. "Recent Studies of the National Character of Great Russians." *Human Development Bulletin*, University of Chicago (February 5, 1955): pp. 39–60.

Kortunov, V. "The Leninist Policy of Peaceful Co-existence and Class Struggle." *International Affairs (USSR)* (May 1979): pp. 85–94.

Legvold, Robert. "Gorbachev's New Approach to Conventional Arms Control." *The Harriman Institute Forum* 1 (January 1988): pp. 1–8.

Lenin, V. I. *Against Boycott: Notes of a Social-Democratic Publicist*. In *Collected Works*, vol. 13. 4th ed., pp. 15–49. London: Lawrence and Wishart, 1962.

———. *Conspectus of Hegel's Book "The Science of Logic."* In *Collected Works*, vol. 38. 4th ed., pp. 85–238. London: Lawrence and Wishart, 1961.

———. Letter to S. I. Gusev of 11 March 1905. In *Collected Works*, vol. 34. 4th ed., pp. 302–3. London: Lawrence and Wishart, 1966.

———. "Materialism and Imperio-Criticism." In *Selected Works*. New York: International Publishers, 1943.

———. "On the Eve of October, 1917." In *The Mind of Modern Russia*, edited by Hans Kohn, pp. 242–45. Rutgers, N.J.: Rutgers University Press, 1955.

———. "A Poor Defense of a Liberal Labour Policy." *Zvezda* (April 1, 1912). In *Collected Works*, vol. 17. 4th ed., pp. 556–61. London: Lawrence and Wishart, 1963.

———. *We Have Paid Too Much*. In *Selected Works*, vol. 10, pp. 301–5. New York: International Publishers, 1943.

———. *What Is to Be Done?* In *Collected Works of V. I. Lenin*, vol. 4, book 2, pp. 89–258. York: International Publishers, 1929.

Lowenthal, Richard. "The Logic of One-Party Rule in Soviet Conduct in World Affairs." In *The Conduct of Soviet Foreign Policy*, edited by Erik Hoffman and Frederic J. Fleron, Jr. New York: Aldine, 1980.

Luard, Evan. "Superpowers and Regional Conflicts." *Foreign Affairs* 64 (Summer 1986): pp. 1006–25.

Lukes, Igor. "Hegel, Freedom and the Ideological Roots of Soviet Foreign Policy." *Fletcher Forum* 5 (Summer 1981): pp. 1278–94.

Meyer, Alfred G. "The Functions of Ideology in the Soviet Political System." *Soviet Studies* 17, no. 3 (January 1966): pp. 273–85.

Moore, Barrington, Jr. "Some Readjustments in Communist Theory." *Journal of the History of Ideas* 6 (1945): pp. 468–82.

New York Times, May 31, June 1, and June 7, 1987.

Nitze, Paul. "Deterring Our Deterrent." *Foreign Policy,* no. 25 (Winter 1976/77): pp. 195–210.

Pipes, Richard. "International Negotiation: Some Operational Principles of Soviet Foreign Policy." Memorandum Prepared at the Request of the Committee on Government Questions, United States Senate Committee print, January 1972.

Ploss, Sidney I. "A New Soviet Era?" *Foreign Policy* 62 (Spring 1986): pp. 46–60.

Ra'anan, Uri. "Soviet Decision-making and International Relations." *Problems of Communism* 29 (November/December 1980): pp. 41–47.

Reddaway, Peter B. "Aspects of Ideological Belief in the Soviet Union; Comments on Professor Meyer's Essay." *Soviet Studies* 17, no. 4 (April 1966): pp. 473–83.

Sergiyev, A. "Leninism on the Correlation of Forces as a Factor of International Relations." *International Affairs (USSR)* (May 1975).

Shakhnazarov, G. "On the Problem of the Correlation of Forces." *Kommunist* 2 (February 1974).

Simes, Dimitri K. "Gorbachev: A New Foreign Policy?" *Foreign Affairs* 65 (America and the World, 1986): pp. 477–500.

Simis, Konstantin. "The Gorbachev Generation." *Foreign Policy* 59 (Summer 1985): pp. 3–21.

Slocombe, Walter. "Negotiating with the Soviets: Getting Past No." In *A Game for High Stakes: Lessons Learned in Negotiating with the Soviet Union,* edited by Leon Sloss and M. Scott Davis. Cambridge, Mass.: Ballinger, 1986.

Sloss, Leon, and M. Scott Davis. "The Soviet Union: The Pursuit of Power and Influence through Negotiation." In *National Negotiating Styles,* edited by Hans Binnendijk. Washington, D.C.: Center for the Study of Foreign Affairs, Foreign Service Institute, U.S. Department of State, 1987.

Sorensen, Theodore. Recorded interview by Carl Kaysen, March 26, 1964, John F. Kennedy Library Oral History Program.

Stoertz, Howard J. "Observations on Soviet Negotiating Practice." In *A Game for High Stakes: Lessons Learned in Negotiating with the Soviet Union,* edited by Leon Sloss and M. Scott Davis. Cambridge, Mass.: Ballinger, 1986.

Tucker, Robert C. "Culture, Political Culture, and Communist Society." *Political Science Quarterly* 82 (June 1973): pp. 173–90.

Ulam, Adam. "Forty Years of Troubled Coexistence." *Foreign Affairs* 64, no. 1 (Fall 1985): pp. 12–32.

Wedge, Bryant, and Curil Muromcew. "Psychological Factors in Soviet Disarmament Negotiation." *Journal of Conflict Resolution* 9, no. 1 (March 1965): pp. 18–36.

White, Stephen. "The U.S.S.R.: Patterns of Autocracy and Industrialism." In *Political Culture and Political Change in Communist States,* edited by Archie Brown and Jack Gray. London: Macmillan, 1977.

York, Herbert. "Negotiating and the U.S. Bureaucracy." In *A Game for High Stakes: Lessons Learned in Negotiating with the Soviet Union,* edited by Leon Sloss and M. Scott Davis. Cambridge, Mass.: Ballinger, 1986.

Zezleslin, V. V. "The Revolutionary Process and International CPSU Policy." *Kommunist* 14 (September 1972): pp. 12–24.

Zimmerman, William. "Elite Perspectives and the Explanation of Soviet Foreign Policy." In *The Conduct of Soviet Foreign Policy,* edited by Erik Hoffman and Frederic J. Fleron, Jr. New York: Aldine, 1980.

INDEX